EDUCATION FOR
PEACE AND JUSTICE

Edited by Padraic O'Hare

1817

HARPER & ROW, PUBLISHERS, SAN FRANCISCO

Cambridge, Hagerstown, New York, Philadelphia
London, Mexico City, São Paulo, Sydney

In Loving Memory of
Vito Del Rosso,
Who Lived a Life of Justice and of Love

FIRST EDITION

Designer: Jim Mennick

Library of Congress Cataloging in Publication Data

Main entry under title:

EDUCATION FOR PEACE AND JUSTICE.

  Includes index.
  1. Church and social problems—Catholic Church—Addresses, essays, lectures. 2. Social justice—Addresses, essays, lectures. 3. Peace—Addresses, essays, lectures. I. O'Hare, Padraic.
HN37.C3E3 1983   261.8'3   82-48418
ISBN 0-06-066361-8

83 84 85 86 87 10 9 8 7 6 5 4 3 2 1

Contents

Foreword

IT IS ONE of the positive "signs of the times" that this remarkable collection of essays should have been gathered, not by theologians or social activists, but by religious educators. Padraic O'Hare is to be complimented for conceiving and executing this project. Theologians sometimes harbor the prejudice that religious education is a second-rate discipline without any coherent foundational theory of its own. And social activists occasionally accuse the educator of being long on theory but short on practice. Too many theologians, however, are unaware of the kind of sophisticated foundational work that has been done in recent years by religious education theorists. In this collection alone, one can point with pride to the achievements of Gabriel Moran, Mary Boys, and Thomas Groome. And social activists perhaps know too little of the work now being done within the field of religious education to overcome the artificial gap between theory and practice. Again, Thomas Groome's ground-breaking work, *Christian Religious Education: Sharing Our Story and Vision* (San Francisco: Harper & Row, 1980), offers a striking case in point.

One can only admire, therefore, the systematic, wide-ranging, and diversified character of the essays that follow. "Peace and Justice Education" does not function simply as a slogan. There are four essays that address the foundational questions, seven that attend to the educational dimension, and four that attend to the ministerial implications. Unlike so many other collections, the contributors reflect evenly the background and insights of both sexes and of various national and ethnic traditions. The medium, in a sense, conveys the message.

What all of the authors do have in common is an abiding commitment to Catholic social doctrine. They reflect from within that broad and rich tradition a distinctive understanding of the nature of the human community and of the individual person within that community. Indeed, these are the twin pillars of Catholic social doctrine. The commitment to social justice is not simply the commitment to the renewal and reconstruction of the world but a commitment to the building of a human community and the enrichment of every person within it.

Catholic social doctrine is to be distinguished always from the social implications of the Gospel. Catholic social doctrine is a clearly discernible body of official teachings on the social order, in its economic and political dimensions. It is concerned with the dignity of the human person as created in the image of God, and with the radically social nature of human existence.

Catholic social doctrine as such did not exist before the end of the nineteenth century, which is not to say that the Catholic Church expressed no official interest in, or concern for, the world outside the sanctuary until Pope Leo XIII's encyclical *rerum novarum* in 1891. But not until Leo XIII did the Catholic Church begin to articulate in a consciously systematic manner a theology of social justice and all that that implies. At first, Catholic social doctrine confined itself to the problems of industrial society. With the Second World War it expanded to take into account the growing material interdependence of the world and the need to provide some moral framework for the political, economic, and strategic issues facing the entire global human community. With Pope Paul VI's apostolic letter *Octagesima adveniens* in 1971, Catholic social doctrine became more deliberately political, in the classical sense of the term. This broader political approach is carried forward in Pope John Paul II's first and third encyclicals, *Redemptor hominis* in 1979 and *Laborem exercens* in 1981. According to Pope John Paul II, what is essential today is the right of citizens to share in the "political life of the community" in service of the common good, whether national or international, and in service of the human person, whose dignity in Christ is the foundation and linchpin of the whole social and political order. "Thus the principle of human rights is of profound concern to the area of social justice and is the measure by which it can be tested in the life of political bodies" (*Redemptor hominis*, United States Catholic Conference, no. 17, par. 7).

The Second Vatican Council, of course, prepared the way for the expansion of Catholic social doctrine to include this political dimension. Among the fundamental principles the Council stressed, especially in its *Gaudium et spes*, are the dignity of the human person created in the image of God (no. 12), the dignity of the moral conscience (no. 16), the excellence of freedom (no. 17), the social nature of human existence and of our destiny (no. 24), the interdependence of person and society (no. 26), the need to promote the common good for the sake of human dignity (no. 26), respect for human beings (no.

27), their fundamental equality as the basis of social justice (no. 29), the value of all human activities because of the redemption (no. 34), the rightful autonomy of temporal realities (no. 36), and the missionary responsibility of the Church to attend to this constellation of values and principles (the document as a whole, especially nos. 40–45). The same insistence on human freedom is sounded in the Council's *Declaration on Religious Freedom*, a freedom that belongs not only to individuals but to groups (no. 4), and that is always subject to the common good (no. 7).

The social mission of the Church is even more explicitly articulated in the synodal document *Iustitia in mundo:* "Action on behalf of justice and participation in the transformation of the world fully appear to us as a constitutive dimension of the preaching of the Gospel, or, in other words, of the Church's mission for the redemption of the human race and its liberation from every oppressive situation" (par. 6).

What is usually missing, however, not only from much official rhetoric on social justice but even from much theological and social activist rhetoric, is a concern for issues of human rights and social justice within the Church itself. Pastoral leaders, not excluding the pope himself, are reluctant to apply the same standards to the community of faith, because that would lead inevitably to a recognition, however painful it might be, of the inevitable gap between our own Catholic ideals and our ecclesiastical performance. The same synodal document, *Iustitia in mundo*, provides a remarkable exception to this. It reminds us that the Church itself must attend to its own household on matters of justice and human rights, for "anyone who ventures to speak to people about justice must first be just in their eyes" (sec. 3, no. 3, par. 2). The Church, which is the sacrament of Christ, is called upon by missionary mandate to practice what it preaches about justice and rights. Significantly, too many social activists talk as if the questions of the ordination of women, the election of bishops, due process in the Church, freedom of theological dissent, and so forth are entirely subsidiary issues. And the Church's official teachers tend also to separate the two arenas. Thus, Pope John Paul II's *Laborem exercens* speaks eloquently of the rights of workers to enter into movements of solidarity, but nowhere is there any explicit application to the rights of workers in ecclesiastical institutions, such as schools, hospitals, and other agencies administered by the Church.

Justice is a universal virtue, to be universally applied, inside as well as outside the Church. Social justice education, therefore, is not only oriented toward the critical examination and reconstruction of the world at large but must also be attentive to the structures and patterns of injustice within the Church itself. If the Church is the sacrament of Christ, then it must practice what it preaches. The principle of sacramentality is as characteristic of Catholicism as is the body of social doctrine produced by the Catholic Church. The one presupposes and depends upon the other.

I hope that those who read through this significant body of articles will never fail to apply what they read to the Church. The Church educates not only in everything it says but in everything it does. It is a matter, therefore, not only of commitment to social justice but of sound educational practice as well. It is at the point of intersection between these two concerns that the following essays emerge.

Richard P. McBrien

University of Notre Dame

Introduction

THIS INTRODUCTION is intended to indicate the purpose of the volume, explain its structure, provide a synopsis of the actual content of each essay, make certain disclaimers, and acknowledge a few of those in whose debt I find myself.

The purpose of the volume is to focus, indeed to linger, on the distinctly educational. By education, I mean joint human action (often, though not always, by people called teachers and students) that leads to change, insight, and motivation to action emanating from conscious and intentional appropriation of new ideas and re-interpreted experience. It is the further purpose of this volume to bring this range of educational wisdom to bear on the imperative need for "a justice which will be less and less imperfect" (*Octogesima adveniens*, no. 15). The volume is divided into three parts: foundational issues, educational issues, and related ministerial issues. And each essay concludes with suggested questions for clarification, reflection, and discussion. Though explicitly educational concerns are raised in the opening section, its primary purpose is to look at certain background issues related to education for social justice. David Hollenbach's essay retrieves a classic notion of courage as a pre-eminent virtue and grace of perseverance in social justice work. Maria Harris's essay is something of an ecclesiological preface to any serious and sustained effort at works of justice within the Church and for a just world. Gabriel Moran provides a penetrating analysis of a taken-for-granted concept in his discussion of the nature of the "social" itself. And, finally, Virgil Elizondo writes on the biblical foundations of Christian ethical responsibility.

In the section on educational issues, Thomas Groome identifies a central theological impetus for social justice education in his reflection on the kingdom of God; he also relates his educational method of "shared praxis" to the goals of such education. Maurice Monette examines the base community. Mary Boys establishes a crucial distinction between proclamation and education for justice and also gives us a fine meditation on a noble notion of teaching. My own essay considers the school as an instrument of education for justice; Margaret Woodward examines the relationship of the development of aesthetic capacities to education for justice; and Russell Butkus brings the insights of John Dewey and Paulo Freire to bear on the enterprise of social justice education. Margaret Gorman does the same with the work of Kohlberg; and Joseph Fahey explores the substance and scope of peace studies programs.

The final section on related ministerial issues contains a series of provocative essays relating the goal of social justice to liturgical engagement (Kathleen Hughes), pastoral care and counseling (Claire Lowery), and spirituality and spiritual formation (Margaret Brennan). It concludes with a highly personal statement by a contemporary social minister, educator, and activist, Ada Maria Isasi-Diaz.

In David Hollenbach's essay, "Courage and Patience: Education for Staying Power in the Pursuit of Peace and Justice," we read a careful exposition of the moral and religious reality of courage (as both daring and enduring) set against the background of a psychosocial sketch of the reality of "burnout." Hollenbach acknowledges that "knowledge of justice does not produce justice" and proceeds to suggest resources "that make courageous staying power more likely in the pursuit of justice." These resources are an experience of the suffering of victims of injustice, a prudent knowledgeability that enables the social justice advocate to be effective and to endure in the face of complexity, a supportive communal environment, some success or knowledge of the success of others and a hope-filled realization of one's limits. This culminates in "a faith in God and love for God as revealed in Jesus Christ" without which the Christian social activist must inevitably grow bitter or frustrated and Christian religious education fall short of the mark.

In her essay, "Education for Priesthood," Maria Harris has looked at what may be the most basic question affecting the Church's ability to be a sacrament and source of healing and justice: the universality of ministerial call. Working in an explicitly Roman Catholic context, Harris portrays the notion of "universal priesthood" and insists, on both ethical and theological grounds, on the need for explicit "education for priesthood" of those who are in truth doing priestly work of mediating, loving, and empowering others. Since the premier priestly work of sacramentalizing all of human existence must take place where people "work, love, pray, and study as well as where they worship," priestly people are needed everywhere.

In his essay, "Social Reform: On the Way to Justice," Gabriel Moran examines the meaning and the reality that is generated by the notion of the social. He considers the way ideas about social education have functioned in general and in religious education in this country, as well as the greatly varied meaning that "social" has for liberals, to whom it connotes solidarity, and conservatives, to whom it implies conformity. Moran re-assesses Hannah Arendt's historical analysis of the social as an ecclesiastical invention that blurs our understanding of the private and the political. In addition, he considers the impact of society on home and politics and concludes with the caution that some modes of social reform do not attend sufficiently to the distinctly political, or provide room for either the idiosyncratic or the deeply contemplative. Moran concludes with a vision of the Church as the pre-eminent example of a social organization that is meant to transform the political reality without itself becoming a political agency.

Virgil Elizondo's "By Their Fruits You Will Know Them: The Biblical Roots of Peace and Justice" is a comprehensive statement of the biblical perspective on humanity, history, and the claims of justice on the Christian. After expressing a somewhat apocalyptic view of the present situation, Elizondo identifies the biblical understanding of life as one that is given meaning by our relationships to mystery and to one another and by a companionship that is essential to humanity. Though he maintains a Catholic emphasis in his approval of the idea of humanity as, ontologically, *imago dei*, Elizondo nevertheless sees the "kingdom of death" dominating human history, as our desire for God is regularly subverted by pride in all its personal and cultural manifestations. Such evil is mastered in the "irruption of the kingdom of life," which is brought about in Jesus of Nazareth who symbolizes and effects an essential humanity in which solidarity with the poor prevents co-option by the world, in which human care is given a place of radical seriousness, and in which the worship of God is our protection against idolatry.

In his "Religious Education for Justice by Educating Justly," Thomas Groome supplies a careful and detailed theological rationale for the importance of justice in Christian life and religious education. This is done by examining the Hebrew and early Christian understanding of the kingdom of God. The educational corollary of the eschatological insight as Groome expresses it is this: "If Christian religious education makes the kingdom of God, as preached by Jesus Christ, its central task, then it must educate for justice." Groome is equally concerned about, and gives us straightforward criteria for, educational practice that endorses an ethical mode of human exchange. The essay concludes with an explicit relating of the author's method of "shared praxis" to education for justice. Groome also identifies certain "secondary principles" of justice education: that it avoid elitism and methods of guilt-inducement and that it steer clear of an excessively psychologized approach to the analysis of moral issues (in favor of a balance with sociological perspectives). The author concludes with the good news that we are not without transcendental resource in our struggle for justice.

Maurice Monette's "Justice, Peace, and the Pedagogy of Grass Roots Christian Community" contrasts a culturally and politically adaptive form of Christianity that embraces a progressive model of "liberal education," with a critical Christian strategy and its "radical educational" model whose goal is transformation. The contrast is set against the backdrop of an analysis of the destructive dynamics of a capitalist organization of society (now grown fully monopolistic and transnational), and the isolation of liberal middle-class society. In this context, Monette argues that the "base community" model of justice education ("educative," rather than "educational" in the traditional sense the word connotes) is the "main vehicle for the transformative pastoral strategy" demanded not only by the destructive individualism and the alienating technological domination of so-called first world societies but, finally, by the gospel.

In her essay, "A Word About Teaching Justly," Mary Boys retrieves a profound understanding of the teaching art against the background of her primary thesis: justice requires that priority be given to education in the Church. She contrasts "ecclesial proclamation" with long-term education. In truly educational activity teachers invite new understanding; they offer conceptual structures; they introduce a variety of views; and they show how classic positions have developed. In addition, the teacher encourages dialogue with other opinions and nurtures appropriation of these experiences by those with whom they labor in this work of searching. Boys looks carefully at Jesus of Nazareth as the true teacher as well as at the signs of the times to which a contemporary religious educator concerned for justice need attend. In the process of investigating the parabolic Jesus as teacher, Boys "models" the biblically literate religious educator who is able to invite imaginative participation and appropriation (through "dynamic analogy") of the ethical world of the Scriptures.

My own essay, "The Renewal of Education and the Nurturing of Justice and Peace," looks at the schooling dimension of education, not from the false belief that this is all of education, but simply because it is one of the most influential of the educational forums and requires our attention. Like that of Mary Boys, my essay is especially attentive to the person and function of the teacher. I place the primary ethical effect of schools precisely in the respect, zest, knowledge, goodness, and magnanimity of spirit that teachers manifest. Second in importance to the personal impact of teachers in promoting an environment of justice is the potential moral effect of a broad and deeply rooted knowledgeability. The knowledgeability emanates from imaginative engagement in the study of the general subjects of knowledge and leads to a depth of understanding and an appreciative world view, which are helpful corollaries to the moral life.

Margaret Woodward's "Cold Animation Is Not Animation" is an evocative study of the aesthetic foundations and impulses for education in justice, and of the practice of education as a just art. Drawing from the experience of aesthetic engagement of peoples around the world, Woodward pictures artistic action and transaction as a disciplined journey filled with the "pain and work" of exercising "the human authority of one's subjecthood." Far from being the effete antithesis of an ethical life, the artistic life is essential to the development of a critical world view, for "aesthetic literacy," as Woodward argues persuasively, has the same revolutionary implications as the achievement of other forms of empowerment and literacy: It defamiliarizes our taken-for-granted world and is the basis of our critique of our own and the dominant ideology. Only the person who engages in aesthetic transactions is able to accept multiple meanings and to live with paradox and ambiguity. These lie at the heart of the moral life, and they are the products of an aesthetically literate and empowering education in justice.

In his essay on John Dewey and Paulo Freire, Russell Butkus has correlated the general lines of the educational thought of these two giants with the explicit goals of education for peace and justice. He describes the major themes in the thought of each and identifies themes common to both (for example, each author's insistence on an experiential, prospective, democratic, and socially transformative kind of education). Butkus's critique of each educator (Dewey, for his lack of a critical principle, and Freire, for possible overoptimism) supplies helpful guidance, as does his concluding set of principles for ethical education.

In Margaret Gorman's "Moral Education, Peace, and Social Justice," we are given a concrete picture of the psychological justification for specific educational strategies for inducing higher levels of moral judgment and action in children, teens, and young adults. Working within Kohlberg's categories, but with a view to the limitations of his work (a view especially informed by Carol Gilligan's criticisms), Gorman deals not so much with social justice as with the psychosocial preliminaries for moral growth and maturity. She suggests explicit strategies for such morally effective techniques as empathy-inducing questions, role-playing, and social service engagement, which, in addition to the service it supplies, leads to growth in self-esteem and in satisfaction of the need to belong.

In the concluding essay of this section, Joseph Fahey supplies a profile of the underlying educational spirit as well as content of programs on peace studies. Fahey insists that such programs be multidisciplinary and problem-centered, engaging a range of academic disciplines within the college or university community. The preferred and central content for exploration in such programs includes the study of war, the arms race and disarmament, social and economic justice, practical methods of dispute resolution (with special attention to empirical analysis of the relations within peaceful societies), the philosophies and strategies of nonviolence (with special attention to hagiography) and, finally, notions and possibilities of world order. Fahey is convinced that peace studies programs must be "reconstructionist" in tone—that is, critical and futurist rather than simply socializing in their method and intent. Above all, Fahey articulates a central theme of fundamental educational concern: the tension that must exist, in all fruitful educational exchange, between moral commitment on the one hand and dispassionate objectivity in the pursuit of knowledge on the other. So long as that tension remains, a false notion of academic objectivity will not lead us to moral neutrality in our educational endeavors.

Section three of the volume, "Related Ministerial Issues," begins with Kathleen Hughes's essay, "Liturgy, Justice, and Peace." This is a remarkably straightforward piece on the intrinsic relationship between authentic liturgical engagement and commitment to justice, set against the background of a droll appraisal of the danger of detached religious ritualism ("playing Church with bells and smells") on the one hand, and manipulation of the liturgy by social activists ("creating liturgy *ex nihilo*") on the other. A striking and persuasive aspect of Hughes's essay is her sympathetic but unyielding criticism of "the superimposition of a theme on the celebration of the liturgy," for the liturgy is an invitation to place ourselves in the way of a summons to transformation, which "is intrinsic to genuine worship." In Christian worship, after all, "we do not gather in the presence of the Holy One in order to discuss what we intend to do but to surrender to God's design for us."

Claire Lowery's "The Pastoral Care and Counseling Relationship" addresses the crucial need to relate the pastoral counseling of individuals to the "needs of the community, [and] the societal ills that frequently cause personal problems and struggle." Lowery rejects a strictly individualistic and psychotherapeutic model of pastoral counseling in favor of an "ecclesial model" in which counseling is seen as part of the pastoral care of a religious community. Practiced with serious attention to the whole life of the ecclesial community, pastoral counseling opens out and attends to the whole context; it becomes the antithesis of the "current temptation to self-groundedness." Instead, pastoral counseling finds its roots in a life of covenant with the God of justice. Lowery tells us that "in the context of the Church's mission, pastoral counseling would not separate love and justice, personal and social responsibility."

Margaret Brennan's essay, "Sing a New Song unto the Lord: The Relationship Between Spirituality and Social Responsibility," defines spirituality as the way a person "more or less consciously relates to God in all the human dimensions of life." And the movement of authentic spirituality is understood as a "kind of dialectical interplay, correlating and calling forth an experience of God on the one hand, with a commitment to social responsibility on the other." Brennan speaks at length, and with great power, of the biblical foundations of a vision of the just life and about the relationship of God with human beings who are "the privileged locus of God's revelation." She relates the relationship in prayer of the Christian with God to a socially responsible life and calls for modes of spiritual formation that are essentially corporate.

Finally, Ada Maria Isasi-Diaz's "A Liberation Perspective on Peace and Social Justice" insists on the absolute identity of one's life commitments and one's ministry of social justice engagement. This insight is the inevitable result of a critical and liberationist perspective on education and on the life of the Church. Of special interest is Isasi-Diaz's linking of excessive specialization and professionalization with approaches to social justice ministry in which personal engagement is missing and the process of conscientizing distorted. Isasi-Diaz offers a concrete case of social justice ministry and the relationship of such ministry to personal commitments and to the critical appropriation of one's own experience in her discussion of her own work in advocacy of justice for women in Church and society.

All of the contributors to this volume are Catholic Christians. It has seemed to me a matter of healthy clarification of the tribal perspective, and not an instance of narrow sectarian feeling, to invite such people to contribute to the volume. And, in any case, all are people of

broad ecumenical sensitivity. I am proud of myself for having conceived the structure and direction of this volume and for having had
the good sense to invite these people to contribute; I am more proud
of the fine contribution of each. I do not, however, agree with everything that is written in the ensuing fifteen essays. But I have not
thought it proper to try to get any of the contributors to alter what
they have written. This tolerance is made easier by the fact that I
agree with almost everything that is written and by the realization that
these highly well developed individuals would have refused such re-
quests in any case. There is, however, one disclaimer that I do wish to
make explicit in this introduction. In a few places throughout the
volume, the question of the relationship of Christianity to its Jewish
roots is rendered explicitly, or implied. In a few such instances, the
treatment is not as sensitive to the integrity and vitality of Jewish
religious tradition as I would like; nor is the treatment in these few
places as free from a discredited supersessionist mentality as contemporary ecumenical relations or scholarship calls for.

I wish to thank all the contributors to this volume. Quite apart
from their willingness to participate in this venture, many of them
have influenced me personally and professionally and four of them are
colleagues of mine at Boston College. I wish, further, to acknowledge
my indebtedness to the former bishop, and the director and the associate director of the Office of Human Development in Rochester,
New York: Most Rev. Joseph L. Hogan and Revs. Charles Mulligan
and Daniel Tormey. During two years working in Rochester, these
men taught me lessons about the Church's social responsibility that
are a continuing source of insight and challenge. Finally, since little
that is creative derives from the unhappy and unloved, my special
thanks to those who love me most specially: my wife, Margaret Ciski
O'Hare, and our son, Brian.

I

FOUNDATIONAL

ISSUES

1. Courage and Patience: Education for Staying Power in the Pursuit of Peace and Justice

DAVID HOLLENBACH, S.J.

IN RECENT YEARS there has been a major renewal of the Church's involvement in the quest for greater justice throughout the world. The importance of Christian commitment to the pursuit of justice is evident on many fronts. It has been strongly emphasized in official church teachings. It is the central theme of liberation theology, one of the most creative developments in Christian thought to occur in our century. The meaning of justice in the North American context has been probed by social scientists, philosophers, and theologians both in the context of interdisciplinary dialogue and that of their Christian faith. These new intellectual developments are partial and incomplete. But they are most encouraging and need to be carried forward vigorously. They deserve the serious attention of all religious educators as new patterns of education for justice are explored. Despite their importance, however, another aspect of the task of education for justice will be the central focus of this essay. We might call it the education of the heart, that part of the person where "the joys and the hopes, the griefs and the anxieties"[1] of the people of our day are experienced and felt by those actively struggling for justice.

Though the idea of justice and the meaning of justice in our society are crucial foci for the educational task, they are not its sole concern. This is so because justice is not an idea. It is an action, a matter of practice, a structured reality that must be created by human freedom and choice. Lack of knowledge of the meaning of justice and of the demands of justice in the concrete situation will surely prevent the Christian community from contributing to the creation of a just society. But though the possession of such knowledge is a necessary condition for effective advocacy of the cause of a more human world, it is not a sufficient condition for such effectiveness. For example, Lawrence Kohlberg has built his model of moral education on the centrality of the norm of justice. Christian religious educators can and should be in full agreement with this emphasis. However, when Kohlberg goes on to affirm that "he [she] who knows the good chooses the good,"[2] both theological and educational questions must be raised.

Much of Christian social thought, particularly in its Roman Catholic form, rests on strongly intellectualist presuppositions that emphasize that *knowledge* of the good is central to the moral life. Thus there is considerable room for agreement between Christian approaches to education for justice and Kohlberg's cognitive approach to moral development. Nevertheless, even in moral theologies that most strongly stress the importance of knowing what is just, like those of Thomas Aquinas and his contemporary disciples, cognition alone cannot guarantee that justice will be done. States of the heart like fear, desire, anxiety, boredom, resentment, anger, sadness, or exhaustion can lead men and women to fail to do what they know will contribute to greater justice. Such states of feeling can even lead them to do what they know to be unjust. By the same token, doing what is known to be just can be greatly facilitated by the presence of confidence, hope, energy, and magnanimity. Knowledge of the good is not in itself sufficient to produce these states of the heart, because human beings are not pure mind. Also, there is a rift or conflict in the center of the human person that Christian theology calls original sin.[3] This conflict is not only within the interior heart of the person but also between the desires of the heart and the good of justice that the mind perceives. This rift is less fundamental than the unity and goodness of the human person as the image of God. It must, however, be taken into account by religious educators, theologians, and indeed all Christians as they rethink their roles and responsibilities in the Christian mission for social change.

In what follows a few modest suggestions about the education of the heart for the pursuit of justice will be outlined. First, a major problem that threatens to undermine much of the personal and corporate progress that has been made in the Christian community's quest for justice will be briefly described. This is the problem of "burnout," or loss of hope and energy, among social justice activists. Second, we will look briefly at a resource in the Christian tradition that can increase our understanding of ways to improve staying power and combat burnout. This resource is the traditional analysis of the virtues of courage and patience found in Catholic moral theology. Third, several suggestions will be made about how courage and patience can be fostered and deepened among contemporary Christians. And finally, a few words will be said about the deeper religious and theological significance of courage and patience in the quest for justice.

The problem of staying power in the commitment to justice has emerged as an important question for the Christian community because of the experience of the lack of it in recent years. Despite the signs of real progress in the Church's social ministry during the last decade, there have also been signs that this work is more arduous and costly than it might have seemed in the early days of renewal. The cost is most tragically visible in the harassment, imprisonment, and even the torture and execution of Christians in a number of countries where the Church is in conflict with economic elites or political ruling groups.[4] In many of these situations injustice is evident and tangible and the needed direction of change is palpable. The struggle Christians face as they prepare to act is an inner struggle between fear and daring, between hope and despair, rather than a struggle to know what justice demands. It is as much an affair of the heart as it is of the mind.

In the North American context the difficulties faced by agents of change are less dramatic but nonetheless very real. Among the hazards that sometimes accompany sustained work for justice are not physical violence or imprisonment, but emotional and psychological exhaustion. Frustration levels among those pursuing the work of justice in North American society seem almost always to be quite high. This is not simply a result of the psychological problems of social justice advocates, it is related to the kind of society they work in. The United States is a highly differentiated pluralist society in which the causes of injustice are neither single nor simple. The patterns of cause and effect in the dynamics of social change are governed by multiple variables. As a result, moral choice is rarely rooted in a simple confrontation between good and evil or between oppressors and oppressed. The complexity of the mechanisms of change make moral choice less a clear-cut decision between justice and injustice than is sometimes the case in less complexly differentiated societies.

The social system that exists in the United States has a distinctive impact on the emotional and affective dimensions of moral choice. Where choices to be made in the pursuit of justice are relatively simple and clear, one can put one's whole heart into one's action without having to exert large amounts of psychological energy to do so. When the choices are less clear or when every choice demands that many factors be held together in balanced tension, we tend to hedge our affective bets a bit. The structures of a complex pluralistic society lead to a certain emotional distancing of social agents from their actions in society. Sociologists call the extreme form of this distancing anomie, a condition in which action loses all normative and affective significance. When such significance is undermined, so is the likelihood of commitment and choice.

This social context exacts a high cost from men and women who pursue the cause of justice over a sustained period of time. All members of advanced industrial societies have problems finding unified meaning and emotional integrity in the chopped-up world in which they live.[5] Those who set out to address the problems of injustice inherent in these societies must carry additional burdens. First, they must deal either directly in experience or indirectly in reflection with the pain and suffering of the victims of injustice. The experience of these negative aspects of social reality make it that much more difficult to maintain an integrated world of meaning and the wholeness of heart that is rooted in such meaning. In addition, the social justice advocate must also regularly deal with the conflicts and contradictions within the social system itself. These conflicts become part of experience and take up residence within the mind and heart of the activist. Finally, deepening awareness of the scope of injustice can combine with frustration over the slow pace of change to produce a smoldering anger. This anger may be the only emotionally effective way that the activist can avoid surrendering to the anomie or loss of affective significance with which modern society threatens everyone.

In short, because the social justice activist is consciously dealing with the negativities of contemporary social reality, he or she is particularly vulnerable to some of these negativities. If they get the upper hand within the heart of a person dedicated to the quest for justice, the final outcome can be a state of emotional burnout that renders further action impossible. Alfred Kammer has described this state as "a physical, emotional, psychological phenomenon—an experience of personal fatigue, alienation, failure."[6] It seems to be a threat not only to Christian social activists but also to people of various beliefs and competencies who are professionally engaged in helping the victims in our complex industrial society.[7] These different emotional dangers are as much a threat to the quest for justice in North America as are the physical threat and danger of violence in other parts of the world. As psychologist James Gill has pointed out, there is deep irony in the fact that people who have the highest level of commitment to helping others in our society are the very people most in danger of disillusionment and burnout. In Gill's words, "Those who altruistically enter the helping professions and devote themselves unstintingly and enthusiastically to meeting the needs of others are the ones likely to experience frustration and disillusionment, find their energy exhausted, distance themselves from people (even friends), regard their efforts as failure, and, in some cases, even abandon their work."[8] This irony is the result of the emotional price that modern industrial society exacts from those who seek to change it. Both the full-time specialist in work for social justice and American Christians in general are in need of help if they are to avoid burnout and develop staying power in their commitment and action. Since the threat is a matter of the heart rather than the head, the defense must address the heart as well.

In the tradition of Christian moral thought the quality of heart that enables people to do what is just in the face of difficulty or adversity is called the virtue of courage. In the writings of Thomas Aquinas, for example, courage is not simply a discrete virtue that a person could develop independent of concern for the doing of justice. Courage is not simply strength of will, fearlessness, or the ability to endure in the face of hardship, it is strength of will in the pursuit of justice. It is the ability to undertake daring action for justice in spite of the presence of well-founded fear. It is patient endurance of either pain or tedium in the pursuit of justice. In Saint Thomas's words, "Now courage in civil affairs establishes a man's spirit in human justice, to preserve which he endures mortal danger; and in the same way the courage which is a gift of grace strengthens the human mind in the good of God's justice, which is won through faith in Jesus Christ."[9] In the Thomistic account of the moral life, then, courage is founded on knowledge of what is just, but it goes beyond knowledge by disposing the spirit to act for justice in the face of opposition.

Courage has two principle forms: daring and endurance. Thomas argues that endurance in the face of adversity is the highest form of courage. Endurance in the cause, even to the point of laying down one's life, is the noblest example of courageous action. Thomas cites the Scriptures to support this contention: "Blessed are they who suffer presecution for justice sake, for theirs is the kingdom of heaven" (Matt. 5:10). This courage of endurance to the point of martyrdom is both the great challenge and the great gift of Christians who are faced with violent opposition in their pursuit of justice.

But Saint Thomas is quite clear that the patient endurance of evil is not the whole of courage. Courage is also vigorously active. As he puts it, "Courage ought not merely to endure unflinchingly the pressure of difficult situations by restraining fear, it ought also to make a calculated attack, when it is necessary to eliminate difficulties in order to win safety for the future. Such action appears to belong to daring. Therefore courage is concerned with fears and acts of daring, restraining the first and measuring the second."[10] Courageous action is daring directed by the norm or measure of justice. It involves passion and even anger. Following Aristotle, Thomas argues that the most natural form of courageous action is an attack against evil provoked by anger. Such rightly directed anger, he says, "is true courage."[11] Thus, in Thomistic thought, assertiveness in the cause of justice is part of the virtuous life of the Christian.

Both the active courage of assertiveness and the patient courage of endurance are needed if Christians are to develop staying power in the quest for justice today. There is no simple psychological or educational recipe for producing such virtues in others, or even in oneself. Just as knowledge of justice does not produce justice of itself, so knowledge of the importance of courage does not produce courageous action. Nevertheless, some suggestions can be made about resources that make courageous staying power more likely in the pursuit of justice.

First, some immediate experience of the suffering of the victims of injustice is important if one's heart is to remain sensitive to the continuing need for action. The effective agent of social justice needs to feel and taste the reality of injustice. This experience is the foundation of the rightly directed anger that Saint Thomas sees as the "most natural" source of courageous action. In American society, some continuing exposure to these harsh realities will serve as an antidote to the experience of social complexity that tends to paralyze the will. People entering into the task of seeking justice need such experience if their hearts as well as their minds are to be attuned to the evil they seek to combat. Those who have been working at the task for a long time, especially if they are in administrative positions in social agencies or teaching positions in academia or the Church, also need some continuing firsthand experience of the struggles of the victims of our society. Such experience can help sustain the affective significance of their work. This suggests that both students and teachers in programs of education for justice need to spend at least a part of their time in personal contact with the poor and other marginal people in our society. This will help develop courage and staying power.

Second, courage depends on what might be called knowledgeability or practical wisdom. This is the quality of mind that has traditionally been called prudence by moral theologians and philosophers. It is the ability to discern the possibilities for greater justice as they exist in the concrete situation. It is therefore more than an understanding of the general principles of social ethics. It depends on an understanding of the conflict and change at work in the area one seeks to address. Since these dynamics are almost inevitably complex and multileveled in our society, prudence includes the ability to live with such complexity, so it is in fact a quality of heart as well as of mind. Having practical wisdom means that one is able to sustain protracted analysis of complex issues without leaping to a premature division of the world into groups of villains and groups of victims. It also calls for a theological awareness that in human history the wheat and the tares are growing together and the task of separating them completely should be left to God on the day of judgment. When humans attempt to do so, they misunderstand the nature of their own abilities and usually fail to promote that form of justice that is within their power to effect. Thus, discerning prudence has the humility, patience, and wisdom to seize the opportunities for justice as they are offered rather than insisting that these opportunities should appear in simpler form. Complexity is a characteristic of the struggle for justice both in social fact and in the proper theological interpretation of this social reality. Recognition of the reality and inevitability of this complexity is a condition for sustained and courageous action.

Religious education for justice should thus resist the frequently strong impulse to reduce this complexity to simple, clear-cut interpretations of injustice. Whether in outlining the politics of an issue or in sketching its theological significance, the fullest possible understanding is necessary if the appropriate action is to be taken. Education for justice thus needs to encourage participants to develop this discerning practical wisdom that rests on an ability to see the world as it is.

A third means that can assist in the development of courage and staying power in the quest for justice is involvement in a supportive community of peers and co-workers. Experience of injustice and a willingness to live with complexity are necessary qualities of the person who is committed to the long-term task of seeking justice in society. But these indispensable qualities can exact a heavy emotional and psychological price. Close friends and trusted colleagues in the work for justice can assist each other to bear these burdens. They can also provide encouragement and a sense of hope to each other. Their mutual support can stimulate both the daring and the patience that the work demands. Advocates of justice are much more likely to sustain the struggle over the long haul if they help each other to do so. The solitary warrior for the cause of right may be a romantic image for some who are dedicated to the tasks of social ministry; those who try to live according to this image, however, are prime candidates for disillusionment and burnout. Indeed, part of courage is the admission that one cannot really even begin this kind of work without a lot of help and guidance from others. Even though every community is touched by the reality of sin and is therefore to some extent in itself unjust, people cannot become effective agents of change without truly communal support. As David Baily Harned has remarked, "Courage is courageous enough to ask for assistance from the same communities and powers that threaten the self with captivity, and it is courageous enough not to desert its responsibilities there."[12]

Courage and staying power depend on the presence of hope. Communal support is itself a powerful source of hope in human life. To the extent that such support is present, even the triumph of great injustice in a particular situation is not the final verdict on the case. Education for justice thus should be education for collaboration, cooperation, and community. It should include collaboration and cooperation between the students themselves in their activities and assignments. Collaboration between students and those outside the classroom who are involved in similar concerns may also be a useful way to foster this goal. And a cooperative relationship between teacher and student will be of great educational benefit as well.

A fourth factor in the development of courage and staying power is the experience that some success in the struggle for justice has been and remains possible. Though the final victory of justice is an eschatological hope, perseverance in such hope depends on seeing signs of its presence already in history. And indeed there *are* victories of justice over injustice in our world. Seeing these victories, hearing the stories of how they came to pass, getting to know the people who made them possible, and participating oneself in bringing them about are all sources of the courage and patience that is so important in the quest for justice. Developing such courage depends in part, therefore, on undertaking tasks where there is at least some hope of success. Estimation of the chance of success is, of course, related to how large one's vision and confidence already are. A magnanimous person will dare much greater efforts than will a pusillanimous one. Those who have already some taste of confidence are thus enabled to risk more and achieve more. From an educational point of view, this suggests that attention to achievements in the history of the struggle for justice is as important as focusing on the most oppressive and violent injustices in the world today. The theological principle that we can only experience conversion because of the presence of grace makes good educational sense as well. We can only develop the courage to dare great things by experiencing the possibility of achievement in our lives and in the lives of others.

A fifth quality of the courageous and patient advocate of justice is a confident and serene acknowledgment of the limits of his or her capabilities, energy, time, and wisdom. Magnanimity is not the same as the effort to ape God by becoming responsible for everything that happens on the face of the earth. Because we human beings are finite and limited creatures, human courage includes the ability to accept our honest limits. Daring and endurance will acquire true focus to the extent that these limits are accepted. Such acceptance is the beginning of the courage truly to be oneself and truly to give oneself to the struggle for justice. Educationally this implies that religious education for justice needs to be education in self-knowledge as well.

All five of these suggestions for ways of fostering courage are a reminder of the fact that the final victory of justice is not fully within our power to achieve. There is a gap between every human effort and the final achievement of true justice. It is precisely because there is such a gap that courage remains a constant necessity. The final source of courage, therefore, is not a trust that one's energy or anger or one's successes and the support one receives from co-workers will finally usher in the kingdom of justice and peace. Confidence in these powers alone is not courage but foolhardy illusion. If courage is truly to be courage at all, it must rest on a movement beyond ourselves, in which we entrust ourselves to God and regain from God the courage to act with steadfastness. As theologians such as Karl Rahner, Paul Tillich, and Leo O'Donovan have pointed out, true courage is ultimately not only rooted in faith but even identical with faith.[13]

Courage is a trust that in the act of self-surrender that all work for justice demands we will not finally be destroyed. Rather, we will be saved, along with those whose burdens we seek to alleviate. As Leo O'Donovan has put it, "Our courage, accordingly, is meant to have the same course as the courage of Christ: for the sake of life into the danger of death and then, through a power which belongs to God alone, through death to eternal life. The price we are willing to pay for our greatest hopes about life can be nothing less than life itself; the love we learn for our fellow human beings and for our world can only be fulfilled if it is put to the test of what seems to be the end of love."[14] Courage is thus not simply a moral virtue to be cultivated by techniques of self-improvement. These techniques, including the five just suggested in this essay, are important parts of every Christian life, but if courage is to have a really trustworthy foundation, it must be founded ultimately on faith in God and love for God as revealed in Jesus Christ. Just as contemporary theologians can identify true courage with true faith, so Augustine saw courage as one aspect of our love of God and neighbor. And the traditions of Christian spirituality, drawing on scriptural sources, have long known that courage is one of the gifts of the Holy Spirit, poured into our hearts by the grace of Christ. Similarly, the enduring courage we call patience is one of the fruits of the presence of the Spirit in our hearts.

From a theological point of view, therefore, we can see that the development of courage in the quest for justice is a religious and spiritual task as much as it is a moral one. This is not to say that religious faith is somehow a substitute for the arduous task of developing the capacity to act in the face of frustration or to endure in the face of setbacks in the quest for justice. Rather, it is simply to point out that education for justice can help foster genuine courage to the extent that it is genuinely Christian education. Its final goal is not to indoctrinate students with the appropriate ideology or to form in them the appropriate instincts. Its ultimate goal is to introduce them to the reality of the God who is revealed in Jesus Christ and whose Spirit is present working for justice in the world today. To the extent that religious education forgets this primary purpose, it seems likely to fail to lead students to either justice or courage. To the extent that it faithfully pursues this primary good, it will be led to undertake all its other tasks in the service of justice as well.

NOTES

1. Second Vatican Council, *Gaudium et spes*, Pastoral Constitution on the Church in the Modern World, translated in Walter M. Abbott, *The Documents of Vatican II* (New York: The America Press, 1966), no. 1.
2. Lawrence Kohlberg, "Education for Justice: A Modern Statement of the Platonic View," in James Gustafson et al., *Moral Education: Five Lectures* (Cambridge: Harvard University Press, 1970), p. 58. This essay has been reprinted under the revised title, "Education for Justice: A Modern Statement of the Socratic View," in Kohlberg, *The Philosophy of Moral Development: Essays in Moral Development*, vol. 1 (New York: Harper & Row, 1981).
3. For a very helpful analysis of the recent theological discussion of original sin, see Brian O. McDermott, "The Theology of Original Sin: Recent Developments," *Theological Studies* 38 (1977), pp. 478–512. Reinhold Niebuhr's critique of John Dewey's philosophy rests on Niebuhr's re-appropriation of the doctrine of original sin. See Padraic O'Hare, "Religious Education for Social Justice," *Religious Education* 75 (January/February 1980), pp. 76–89. Contemporary justice-oriented education could well benefit from a similar re-appropriation, though that is a task that goes beyond the scope of this essay.
4. For moving narratives of the lives of five Christians who gave their lives in

response to the Christian vocation to promote justice, see William O'Malley, *The Voice of Blood: Five Christian Martyrs of Our Time* (Maryknoll, N.Y.: Orbis Books, 1980).

5. See Peter Berger, Brigitte Berger, and Hansfried Kellner, *The Homeless Mind: Modernization and Consciousness* (New York: Vintage Books, 1973), especially chapter 3.

6. Alfred C. Kammer, S. J., " 'Burn-out'—A Contemporary Dilemma for the Jesuit Social Activist," *Studies in the Spirituality of Jesuits* 10:1 (January 1978), p. 1.

7. See Jerry Edelwich and Archie Brodsky, *Burnout: Stages of Disillusionment in the Helping Professions* (New York: Human Sciences Press, 1980).

8. James J. Gill, S. J., M.D., "Burnout: A Growing Threat in Ministry," *Human Development* 1:2 (Summer 1980), p. 22.

9. Saint Thomas Aquinas, *Summa Theologiae*, II^{a}II^{ae}, q. 124, art. 3, ad 1. The translation is that of the Blackfriar's edition, vol. 42 (New York: McGraw-Hill, 1966).

10. Ibid., q. 123, art. 3.

11. Ibid., q. 123, art. 11, ad 3.

12. David Baily Harned, *Faith and Virtue* (Philadelphia: Pilgrim Press, 1973), p. 143.

13. See Karl Rahner, "Faith as Courage," translated by Rosaleen Ockenden, in *Meditations on Freedom and the Spirit* (New York: Seabury, 1978), pp. 5–29; Paul Tillich, *The Courage to Be* (New Haven: Yale University Press, 1952); Leo J. O'Donovan, "The Courage of Faith: An Essay in Honor of William F. Lynch's Seventieth Birthday," *Thought* 53 (1978), pp. 369–83.

14. O'Donovan, p. 382.

QUESTIONS FOR REFLECTION AND DISCUSSION

1. What are the main causes of people's fear or apathy about becoming involved in the Christian struggle for justice?

2. What are the chief threats to long-term commitment to the work of justice for North American Christians today?

3. How would you distinguish courage from foolhardy aggressiveness? What makes patience different from lethargy and apathy?

4. How can courageous and patient work for justice be supported by families, by educators, by friends, by parishes, and by religious communities?

5. What are some of the ways that Christian faith is a source of courage and patience in the quest for justice?

2. Education for Priesthood

MARIA HARRIS

Introduction

Several years ago, as a member of an ecumenical group, I was asked to introduce myself in terms of my religious tradition, naming as I did so that element in the tradition most important to me. I did not have much difficulty: a born and bred Catholic, I related that fact and then chose the central element. "Eucharist," I said. I remember the incident clearly because what struck me at the time was that of a group of thirty-six people, only six of whom were Catholics, each of those six chose to identify exactly the same reality as central. Without any prior knowledge of one another, all of us gave "Eucharist" as our response.

The story illustrates an understanding we tend to have of ourselves as Catholics: we are a sacramental people. Sacrament, and especially the sacrament of the Eucharist, defines who we are religiously.[1] And that understanding spills over into our daily lives. We are a people of ritual and gesture. We are proud bearers of an artistic tradition that includes painting, sculpture, drama, and music. We take easily to the notion that the divine reveals itself in flesh and blood and oil and water and fire. We rarely need an excuse for a party and rarely have a party without wine—in part because our religious leaders drink wine publicly in our most important rite. Ours is, to use a passage from Nathan Scott, the "persistently central assumption" that "certain objects or actions or words or places belonging to the ordinary spheres of life may convey to us a unique illumination of the whole mystery of our existence, because in these actions and realities . . . something 'numinous' is resident, something holy and gracious."[2]

Wonderful, as far as it goes. Fine. But there is a shadow side to all this, a shadow that is growing. Ultimately, the shadow points to an issue of justice. I refer to the developing awareness among the most active people in the Catholic church of a boundary with reference to sacrament; a line not to be crossed; an awareness that getting too close to the meaning of sacrament and to the exercise of sacramental power, as many are doing, is raising many questions that if put to the tradition will ineluctably change it in the most fundamental way. The issue might be called Education for Priesthood.

Do not understand me too quickly. I am not writing here as an advocate for sacramental ordination of women, although the Catholic church's present practice in this regard seems to me patently and sinfully unjust. And I am not only writing of the much publicized and openly acknowledged celebration of shared bread, wine, and memory taking place throughout the world without benefit of clergy.[3] These are certainly elements in the situation. Nonetheless, I am speaking of a much wider set of activities, engaged in, as far as we know, by people of both sexes, of every age, race, and nationality.[4] Catechists and teachers everywhere are initiating people into sacramental life, whether that is baptism or confirmation or Eucharist; DRE's, counselors, and pastoral "ministers" are engaged in healing of brokenness and failure and sin—indeed, they are "hearing confessions"; members of the laity are witnessing marriages with the approval of the Holy See.[5] All of these activities—initiation, reconciliation, forgiving sin, celebrating marriage, remembering with bread and wine—are traditionally sacramental actions or, put another way, priestly activity. *Implicitly*, education in this priestly activity is going on everywhere. But *explicitly*, education for priesthood is still spoken of as the exclusive right of a diocese or a seminary, and *priest* is still thought of as a term referring exclusively and univocally to an ordained, male celibate publically granted faculties by a bishop. My argument here is that this situation needs to be challenged and changed. And my thesis is that as long as we continue to convey, by word and action, that only one form of priestly education, one definition of priest, one repository of sacramental power, exists, we perpetuate an educational system that is dishonest, unfair, and injust. Put positively, education for priesthood is an issue of social justice. How this issue might be addressed is the burden of this essay.

Models of Priesthood

The first item on the educational agenda is an exploration of the meaning of priesthood. Here I would offer as illuminating the superior study by Walter Burghardt, "What Is a Priest?"[6] He points out that in different periods of the church's history, several different theologies and models of priesthood have come into prominence, and mentions five. First is the *jurisdictional* model, which sees the priest holding a fullness of authority, where the meaning of "to teach" is to impose authoritative doctrine as a matter of obedience. In this model, admission to and denial of sacraments are quasijuridical actions. Second is the *cultic* model, found in much patristic and medieval theology, in which the priest is regarded as the hierophant, the performer of sacred mysteries. In this model, the priest offers sacrifice in the place of the community. Third is the *pastoral* model, evident in much of the New Testament but recovered in Vatican II, in which the priest is viewed primarily as pastor or community leader. A fourth model is the *prophetic* model. Here, a person is seen predominantly as proclaimer of the word of God, the role being based on the conceptions of prophet and apostle found in the Hebrew and Christian Scriptures. This is a model especially evident in Protestant theology, in which the term *priest* is often shunned as too heavily weighted with cultic overtones. Fifth, and finally, is the *monastic* model, in which the priest is viewed primarily as a holy, sacred person, a guru, or a spiritual director. In this model, monastic spirituality is in great part imposed on diocesan seminaries and diocesan priests and practices like meditation, recitation of the office, community life, and celibacy extended to all. The priest, in this model, is expected to be withdrawn from the world and its vanities.[7]

Among the many values of the Burghardt typology is its illumination of the historical reality that in the course of church history, not one but many models of priesthood have existed and, in several cases, overlapped. This suggests to me that although models of priesthood develop, even with the guidance of the Spirit of God, no one meaning can be canonized or considered forever normative. Different historical and social reality calls for different and more appropriate models and meanings. The New Guinea missionary William Burrows, for example, points out that all five of these understandings of priesthood arose in the Second Church, that is, in the church of western Europe and North America.[8] Had priesthood developed from the lives of the people of the Third Church (the churches south of the equator, who will comprise 70 percent of the world's Catholic population by the year 2000)[9] we would undoubtedly have come to different understandings of priesthood. Those of us who are feminists make similar claims; these models arose almost exclusively out of male experience. If women had, as they did in the early church,[10] continued to exercise priestly roles, we would understand priesthood differently today.

But Burghardt's essay is instructive in another area. Having noted the universal priesthood of all Christians, his point of arrival is the specialized ministry of the ordained priest. The title of the essay, "What Is a Priest?" could as easily be "What Is an Ordained Priest?" The unquestioned and underlying assumption appears to be that the real meaning of priest and priesthood, put more directly, the *real* priest, is the ordained male clergyman. Acknowledgment is made in passing of the priesthood of the entire people, but the focus tends not to see that universal priesthood as primary or normative. I find this point of arrival pervasive in writing and teaching on priesthood, and it is precisely the point I wish to challenge. My claim is that the meaning of priesthood that needs to be stressed in today's Church—or the model of priesthood toward which all people need to be educated —is not that of the specialist; it is their *own* priesthood that needs to be taught. It is the universal priesthood that is normative, and it is precisely the neglect of this wider, more inclusive and historically grounded understanding that is unjust. And note well: A charge that I am Protestantizing the tradition will not work here; the claim to universal priesthood is a deeply rooted Catholic reality.

Warrants for Universal Priesthood

For those of us who would teach this universal priesthood with utmost seriousness, the warrants are extensive. The First Epistle of Peter states it thus:

> Come to the Lord, the living stone rejected as worthless by humans, but chosen as valuable by God. Come as living stones, and let yourselves be used in building the spiritual temple, where you will serve as holy *priests.* . . .

> You are the chosen race, the King's *priests*, the holy nation, chosen to proclaim the wonderful acts of God, who called you from the darkness into the marvelous light. [2:4–5,9]

Chrysostom, on baptism, also stresses this theme: "So art thou thyself made priest (and prophet and king) in the laver,"[11] although this understanding is lost in the following centuries. Rekindled with the Reformation, the universal priesthood is emphasized in our century prominently in Congar's *Lay People in the Church.*[12] The Vatican II decrees on the Church (pp. 31–34) and on the Laity (p. 2) are especially explicit: All share in the priestly ministry of the Christ. To quote paragraph 31 of *Lumen gentium:* "These faithful are by baptism made one body with Christ and are established among the people of God. They are in their own way made sharers in the priestly, prophetic and kingly functions of Christ."[13] More recently Hans Küng explicates a discovery now taken almost for granted: the term *priestly ministry* is not true to the Christian Scriptures when it is used for particular church ministers, but only when it is used with reference to all Christians.[14]

What I am suggesting to educators for justice, however, is not only because of grounding supplied by Küng or Congar or Vatican II or even Peter. I am also suggesting that we are impelled to teach people their priesthood because of an important category in the Christian tradition, that of the *sensus fidelium*. This category, which refers to the sense of faith residing in the Christian community, can be interpreted as the tradition alive in the contemporary experience of the community.[15] In this discussion I am claiming that the contemporary experience of innumerable members of the Catholic community is their own involvement in priesthood, an experience supported by, and grounded in, the tradition. More and more of us discover ourselves in the role of loving and trusting grace to one another, mediating the presence of God to one another, empowering one another to our own best possibilities. Such mediation, such love, such empowering is accurately understood as priestly work. And even more to the point, the one engaged in such activity is legitimately and accurately—not only metaphorically—called a priest. In other words, far more of us are priests to one another than is usually recognized. And since this is true, justice impels us to educate to this awareness by beginning to use the term *priest* not only for one another, but for ourselves. Such is the responsibility of any education to priesthood that claims to be just.

Re-membrance and Presence: The Content of Priesthood

If priesthood is a universal vocation for all in the Church, then the community as a whole, but also individual teachers within the community, must translate the meaning of priesthood into daily activity and articulate what priesthood looks like in ordinary life. Although what follows is not inclusive, it does suggest a starting point.[16] Priestly work can be characterized as living fully in the present, out of the past.[17] The first of the priestly roles, then, becomes the task of re-membering, not only in the sense of exercising the mental faculty of memory but in the sense of bringing-forward-into-membership-once-again that which and those who may have been forgotten. Most explicitly, re-member the tradition, which is not dry, verbal lore, but the people on whose blood and bones and bodies we stand. "Tradition," wrote Chesterton, "is the extension of the franchise to that most obscure of all classes, our ancestors. It is the democracy of the dead. Tradition refuses to submit to the small and arrogant oligarchy of those who merely happen to be walking about."[18] It needs to be stressed that we re-member in three ways: (1) by telling the stories of the people who are the tradition; (2) by incorporating the nonhuman universe—the trees, and animals and rocks and sky—into the stories as our brothers and sisters, refusing to dis-member the earth; and (3) by ritualizing the Story of the Death and Resurrection of Jesus, which is sign and sacrament for all people of their own death and resurrection, or what in liturgical language is called anamnesis. Universal priesthood is the guarantor that the entire story will be re-membered, the entire tradition, the entire earth. A too narrow and specialized priesthood has in the past too often resulted in the impression that the entire story is one of popes and bishops and clergy and founders of religious orders; of virgins and martyrs and widows.[19] A wider concept of priesthood could result in a more complete rendering of the story of the women and men who are our past in a beautiful and welcome revisionist history.[20]

The complement to re-membering the past is creating the present, more accurately, the priestly work of creating presence itself. For priesthood is not only the saying of the word, "Re-member." It is a symbolizing capacity as well, a sacramental act in which that which graces us is the ability to make present the divine. The sacramental imagination at the heart of Catholicism rests on the conviction that any reality, but especially material, physical, tangible reality, can embody the holy. The Christ is the sacrament of the encounter with the presence of God; the Church is the sacrament of the encounter with the presence of the Christ; the people who are the church are the sacraments for the encounter with all of these—and with much else besides. "The range of the Christian sacramental imagination is not restricted to the seven traditional sacraments. It is capable of seeing in the whole cosmos and in all human relationships a kind of symbolic realization of God's covenant with humanity."[21]

The invitation to priestly activity is intensely practical, yet intensely poetic. It can refer, for example, to attentiveness to environment as a necessary component of human work, with special awareness of the diversity of settings where the divine is present. This invitation to priesthood ought not be conceived, however, as an invitation to a dilettante game. Dilettantism, as most people realize, is the nonserious dabbling within a presumably serious area. The invitation is instead, to use a phrase of Elizabeth Sewell, "an invitation to the universe."[22] It depends on the mind and body working seriously with the imagination, "being keenly alive to every possible sense impression, feeling and intuition, observing passionately and with joy by means of its five senses everything that is going on inside and outside itself, and ready always to relate sensations, feelings and images, not just out of a vague experimentalism but because of a realization this is a wonderful means of discovering new meaning."[23] The areas of human life most obviously open to this priestly or sacramental activity, in which people engage and are engaged by the earth, one another, and God are those where they work, love, pray, and study, as well as where they worship. Thus, the priestly person must be everywhere. Those who speak of their lives as engagement in a "ministry of presence" are deeply aware of this. They are priestly people who recognize that every limited reality can communicate, reveal, and disclose the presence of divinity, who know that although God never leaves identical fingerprints, the divine trace is everywhere.

Agencies for Priesthood Education

Currently, at least in the United States, four agencies are engaged in education for universal priesthood in the sense described thus far. Although this is usually not explicit or openly asserted, the courses, curricular patterns, ministerial activities, exercise of authority, and sense of self being developed in such agencies point inexorably in this direction. For these agencies, what might be advocated by those of us encouraging universal priesthood?

1. *Seminaries.* Some Catholic seminaries offer a Master of Divinity degree without discrimination. It could be made very clear in these institutions that an identical course of study and an identical preparation are being offered to those who are candidates for ordination and those who are not, and that the terms *priestly activity, common priesthood,* or simply *priesthood* can be claimed by all. The only distinction to be made for graduates will then be that all are priests though some are ordained priests. Those Catholic seminaries that admit only unmarried men as degree candidates have a somewhat different, although related, task. For, in addition to clarifying the distinctions just made, these schools need to make it clear to their students that the training they are receiving is in no way exclusive to their institution and that upon graduation they will undoubtedly be working with both female and male colleagues with the same academic credentials. Many newly ordained Catholic clergymen are apparently unaware of this reality, and authority conflicts in local settings thereby arise unnecessarily. Realistic and honest preparation in seminary could obviate such occurrences. Those Catholic students (whose number grows yearly) currently studying in nondenominational or Protestant seminaries need some Catholic community in those settings in which their own priestly identity is studied and explored. Often, without reflection and in their desire for active ministry, such stu-

dents choose membership in another Christian communion without giving serious consideration to naming and exercising the priesthood that is theirs by reason of baptism and confirmation.

However, the point of all this is not primarily for students in seminary to come to an understanding of their own individual priesthood. The salient and critical point is that the opportunity to focus on priesthood through study ought to impel such students to empower the priesthood of the people with whom they work, and to educate communities to their universal priesthood. It may even lead to the realization that seminaries as institutions, in the long run, may be counterproductive to such education and empowering.

2. *Graduate Schools of Pastoral Ministry.* The last decade has witnessed a remarkable growth of programs in pastoral ministry, almost all of which are situated (in this country) in large metropolitan areas and attended by women and men from all over the world as well as from the United States. Boston College, Fordham, Seattle, Loyola-Chicago, and the University of San Francisco, for example, continue to graduate people skilled in Scripture, religious education, theology, and pastoral ministry. However, these programs (which tend to be administered by, or under the jurisdiction of, ordained men, and whose faculties are still largely clergy) do not describe themselves as programs of priestly ministry or priestly education. Obviously, the term *pastoral ministry* is intended to connote a set of works beyond the priestly—especially prophetic, educational, and political work. Nonetheless, in the exclusive use of *pastoral* and avoidance of the term *priestly* there may be a too easy or an unexamined acceptance of the narrow and univocal meaning of priesthood I am questioning here. This could be construed as a reluctance to face the enormous institutional and systemic changes for which such places are at least in part responsible. Since some opponents of the formal ordination of women and/or married people have been quite articulate in pointing out that ministry can be as universal as anyone wishes but priesthood is a special prerogative, it remains problematical that graduate schools have chosen the term *pastoral ministry* for their work and thus far avoided *priesthood*. It may be an astute, temporary decision, but somewhere the education for priesthood implicitly occurring in these schools will have to be acknowledged, named, and faced directly.

3. *Diocesan Agencies.* The people who graduate from seminaries and graduate schools of pastoral ministry often go on to take diocesan positions as directors of religious education or directors of pastoral ministry. Their understanding of their own priestly vocation can have a direct effect on those with whom they work, especially in two areas.

The first is the hiring and appointment of personnel; the second is education. I would contend that the power of these two functions lies in the influence wielded with reference to church order. Appointment of personnel to local positions is the activity of creating order in the church. "In looking for the meaning of order in the church, it is necessary to leave behind the theological and canonical system which had its point of departure in the hierarchy and look instead to the reality of the unit which is the people of God in Christ and locate grace and discernment in that body."[24] That is precisely what is happening; the perspective of diocesan agencies is more and more "the reality of the local unit" with its particular needs and gifts, and assignments are routinely made with this as the focus. This is especially true of assignments of nonordained people.

Educationally, it falls to the diocesan agency, because of its more extensive view, to summon local communities to their own exercise of priesthood. The diocesan agency is called to offer resources, to be a consultant where appropriate, and to help local units in forming alliances with one another. As such, the diocesan community can become a demonstration community of communities with the local church as the basic unit, reminding all that the world Church exists only as such a communion of communities, each of which is called to respond to the needs of its own particular people, who are called, in turn, to act on their own priestly vocations outward to the world. The diocesan Church, even more than the national or international Church, can educate the local Church to embodiment of this possibility.

4. *The Local Church.*   More than seminary or graduate school or even diocese, the local church exists as the primary unit of education for priesthood. In referring to priesthood several years ago, Rosemary Ruether suggested that the processes of selecting and educating for such ministry should arise from within the community itself. "The community should be engaged first of all, in theological self-reflection on its own mission. Out of this process especially talented and committed persons develop who are designated by the congregation for more specialized training to be equipped to become teachers and pastors."[25] Although concurring with Ruether that the congregation should be the locus for religious self-reflection and the place where people come to a realization of their own particular roles, I think it necessary to stress that the local church, as the place of baptism and confirmation, is the setting where one learns the intention of these sacraments. They are directed toward the involvement of the Catholic

Christian in her and his own priesthood. For the local community is the natural place where priesthood begins: initiating, healing, forgiving, celebrating, and engaging in sacramental life. Here is born that "invitation to the universe" whose acceptance is the fullness and completion of priesthood.

Conclusion

At the Detroit Ordination Conference in 1975, Carroll Stuhlmuller suggested that if the Roman Catholic Church continued to restrict priesthood to celibate male Christians, then pastoral activity—like teaching, preaching, healing, counseling, re-affirming forgiveness, inspirational leadership at prayer—would become more and more noneucharistic.[26] For a while during the past decade, it seemed his prediction was coming true. As always, people who did not have access to an ordained clergyman chose not to celebrate the Lord's Supper, whereas places that had always offered a time for daily mass began to schedule "nonliturgical" or "paraliturgical" services in place of liturgy. Recently, however, that seems to be reversing. My own conviction is that the implicit education in priesthood occurring today is the major reason, and that if that education were more conscious and intentional, the reversal would be even more rapid. The movement has been inaugurated, in addition, by "a growing sense that the existing institutions have ceased adequately to meet the problems posed by an environment that they have in part created."[27] Along with increasingly well educated parishioners, graduates of seminaries and schools of pastoral ministry are theologically and academically astute enough to realize that they, along with the official hierarchy, are *also* the Roman Catholic church. They are realizing that when the rules and conceptual understandings that keep a particular group in power are made exclusively by that group, such rules and understandings are inevitably called into question.

At the deepest level, however, the truth is burgeoning that priesthood is the gift and grace and glory of the entire people, and that instead of being false to one's tradition in performing sacramental action, universal priesthood mandates such action in simple justice. And this includes eucharistic action as well: chastened, simple, reverent action in which people know their own participation in mystery with continual yet joyful surprise because it is constant gift, rather than secure possession. The Catholic sacramental identity is holding firm, for today as repeatedly in the past, the primary place we recognize both ourselves and one another is in the breaking of the bread.

NOTES

1. See Richard McBrien, *Catholicism* (Minneapolis: Winston Press, 1980), vol. 2, p. 722. Here McBrien asks what is *characteristically* Catholic, and after listing grace triumphant over sin, tradition, and peoplehood, writes, "Most significantly, its sense of *sacramentality* and its correlative sense of the importance of *mediation*. God is present to us through signs and symbols, and the presence of God is effective for us through these same visible signs and instruments." The italics are his.

2. In *The Wild Prayer of Longing* (New Haven: Yale University Press, 1971), p. 49.

3. See for example *National Catholic Reporter*, 17:35 (July 17, 1981); see David Power, *Gifts That Differ: Lay Ministries Established and Unestablished* (New York: Pueblo Publishing, 1980), who writes, "Many persons today exercise the role of presidency in community and liturgy without ordination," p. 131.

4. Read for example Edward Schillebeeckx, *Ministry* (New York: Crossroads, 1981), especially some of the speeches of bishops throughout the world, found in chapter 6, pp. 105–126; William Burrows, *New Ministries: The Global Context* (Maryknoll, N.Y.: Orbis Books, 1980).

5. Power, p. 23.

6. In Michael Taylor, ed., *The Sacraments* (New York: Alba House, 1981), pp. 157–70. First published in the Jesuit periodical of spirituality, *The Way Supplement* 23 (Autumn 1974).

7. Pp. 162–64. Another, perhaps better known, typology is the threefold model of bishop-priest-deacon. See also Geoffrey Kelly, "Priesthood in the Context of Brotherhood" in *Priestly Brothers* (Wheaton, Md.: National Assembly of Religious Brothers, 1975), pp. 5–19. Kelly writes, "It would seem that the early church had three models of the priesthood: the hierarchical (apostles and the episkopos-presbyteros), the charismatic-prophetic (a case might be made for including 'teachers' from *Didache* XIV–XV and from Acts 13:2–3), and the communitarian in which the natural or appointed leader would preside."

8. Burrows, p. 118.

9. See Walbert Buhlmann, *The Coming of the Third Church* (Maryknoll, N.Y.: Orbis Books, 1977).

10. See Elisabeth Schussler Fiorenza, "Word, Spirit and Power: Women in Early Christian Communities," in Rosemary Ruether and Eleanor McLaughlin, eds., *Women of Spirit* (New York: Simon & Schuster, 1979), pp. 29–70; see Elisabeth M. Tetlow, *Women and Ministry in the New Testament* (New York: Paulist Press, 1980).

11. Cited by Hans-Ruedi Weber in "The Spontaneous Missionary Church," *Laity*, reprints from nos. 2–6 (Geneva: Department of the Laity, World Council of Churches, 1962), p. 78.

12. (Westminster, Md.: Newman, 1959).

13. *The Documents of Vatican II*, Walter Abbott, general editor (New York: The America Press, 1966).

14. See *Why Priests?* (Garden City, N.Y.: Doubleday, 1972), p. 42.

15. See James D. Whitehead and Evelyn Eaton Whitehead, *Method in Ministry* (New York: Seabury, 1980), p. 17. This theme is developed by the Whiteheads throughout this book. See, for example, pp. 18–19, 56–57, 86.

16. For a more developed description of priestly ministry, especially as related to teaching, prayer, and community, see my *Portrait of Youth Ministry* (New York: Paulist Press, 1981).

17. In contrast to prophecy, which can be thought of as "living fully in the present out of the future." I am indebted to David Reid, in *What Are They Saying about the Prophets?* (New York: Paulist Press, 1980), for this distinction. See p. 16.
18. Gilbert K. Chesterton, *Orthodoxy* (Garden City, N.Y.: Doubleday Image Book, 1959), p. 48.
19. "So far, history of the church has been written as the story of bishops and priests and popes. They are the holders of power, and the story of a society is told in terms of the exercise of power. The story of 'other' ministries is usually limited to narrating their subordination to priesthood. Perhaps history is now taking a new turn. What has been on the edges may move toward the center. Such a history would be written with different views of the church community, different images of power." Power, p. 83.
20. Of such historical necessity, historian Mary Kay Thompson Tetreault notes "we are socialized to attribute historical significance to certain activities rather than others. The process of including women's experiences in our histories does not mean simply adding materials to traditional histories. It means rethinking much of . . . history," See "Women in U.S. History: Beyond a Patriarchal Perspective," in *CIBC Bulletin*, 11:5 (1980), p. 10.
21. David Hollenbach, "A Prophetic Church and the Catholic Sacramental Imagination," in John C. Haughey, ed., *The Faith that Does Justice* (New York: Paulist Press, 1977), p. 253.
22. "The Death of the Imagination," reprinted in Nathan Scott, ed., *The New Orpheus* (New York: Sheed & Ward, 1964), p. 375.
23. Ibid.
24. Power, p. 116.
25. See *New Woman, New Earth* (New York: Seabury, 1974), p. 81.
26. See "Women's Place: A Biblical View," in *Women and Catholic Priesthood: An Expanded Vision*, edited by Anne Marie Gardiner (New York: Paulist Press, 1976), p. 28.
27. Thomas S. Kuhn, *The Structure of Scientific Revolutions*, rev. ed., (Chicago: University of Chicago Press, 1970), p. 92.

QUESTIONS FOR REFLECTION AND DISCUSSION

1. How would the question, "But what about ordained priests?" prove the thesis of this essay?

2. How might the experience of women or a southern hemisphere Christian change the meaning of priesthood?

3. In what ways is pastoral ministry the same as priestly ministry? In what ways different?

4. What are some reasons for sharing Eucharist without benefit of clergy? What are some reasons for *not* celebrating Eucharist without clergy?

5. What are some examples from your own life that demonstrate your engagement in sacramental and priestly activity?

3. Social Reform: On the Way to Justice

GABRIEL MORAN

IN THIS ESSAY on the need for social reform I begin with the admission that I have always been puzzled by the word *social*. I could never understand the frequent use of the word in terms like *social welfare, social work, social programs, social justice*. I suspected that the modifier *social* gets in the way of our perceiving the problem before our eyes. Often the word *social* seems merely to be a badge by which people who are called liberal can recognize one another.

I think I have discovered something about the use of the word *social*, and I would like to share it. If my discovery has any validity then undoubtedly other people already are aware of what I have to offer. Even if that be the case, it may still be worthwhile to play with the ambiguities of the word *social* so as to understand better the need for reform and a role for churches. What I wish to suggest is that the range of contributions needed may be wider than what religious and political liberalism assumes is social reform. I will begin with a case study in the use of *social*, namely, the religious education movement in the early twentieth century. I will then trace the rise in history of *society* and *social*, relying mainly on the writing of Hannah Arendt. Then I will draw three conclusions about social reform and the struggle for social justice.

I

The literature of progressive education early in this century used no word more frequently than social. The religious education movement, springing from common roots and reaction to common enemies, kept pace with the rest of educational literature in trumpeting the idea of social education. The religious, mostly Protestant, leaders of the time drew inspiration from the Social Gospel movement and also from the emerging social sciences. George Albert Coe's great book in the movement is entitled *A Social Theory of Religious Education*.[1] Coe would have agreed with H. Hartshorne's defining the end of religious education as "character that eventuates in social functioning."[2] Coe, Hartshorne, and many other Christian writers thought they had discovered something new, namely, that Christianity is a social religion.

The religious education movement had limited success in convincing either church or nonchurch world that they had found in the social the key to Christianity. Some of the opposition to the religious education movement is not difficult to understand. People with a fundamentalist mentality, especially if they are rich, have little use for the social, whether in 1900, 1940, or the 1980s. Other objections are not so easily dismissed. One book written in the 1930s, *Education for Life with God*, deserves notice. The author, W. Evans Powell, was very critical of religious education "as a sort of emotionalized social education."[3] However, he was not advocating biblical fundamentalism or individualistic morality. Instead of claiming as the right wing did that social education goes too far, Powell claimed that it did not go far enough. Specifically, it did not include the cosmic, the metaphysical, and the symbolic that are inherent to religion.

A better known writer, Reinhold Niebuhr, took on the movement in the late 1930s and early 1940s. He was generally critical of the liberal church and took particular aim at educators who "have given themselves to the fond illusion that justice through voluntary cooperation waited only upon a more universal or more adequate educational enterprise."[4] Any church educator who advocates social reform and social justice has to ponder Niebuhr's strong attack upon the social aims of religious education. Why would Reinhold Niebuhr, who was so involved in the political events of his day, be so suspicious of social religious education? Niebuhr resists all talk of social reform on the premise that we are individually and collectively caught in sin. For a long while I just could not see why Niebuhr makes the jump he does. He constantly implies that advocacy of the social is equivalent to denial of sin. Harrison Elliot, who tried to debate the issue with Niebuhr, could never convince him that the social aim of religious education did not preclude a Christian doctrine of sin.[5]

After reading many times the exchanges of Elliot and Niebuhr and after listening to many contemporary church debates I have come to this conclusion: Liberals hear a set of connotations in the word *social* that is very different from what conservatives hear. When liberals say "social" they mean "nothing less than social"; when conservatives say "social" they mean "nothing more than social." The liberal's use of *social* presumes that the enemy is individualism; thus, to be social is to be really getting to the problem not only of the individual but of the institutional patterns in which the individual lives. The conservative's use of social has a sense of the restriction of social to mere behavioral conformity. Obviously no religious group can accept "sociability" as the measure of their convictions and commitments. A mere social answer is not getting to the difficult spiritual, metaphysical, cosmic issues.

I am presuming good faith on the part of the conflicting positions. I am trying to explore what has been a controversy of many decades' standing that no doubt involves ignorance, selfishness, and lack of love. Nonetheless, much of the problem may be a genuine misunderstanding. John Henry Newman wrote: "Controversy, at least in this age, does not lie between the hosts of heaven, Michael and his angels on the one side, and the powers of evil on the other; but it is a sort of night battle, where each fights for himself, and friend and foe stand together. When men understand each other's meaning, they see, for the most part, that controversy is either superfluous or hopeless."[6]

In a recent Woody Allen movie there is a scene in which a young woman is telling Allen about the profound social message of the movie *Bicycle Thieves*. He responds by saying that he thinks the movie's meaning is far more profound than one of social message. He says it has to do with death and great cosmic issues. That scene reproduces for me much of church discussion in the 1930s and 1940s, and it is a conversation that continues in churches today. How did the word *social* come to occupy this confusing place in religious and secular discussion?

II

In trying to answer that question one is driven back into the origin and history of the idea of the social. These days people run together words like social, cultural, political, public, institutional, and so on, but each of these terms has its own history. The social sciences are not a great key to understanding on this issue because sciences have to presuppose some axioms, including the existence of whatever they study. Social sciences purport to tell us all about the social, but where did this construct come from?

In Hannah Arendt's interpretation, the Greeks divided life into the public and the private.[7] In the *polis*, which she seems to take as the ideal setting, there was the privacy of the household and the public domain of politics. The family household was caught up in the necessities of life and was regulated by the power of the father. The family was radically unequal in its members and, insofar as it was forced to labor for survival from day to day, the family was the realm of privation; hence the word private.

The public, in direct contrast, was the place of freedom. Those citizens who could leave behind the necessities of the household and step into the arena of political speech were the free men of the *polis*. Here there was radical equality with one's peers, a fact that did not exclude a struggle for excellence by individual men. Aristotle's definition of the human as the animal capable of speech directly refers to this realm of politics in which speech rather than violence shapes our lives.

Our word for society/social comes from the Latin and originally referred to a grouping for a specific purpose. That meaning is still present in our word associations. The Greeks did not have a corresponding term, or at least they did not have a term for the generalized meaning of society that eventually emerged among the Romans. Arendt credits—or blames—the Christian church for a major part in the rise of society/social.

The Christian church set out to create a bond among people that was neither private nor public. Christianity was not to be confined to the shadow life of the household. It brought the household into relation with other households and into relation with the powers and principalities of the universe. On the other hand, Christianity was not a political movement in the public realm. It claimed to unite people by a bond of charity or fraternity that does not deal in political factions. The church could see itself as a mystical union that transcended the struggle for political unity.

This distinctive rise of society/social with the church became blurred during the early Christian centuries. The church had to cope with the secular political powers that were and with a kind of intramural politics that grew up within church organization. When Aristotle was rediscovered in the West, the difference between social and political had become unclear in Latin, so that Aquinas could write: "*Homo est naturaliter politicus, id est, socialis.*" His mentor, Aristotle, would surely have agreed that the human being is by nature political, though that would have meant to Aristotle something more specific than, or at least something different from, the fact that humans associate together.

When the modern world came to birth in the seventeenth and eighteenth centuries, society/social was thoroughly established. So well established was society that it threatened to engulf the family household on the one side and the distinctive realm of politics on the other side. I will return to that point presently. What I would stress here is that society was a kind of church without Christ, where all were to behave with proper decorum and achieve a mystical harmony. The struggle for freedom in Europe and North America included the over-throwing of political despotism, but there was also a struggle for free-dom from the pressure of "social conformity." Over against the more fully conscious individual was the collective unity of the social. The hope for freedom became located in the inner life of the individual; outside in society one had to conform according to "roles."

Karl Marx was critical of the fiction that earlier economists had offered, namely, the belief that an invisible hand harmonized society. Marx perceived that conflict is as real as the harmony. However, he accepted all too readily the assumption that man should be socialized. We should be able today to recognize the dangerous meaning as well as the positive possibilities in the "socialization of man."

Robert Heilbroner's fine book *Marxism: For and Against* distin-guishes good and bad aspects of Marxism.[8] On the good side, Heil-broner finds that "the laudable element in Marxism is its declaration that the only 'meaning' to be ascribed to history is its moral unfold-ing, or more precisely, its orientation to human freedom."[9] Is such a declaration laudable? A concern to increase rather than decrease hu-man freedom is undoubtedly laudable. But is that aim best achieved by making moral unfolding to be the *only* meaning in the world?

Marxism proposed to overcome class conflict and make us into one big society. Arendt thinks that Marx's real obstacle to the project was the nation-state rather than class conflict. In any case, many other people besides Marxists dream of the "socialization of man." All men will be free when and only when this social harmony is realized. The sexist ring in the statement of the project is not accidental. Women offer a resistance to socialization in ways that Marxism and some of social science had not attended to in the past. Religion should also look carefully at any scheme to unite us all that is not acutely aware of the self-deception that infects the human race.

III

This last comment leads into a consideration of the positive and negative possibilities in the rise of society/social. As I understand Arendt's treatment, she seems almost wholly pessimistic and despair-ing about the modern emergence of society. Perhaps the effect has been for the worse, but I think we should consider the actual and potential goods in the rise of society/social during recent centuries.

The public and private realms divided life in the *polis*. Society arose not exactly as a third element placed between the two. Rather, society or the social came between the two by overlapping both of them. On the one side, the family household becomes part of social reality; on the other side, politics becomes a function of society. If that is true, what are the good and bad aspects of this development?

From the family household side, the good news is that labor is brought into the light. The people who did the toilsome tasks throughout the centuries have their lot improved. Slavery is almost bound to disappear once it is subjected to social criticism. Others who were not slaves but have carried the burden of necessary labor get some help from the social light.

I cannot imagine glorifying a situation in which the majority of people were not citizens or "free men." Before the rise of modern technology the necessities of life may have seemed to require that most people live poor, laborious, and unfree lives. We can no longer abide with the assumption that God established this order and that it is unchangeable. Today society with its technology provides the possibility that a more humane order is possible, one in which women would be fully recognized as persons and children would also be acknowledged as persons, albeit with a different set of protections than adults need.

The bad news for the family is that the distinctive character of family relations can be blurred. I am referring to the current lament that the family is disintegrating or has just disintegrated. I consider that claim—and it is a claim that has gone on for centuries—to be spurious and diversionary. Families will continue so long as the human race continues; there is not even a serious competitor to the family. Rather, the threat comes in the conformity that society demands of families. The family may not do its tasks as well as it might because its distinctive relationships, especially that of parent and child, can be sunk into the fuzziness of "social relations."

I think that Christoper Lasch's attack on social sciences/social workers as the real enemy of the family is overstated.[10] The family is not in the dire condition that Lasch assumes it is. Nonetheless, the family needs to resist the embrace of its friends and helpers, and the social experts who wish to fix up the family according to society's image. Each household has a television set that on the average is turned on for six and a half hours per day. Such an instrument is a special sign of society's conformity. Even without Big Brother watching us all in our homes (a feat now becoming technologically feasible) we may all feel a pressure to conform to whatever TV says is the right clothing, the right speech, the right way to raise children.

What happens to the political realm with the rise of the social? As with the private household, one can imagine both good and bad effects. On the positive side, the public sector can be stabilized and ordered by means that are complementary to the state and its politics. The theory that founded the United States of America supposed that local and federal governments would be limited because social organizations would be there to help. Jefferson's famous motto that "government is best which governs least" presupposes family, church, school, neighborhood, and voluntary associations.

Among these social groups are the university and the church. We seem to be clearer about the university's role in contributing to the political order without itself being political. We reserve the word *politicize* to describe the university being turned into an arm of state politics. The distinction is a crucial one, and the contribution of the university to the political health of the nation is no small issue. I think something similar should be said of the church, and I will come back to that in my conclusions. Here, I would like to note one other social group that is important to U.S. cities, namely, sports teams. A baseball or basketball team may be able to do more for racial harmony than any number of government decrees. Sports teams can be an escape from the serious issues of politics, but sports can also be a means by which people learn to cope with life and find an outlet for energies that could turn violent.

The negative side for the political in the rise of the social is similar to the family's; that is, the social swallows its friends. Politics becomes a function of society's maintaining its behavioral patterns, politics as a kind of national housekeeping. The executive branch of government comes to be called "the administration," taken up the with administering the affairs of a superhousehold. Where can one find a political body articulating the nature of our lives as political animals? Is the U.S. Senate a body for political debate or a social club of rich men? The fact that half of the U.S. Senate's members are millionaires could mean that these men are freed from life's necessities to engage in high-powered political debate. However, the absence of women and of minority groups in such a body makes one wonder if this body is not a social club for those who have enough money to get elected.

Using the above yardstick, the record of communist governments is no better and is probably worse. The Soviet government does not have men and women regularly engaged in political debate. Their political picture is an almost endless string of male administrators engaged in national housekeeping. Marx's prediction of the "withering away of the state" is often ridiculed in light of the gigantic bureaucracies in communistic countries. However, Marx may have been right in an ironic way. The state and politics have indeed withered away by being absorbed into the social form called bureaucracy. Marx had assumed that when the state withered away everyone would be free. He did not count on the state/politics withering away into a social system that is not very conducive to the freedom of the individual. Bureaucracy is a system of authority in which nobody is in charge, but that can be a coercive form of authority.

Debate, compromise, voting, and decision have a terrible fallibility about them. People who are free to decide about their lives sometimes makes serious mistakes. Some people even have to be restrained by law from criminal activity. Nonetheless, the alternative today is to turn over human life to the machinelike image of bureaucratic organization. This kind of organization may be helpful in some areas of life, but it is hardly adequate to the political life.

IV

Some of my conclusions have so far been hinted at; I have three points of summary.

First, concern with the social is on the right track, but the social has its place as means more than end. When liberal church people talk about social reform or social justice they may not be successful in escaping a parochialism. The social has to be connected to the political; if the political realm is dormant, then the social needs to be used to re-invigorate the political. The liberal assumption, as I said above, is that since the social transcends the individual, then involving oneself in the social is to have reached the real issues of the world. I am afraid other people do not hear it that way. For them social carries the meaning of a mere voluntary association of which church is, in their minds, a primary example.

Political and business leaders may be all too ready to let church people engage in social welfare and social reform. Such leaders may use a meaning of social that allows them to evade their own responsibilities for a just world. John Edgerton, president of the National Association of Manufacturers, said in 1930: "Why, I've never thought of paying men on a basis of what they need. I pay men for efficiency. Personally, I attended to all those other things, social welfare, in my church work." The connection is seldom made that explicitly. Nevertheless, government officials and business executives often do have a vague sense that the social is historically related to church work.

This attitude on the part of business and government leaders may seem disingenuous. Whether or not it is, one must know of it to make sense of much of their discussion. The secretary of housing and urban development in 1981 complained that under his predecessor the department "was strictly a social agency, not properly managed for years."[11] Many people would assume that the social is what a Department of Housing and Urban Development is for. Secretary Samuel Pierce, Jr., seemed to carry over the historical meaning of social described above. When the government began tampering with social security the assumption seemed to be: The government should probably not be in the business of providing for a social kind of security. Insofar as the government does give out money to the old it is a benefit to which no one is entitled. The poor have no right to social welfare from the government and the old have no right to social security; the government's involvement in this area is assumed to be peripheral and dispensable.

I spoke above about the danger of the social swallowing the political. Now I seem to be indicating that the political remains clearly distinct from the social. What in fact seems to have happened is that the social did eliminate most political discourse and decision, leaving the government to those who would "administer" it, namely, business officials. Thus, we have a constant traffic of men between positions in the business corporation and positions in the government. Politicians, it is thought, are the realistic hard-nosed businessmen, whereas the social realm is for pious contributions to the soft part of the economy.

Some church people in Latin America have become very aware of what is described in the preceding paragraph: the relegation of the church to social causes while an entwinement of economic and political power remains oppressive. The Latin American priests in their letter of July 1980 to Pope John Paul II wrote: "One cannot call the cause of this situation 'humanitarian' or 'social.' It is a political cause because there must be a radical transformation of structures which will put an end to the privileges of a small minority which maintains itself through great political and economic power."[12]

In sum, I am expressing caution about using the phrase "social justice" when the first question is simply justice. Putting the word social here may encourage the forming or using of associations to work for justice. The word may also help us to see some of the specific needs of people. What one has to resist is a usage of social that is closed off on the side of the political and the questions of government. At its best, our social activity mediates our exercise of power beyond social organization to economic and government strongholds.

My second point refers to the other side of the social. If, as I have just said, the term *social* could mediate between our private, personal, inner lives and institutional change, then social reform does not exclude spiritual and personal transformation. Within this framework I wish to comment on two distinct but related points: (a) making alliances with people who seem not very social-minded, and (b) the importance of what gets called spirituality. The two points are connected in that groups who are not socially active often have distinctive programs of spiritual formation.

By referring to people who do not seem social-minded I am playing upon the connotation of behavioral conformity. That meaning is highlighted if one uses the related word *sociable*. Full acceptance into society requires one to be sociable and to observe the rules of etiquette. In U.S. society the standards were largely established by early Protestant settlers. From the beginning and to this day, particular groups have rebelled against the etiquette. Catholics, blacks, Jews, and dissident Protestant groups have at times not been very social or sociable. They were resisting assimilation into the society that they found here. They might possibly be concerned with social causes (e.g., poverty, racial discrimination) though not being very social-minded (e.g., ready to join a civic club's efforts in behalf of local harmony).

What this means for people active in social programs is not to write off people because they are not social activists. Some people who seem to be cranky individualists are good reminders to planners of social programs that there are many ways to fight injustice. Those who go their own idiosyncratic way and are not very good at socializing may have a sense of that negative meaning of social, that is, conformity of everyone's behavior before the all-seeing eye of society.

My other comment that I said is related is one about the place of the inner life. What is one to make of a spirituality that is suspicious of social reform? Much of the last decade seems to a have been a withdrawal from social engagement to looking into oneself. The new interest in spirituality could mean one of two things; a narcissistic turning away from the issue of injustice in the world *or* a deepening of energies so that the passion for justice reaches not only social programs but the great cosmic issues like nuclear war and world starvation. People who are skeptical of social reform may be reminding us with the wisdom of the ages not to put our trust in human remedies. At the same time those people need reminding that many of the Church's greatest contemplatives (e.g., Eckhart, Merton) were passionately concerned with injustice.

A book that attracted considerable attention in England a few years ago is *Christianity and the World Order*. The author, Edward Norman, writes: "The wise aspirant to eternity will recognize no hope of a better social order in his endeavors, for he knows that the expectations of men are incapable of satisfaction. . . . Christians are those who act under the permanent rule that the ways of God are not the ways of men."[13] A partial truth in this statement is offered as an excuse for doing nothing to reduce the injustice in the world. True, "the ways of God are not the ways of men" (the sexist language is not an accidental feature here). Jews and Christians believe they can never identify their programs with God's. The ways of some men are indeed not the ways of God, which is why other men, women, and children must resist those humanly created injustices. Wise aspirants to eternity ought to know that we can always hope for, and we can constantly realize, a better social order even if it is still immeasurably distant from whatever God has in mind.

One can helpfully contrast Norman's glib pronouncement with the statement of a man who was also rather unsociable to the social planners of his day. In *Concluding Unscientific Postscript*, Kierkegaard wrote: "All paganism consists in this, that God is related to man directly, as the obviously extraordinary to the astonished observer. . . . Christianity consists in an eruption of inwardness which corresponds to the divine elusiveness that God has absolutely nothing obvious about him. It cannot immediately occur to anyone that he exists, although his invisibility is again his omnipresence."[14] The eruption of inwardness no doubt makes one skeptical of programs to make right this world. The inwardness, however, corresponds to a divine elusiveness that affects the smallest personal detail and the greatest cosmic design. Those who have an inwardness that cuts them loose from the obviously extraordinary are set free to engage in daring activity for an invisible but omnipresent God.

Third, and finally, it should be said that a religious organization, specifically here the church, is the outstanding case of a social organization whose mission is to transform the political order without itself being politicized. The line dividing these concepts can become very fine, which only means that we must be constantly attentive to the question. The built-in ambiguity of the word *social* that I have described in this article should at least indicate why there is confusion in this area.

The Church, like the university or the sports team, has a mission to influence the public sphere in a way that is always distinct from party politics. These social organizations have to work their influence while observing rules of fair play. Sometimes those rules are not entirely clear. Anyone who does not like what is on TV can send a letter to the producer or advertiser. Such action is encouraged as civic responsibility. If many people organize their voices to be better heard, the tactic is legitimate. At some point, however, when the pressure is too narrowly focused and producers are under pressure to accept a code of censorship, the rules of fairness have been broken. No one knows exactly where and how to draw that line.

In similar fashion a church official has a right to speak out on political issues during an election campaign. Not only as an individual citizen but as a spokesperson for the Church, he has a right and sometimes a duty to make his views known. The Church in its various organizations can be an instrument for political education. Obviously the Church will view political choices with its own good a concern, as do labor unions, universities, and business corporations. The Church has a special obligation to organize its resources where it sees a grave peril to public morality. Nonetheless, there are always rules of fairness to be observed. If millions of dollars flow into a congressional district to get a "targeted" representative, the victory for a single interest lobby may not be worth the price. If a church leader issues a letter telling people how to vote, the tactic may be unwise both politically and religiously. Our political system is by no means perfect. Compared to other available systems, however, it is worth preserving and trying to reform with activities that do not violate its balances, compromises, and restraints.

An unfortunate consequence of violations of fairness is that they lead to a call for churches to stay out of the political order. During the 1980 campaign the *New York Times* ran a lead editorial entitled "Private Religion, Public Morality."[15] As that title indicates, the *Times* advised the churches and church people to get out of the public forum and stay where they belong: in private. "The proper boundary between politics and religious advocacy... can be found only when secular morality is given precedence over all religious moralities." Jefferson's wall of separation is, of course, invoked, and the wall cannot stand "unless religions respect the primacy of a secular morality in law." The *Times*' distinction is charmingly clear, but the United States of America is not the *polis* of Aristotle. The choices for the Church are not the private household on one side and party politics on the other.

The Church has the right and the duty to be a social reformer. By helping to create the social as a third force, the Church has another ground to stand upon than private religion or public morality. The Church shares the word *religious* with other groups, and it also shares in the word *secular*. The Church has to be careful about how it throws its weight around because in this country today it must respect the freedom of individuals and the diversity of culture. Nevertheless, the church has a mission in this world and in the public sector of this world. Its mission concerns the realization of justice—or at least the struggle against injustice. With organized voices, and sometimes at the risk of money and life, the church has to speak to whomever can hear. Justice will finally be of God's own defining, but meanwhile, central to the Church's existence is social reform and social justice.

NOTES

1. George Albert Coe, *A Social Theory of Religious Education* (New York: Scribner's, 1920).
2. Quoted in E. G. Homrighausen, "The Real Problem of Religious Education," 34 (January 1939), p. 14.
3. Wilfred Evans Powell, *Education for Life With God* (New York: Abingdon, 1934), p. 39.
4. Reinhold Niebuhr, *Moral Man and Immoral Society* (New York, Scribner's, 1932), p. 3.
5. See Harrison Elliot, *Can Religious Education Be Christian?* (New York: Macmillan, 1940), chap. 10.
6. John Henry Newman, *University Sermons* (London: Longmans, Green, 1918), pp. 200 f.
7. Hannah Arendt, *The Human Condition* (Chicago: University of Chicago Press, 1958), pp. 22–78.
8. Robert Heilbroner, *Marxism: For and Against* (New York: Norton, 1980).
9. Ibid., pp. 80 f.
10. Christopher Lasch, *Haven in a Heartless World* (New York: Basic Books, 1977).
11. *New York Times*, July 16, 1981, p. A20.
12. Quoted in Edward Schillebeeckx, *Ministry* (New York: Crossroads, 1981), p. 134.
13. Edward Norman, *Christianity and the World Order* (New York: Oxford, 1979), p. 79.
14. Sören Kierkegaard, *Concluding Unscientific Postscript* (Princeton: Princeton University Press), p. 125.
15. *New York Times*, October 5, 1980.

QUESTIONS FOR REFLECTION AND DISCUSSION

1. What does the term *social* mean to you?

2. Why did Reinhold Niebuhr see a conflict between the social aim of religious education and the Christian view of the human condition?

3. What are guidelines of fair play for social reformers in a pluralistic setting?

4. What is the relationship between contemplation and social reform in the medieval Church and in the Reformation?

5. What is the role of the Church in society?

4. By Their Fruits You Will Know Them: The Biblical Roots of Peace and Justice

VIRGIL ELIZONDO

Introduction

Justice is a beautiful concept, the foundation of peace and the very core of Christian existence in today's world.[1] Biblical justice goes far deeper than merely righting the wrongs of an evil world. The justice of God goes to the very roots of evil itself, to the very roots of the injustice that guides today's world into destruction. Biblical justice, especially in the New Testament, is concerned with much more than mere reform of society. In brief, it is concerned with the re-creation of human beings and of the world as it has been created by human beings. It is concerned with a total re-creation of society, of culture, of religion, and of people.

Christianity is about life. "I came so that they might have life and have it to the fullest" (John 10:10). It is concerned with the elimination of death and everything that produces death. One need not be a great scholar, theologian, or social analyst to recognize that humanity uses the best of its creative ingenuity to produce death and produce it in abundance. We do not in any way deny or cease to admire the great advances and unanticipated breakthroughs in science and medicine. But our scandal is even greater at the destructive power that humanity is producing. Today we live in a death-bearing world.

Millions of people who live in continents rich with natural resources are living in misery while their wealth is exploited by their own powerful rich, and even more by the powerful of the great and dominant nations of the world. Exploitation is often masked by the title "aid and development."[2] The production of weapons for the destruction of humanity is justified and promoted under the guise of the national defense. We justify the buildup for war by speaking about our need for peace. Humanity is threatened by annihilation by the very modern weapons of war that are created in name of peace. Manipulation of the masses is seen as information and entertainment. Crime and violence are on the increase, especially in the traditional "civilized countries of the world." Our prison population increases rapidly each day. Liberty is confused with licentiousness as people destroy themselves in their unending search for new pleasures. It seems that humanity cannot wait to destroy itself!

Whether we affirm that sin perverted human nature itself or that it merely wounded it appears somewhat of an academic distinction. In the present world order, it is evident that confusion permeates human norms, values, institutions, thought, science, and religion itself. Even our interpretations of the Bible are often done in a way that justifies the death-bearing ways of the dominant society. We can achieve great scientific discoveries, but do they serve humanity and improve human life? Hiroshima, Nagasaki, today's nuclear bombs! Whether in capitalism, socialism, dictatorships, or communism, the principle of survival and advancement of the fittest through the unscrupulous manipulation of the masses seems to be basic law for those who want to succeed and find "happiness" in this world.

In the present world order, there seems to be no way out, save that of global annihilation. One does not need a crystal ball that foretells the future to read the signs of the times. Individualism, fear of others, egoism, materialism, inflation, drugs for legal or illegal purposes, and weapons will surely destroy us.

Are we then to give up? Shall we become pessimistic and just wait for the day of doom, or is there hope? As Christians we dare to affirm life and to hope for the fullness of life. We dare to hope not only for life but for life in abundance in spite of the perversion and confusion that reign in today's world order. The Bible is the word of life. Jesus alone has the word on definitive life: "Lord, to whom shall we go? You have the words of eternal life" (John 6:68).[3] As Christians we go to the roots of our Judeo-Christian tradition to discover life and, by contrast, to discover the causes of death. We dare to believe that as Christians we have received life and we have received the light of life. We are the bearers of this light and this life. We must then be able to see clearly and to name the demons that bring death to our world so that we might exorcize men, women, society, culture, and religion itself of everything that destroys life. This is our originality. This is our mission. This will be the cause of our rejection by those who seek to live through the ways of death.

As one goes through the pages of the Bible, it becomes clear that there is a fundamental affirmation running from beginning to end. God is the essence of goodness. God's creation is good, and of all creation, it is only men and women who are the image of God and thus very good. Yet throughout the Scriptures there is also the fundamental affirmation that in spite of God's goodness and of the fundamental goodness of men and women, human beings sin, and through sin, suffering and death have entered the world. From Adam death has reigned in the world (Rom. 5:12).

The first eleven chapters of Genesis present a visually magnificent summary of life as intended by the creator and life as determined and shaped by humanity. It is only in the contrast of these two ways of life that we can appreciate the new way of Jesus of Nazareth and of Christianity today. These then will be the three major topics that we will develop in this essay: the biblical notion of life, the development of the kingdom of death, and the irruption of the kingdom of life.

The Biblical Notion of Life: The Garden

There is no clear-cut definition of life in the Bible, but there is an abundance of images that together bring out the true meaning of human life. From the beginning we might say that life consists in living in the proper relationship with each other, with nature, and with God.

Relationship of Creative Mastery

In Genesis 2, man is modeled out of the dust of the earth. Surprisingly, without attempting to see the Bible as a scientific document, we see that this early description of the creation of man is, anthropologically speaking, very accurate. The more we study about the development and evolution of human groups, the more we discover how the land, vegetation, and climate condition the development of the peoples' way of life—their norms, their values, their aspirations, and their world vision. We are not affirming a geobiological determinism, but we do recognize the strong influence of the environment upon the development of the culture of people.

Yet men and women are not just created out of the earth, they are told to *cultivate* and to *take care of* the land (Gen. 2:15). Human beings are placed in the *garden* where they are free to eat of its fruit and to enjoy it (Gen. 2:16). But human beings find their authentic greatness to the degree they cultivate and humanize the environment. It is not just the enjoyment of it that humanizes, but the very cultivation, the working with our minds and our hands to improve that which has been given to us. We are called upon to give order, meaning, and direction. The earth belongs to us, but it is our sacred task to cultivate it. We must observe it carefully, study its ways, discover its potential, and determine its use so that we might be able to *name* it correctly according to God's command (Gen. 2:19). It is in the naming of the various elements of creation that we as human beings give a specific reality, function, and orientation to creation itself. For example, when we name the medicinal qualities of one plant and the poisonous effects of another, when we shape a metal and call it a knife and determine its use, this activity leads to the development of a language that names and expresses the meaning we have given to reality. It leads to the ordering of society, to the determination of priorities, and to the use of reality itself. This process allows us to live in a cohesive and meaningful way.

It is in fidelity to the God of life that men and women, by cultivating the environment, develop their culture, which in turn develops a specific type of humanity. By elevating the best of what they are and offering it to the Creator of life they develop their cult, which is the highest expression of their being and of their communion with the ultimate. Thus, culture and cult are an act of fidelity to the creator.

The image of men and women as cultivating, taking care of, and naming creation as it appears in Genesis 2, along with the image of men and women as subduing creation and having dominion over it in Genesis 1, gives us the first element of what it means to be alive: Men and women are to be the masters of creation; they are to work it, to cultivate it, to improve it, to humanize it, to name it, and to enjoy it. The relationship of mastery of men and women over the rest of creation is the first life-giving relationship of God's creation.

Relationship of Companionship

Genesis 2 brings out another important aspect of life. Human beings can possess the entire universe and lack absolutely nothing, but they will not be satisfied, fulfilled, or happy. To be alive, more is needed than material objects, wealth, or riches. It is not good for man to be alone. Thus the Bible presents man in need of other people. God gives man a woman, not to be the servant or a mere object of pleasure but to be a companion and a friend. It is precisely in the context of personal relationships that we are called forth to life. To the degree that we become someone to someone and that others become someone to us, we come to life. When sometime affectionately calls us by name, that, in effect, calls us to life.

And furthermore, it is in the free intercommunion of people that the image of God in the human is mirrored in its most authentic form. It is in the interrelationship of people that men and women truly live and radiate the image of God. People in isolation from one another are not the fullness of the image of God. It is in the relationship itself, as in the Trinity, that the fullness of the *imago Dei* comes through. The image of the God who seeks to communicate God's own life to humanity comes through in human beings seeking to enter into the interrelationship of communion with one another.[5]

God creates each person to be unique: Adam, Eve, Cain, and Abel. None is a copy of any other. Each is an original production. Yet they all have one thing in common: They cannot live-alone. They need one another. In the relationship of love, friendship, brotherhood, and sisterhood they give life to one another. We are co-creative of each other. It is precisely in the context of the relationship of friendship that the blindness of stereotypes and the fear of strangers is dispelled so that we are able to become persons to one another. The relationship of companionship is the second life-giving relationship of God's creation.

Relationship of Friendship with God

The third fundamental image of life is intimacy with God. Genesis 3 gives a very beautiful and simple image of the intimacy of God with the favorite of creation. God is presented as walking around in the garden in the cool of the early evening. This image brings out the close familiarity and intimacy between God and man and woman. Human beings are not intended to live in fear of God or distant from God but in a filial and liberating obedience to the God of life. True intimacy comes out of absolute trust, and only upon trust and fidelity can intimacy continue. Men and women are certainly creatures, but they are not created to be distant from the source of life. In fact, it is precisely through this intimacy with the creator that they will reach the fullness of life. Walking in the garden with God who walks together with them, men and women will be able to obtain and to experience the fullness of life. Faithful intimacy with God is the third life-giving relationship and the ultimate basis of the others.

Because men and women are unique, life cannot be reduced to mere existence. The all-important question is whether existence is life-bearing or death-bearing. For the Bible, life is existence in the proper relationships as ordained by the Author and Giver of life. Men and women are fully alive when they are the masters of material creation, brother and sisters of one another, and faithful friends of God.

Thus life is the proper relationship with each other, with nature, and with God. In the garden, men and women, lesser creatures, and God exist in harmony and peace.

The Kingdom of Death: The City with Its Towers

The incredible, devasting mastery of inequity! Men and women are good, but the evil and destructive actions invented and perpetrated by human beings are astounding. Not only do people commit crimes against one another, upon closer and more penetrating analysis, we discover that evil values are often masked as good. They become an integral part of the values, language, civilization, and even religions of the people. Evil becomes ingrained in the culture of the people and thus appears as good. It is transmitted as part of the wisdom of the group, and even of the group's image of the way of God. To question it appears as blasphemy.

We affirm that God is the absolute and perfect good, that God's creation is good, and that men and women, the image of God, are very good. But we cannot deny that perversion, corruption, fratricide, violence, crime, and war reign in the world. Saving grace has indeed entered our world, but the reign of evil and death continues to have a strong grasp and a determining role in the affairs of the contemporary world. The heroes of the world are those who conquer and kill, those who enslave and dominate, and those who exploit and manipulate. The ones who obtain power proceed to name reality, to judge it accordingly, and to legitimize their way of life and their actions. The weak are called backward and untouchable, the violated are called whores and sensous creatures, and the enslaved are called uncivilized savages in need of supervision![6] Truly, in a sinful world might makes right.[7]

The present world order is that of darkness, confusion, blindness, perversion of thought and values, enslavement, and death. In such a condition, good people will do evil things while being convinced they are doing good. If there is to be a way out one must go to the very foundations of evil, that is, to the very foundation of an unjust world. We will never fully understand the question of evil, but the Bible presents some penetrating and realistic aspects that are certainly verified in today's society. Evil comes through the perversion and inversion of life-giving relationships as intended by the creator.

Slaves of Creation

Men and women were created to be the masters, but they have abdicated and become the slaves.

I am conscious of the various possible interpretations of Genesis 3. However, in doing a cultural reading of the Bible, one strives to see the core images and to discover their function. In Genesis, Adam and Eve are pictured as having everything they needed for a happy life, but they were not satisfied. In the center of the garden of the delights was the fruit tree that they did not possess. The fruit tree exists in the midst of the lives of every one of us. It is the desire to stand beyond good and evil, that is, the desire to use things, and even people who are looked upon as things, for one's own enjoyment without any sense of responsibility or even willingness to ask the question about responsibility. Adam and Eve had everything, but they still wanted more. The forbidden fruit confuses happiness with having and can easily turn creation itself into the chief idol of the religion of materialism. The more one has, the more one wants, and the less satisfying one's possessions become! One becomes possessed with the desire for more. The end product of such a fundamental attitude is that one ends up being a slave of the world. In this way of life human beings abdicate their position of mastery. They are no longer in control of the world, but rather, the world is in control of them. Wealth and material possessions become the all-important values, and everything and everyone else is subordinated. The supermarkets become the cathedrals of such a religion.

In this enslavement, the earth is no longer cultivated with great care, but exploited, wounded, and polluted. The earth and its wealth are not appreciated as the great gift of the creator for all humanity to enjoy, but reduced to raw materials that can increase the profit of those who have taken over for themselves what, in fact, belongs to everyone. Furthermore, the poor countries of the world become the trash cans for the dangerously radioactive chemical waste products of the rich countries of the world. What cannot be dumped in the United States is carried to the other countries to be dumped. Our land is sacred, but their land can be desecrated. Chemical fertilizers, too dangerous to be used in our own country, are readily and easily sold to the poor countries of the world. Are we, in effect, poisoning their food products, many of which paradoxically are then imported into our own country? Exploitation for profit becomes the unquestioned rule of the land and of the so-called progress of humanity! Who will die in the process seems to be of little or no concern to those in control. At least the gas chambers of Germany were clearly for the destruction of life, but in today's more subtle society, we are selling and transporting many death-bearing materials to the masses of the poor of the world under the label of fertilizers, chemicals, medicines, and nutriments. Under the label of life, we export death! In the opinion of this writer, this is the worst of the confusion of Babel—to send death-bearing gifts disguised as gifts of life.

Even worse than the irresponsible exploitation of the earth is the measurement of human dignity in terms of material wealth. The poor, according to this world's values, are worthless, untouchable, without dignity and even without the right to life itself. They can therefore be easily exploited and disposed of when they are no longer needed. They do not even count. When they die, or are killed, their names are not even mentioned. They are the millions of nameless victims of today's economic wars. They are the faceless masses whose broken bodies and spilled blood produced the fine dining and wining of the rich nations of the world. Even the bread and wine that is offered in our religious assemblies is truly the body and blood of those whose life is being taken so that the sinful world might continue to live. Human beings are reduced to material objects and used without scruple for the benefit of the powerful.

Once material possession has become the god of our heart, we will stop at nothing to obtain communion with the god. We will measure everything in terms of our god and structure our values, our world of meanings, language, symbols, and religion in relation to our created sacred image. The great tragedy is that in seeking to possess, we become possessed, from being the masters we become slaves and the servants (not the stewards) of creation. In trying to possess the world we abdicate our position as creative cultivators of the garden of delights. We leave the garden to build our cities and towns.

Enemies of One Another

The beauty and magnificence of God's creation is that God has made each individual person an original masterpiece. There are no two persons who are the same. To appreciate what one is, to develop one's abilities to the best degree possible, and to offer to God the best of one's work is the true greatness of the human being and the glory of God. This is truly men and women fully alive. Each of us developing what God has given to us to the best of our ability and offering what we are to our creator.

The difficulty comes when we begin to appreciate ourselves, not in terms of our uniqueness, but rather in terms of someone else. Once we begin to compare ourselves to others, jealousies begin and our imaginations go wild. We go to the point of convincing ourselves, as Cain did, that God has blessed the other but rejected me. Often I am so concerned with what God appears to be doing for others that I fail to appreciate what he is doing for me. It goes to the point of feeling and being convinced that only the other is blessed whereas I am rejected and cursed.

These comparisons are one of the root causes of the perversion of human relationship. It is clear in the Genesis story that God tells Cain that he has no reason to be jealous. In God's response to Cain, it seems that it was more Cain who thought that God has favored Abel. God clearly tells Cain, "Why are you so resentful and crestfallen? If you do well, you can hold up your head; but if not, sin is a demon lurking at the door: Its urge is toward you, yet you can be his master" (Gen. 4:6). It is clear that we should not be judging whether God has blessed someone else and not me. The important thing God wants us to do is to do what we have to do well. If we do it well, we can hold our head up high. That means we can have a legitimate pride in what we have done and a profound sense of satisfaction that if we have done well, it has been pleasing to God. However, jealously leads to intrigue, lies, destructive actions, and even murder. The moment we are jealous of another, that other controls our life. In many ways we will seek to get rid of or even to destroy the other. These motivations turn every person into a potential enemy. Furthermore, these comparative attitudes destroy our innermost freedom, for our lives will be constantly shaped and conditioned by what is happening to others. We will never be free to be ourselves, for we will always be seeking to imitate and outdo others. We become so concerned with what others are accomplishing that we fail to appreciate what we are and what we ourselves can and are accomplishing.

In such a state of existence, "to be" means "to be better than others." It appears that only by becoming superior to others can one come to the fullness of life. One constantly needs lesser others to affirm one's humanity. It is this attitude that is one of the root causes of racism. We need to define metaphysically inferior peoples to allow us to have an existential sense of well-being. The concrete consequences of this mentality are devastating. Once this attitude has been engraved in us, we might even exercise heroic charity and dedication in relation to the poor, the suffering, and the miserable of society but, in effect, we need those socially defined lesser or inferior human beings in order to affirm our own humanity. With this frame of reference, the criminals and the charitable persons both see their fulfillment through the affirmation of a lesser other! True, one exploits them whereas the other seeks to serve them, but in the ultimate analysis, both continue to subjugate them. Subjugation gives life to those who seek to be by being better than others or superior to others.

People become psychological and sociological vampires who need victims in order to survive.

Although personal advancement and the enjoyment of the fruit of one's labor is a great and humanizing virtue, advancement at the cost of others and the enjoyment of the fruits of the labor of the exploited other is a dehumanizing and destructive vice. To the degree that this attitude of egocentric individualism becomes ingrained in the culture of a people, authentic personal relationships and cooperation between people becomes impossible. Each one is out for his or her own self! May the best one win! We glorify agression, justify violence, and canonize the winners as the heroes and the saints of a society built, not upon God, but upon the foundations of Cain. Authentic fellowship becomes either superficial or impossible, and every person becomes a potential, if not a real, rival and eventual enemy of every other.

One of the greatest sources of indignation to a conquered group is that the women of the oppressed group, especially those of the indigenous ruling class, will be offered in marriage, or will offer themselves, to the men who now appear to them to be the gods or giants of this world. It is the ongoing story that the conquerors appear as the sons of heaven who become wonderful and appealing to the daughters of mere earthly men (Gen. 6:1–4). The Bible is quite clear on the final point in speaking about the sons of heaven: "They were the heroes of old, the men of reknown" (Gen. 6:4). They will bypass their own men, who now appear as inferior, unworthy, and not even beautiful, for the sake of the gods! And these human gods will use the women and easily leave them behind. They have children with them but will also find it quite easy to leave them behind. The conquered are seen as "senuous" and easy prey, but seldom as human beings, as partners in life and as equals in society. They are used and abused easily, and children are conceived without concern and then left behind, for they do not count.[8]

As cultures and societies develop and evolve along the way of Cain, the image of the conquerer and the dominant is projected as the only authentic representation not only of beauty and charm, but even of God. Even sacred art will use the faces, the figures, the features, and the color of the dominant group to mirror the image of the divine. People in western civilization today become quite easily scandalized to see a black image of Christ, or a brown baby Jesus, or a fat Blessed Mother.

The interiorization of the idea that only the powerful are beautiful and bearers of the *imago Dei* is one of the most painful and destructive elements of the ways of Cain. This internalizes self-hatred amongst the dominated and conquered. This attitude continues today and is re-inforced by the media of communication. The men and women look down upon themselves! The women go off in search of their new trophies, and as the men begin to develop, one of the greatest trophies is to marry a woman of the oppresser group. This seems to be the outward sign that they have been accepted.[9] This is the ultimate oppression and degradation of the human spirit, for to be human now means not only being better than the other, even prior to that, I must cease being myself and become the other, for it is only the other who appears to be human in the image of God.

Antagonistic Rivals of God

The third perversion comes through clearly in the imagery of the city and tower of Babel in Genesis 11. It is evident in Genesis 9 and 10 that the great diversity of families, of nations, and of languages is the great blessing of God after the flood. It is only in Genesis 11 that we come to the perversion of this God-intended diversity. One group decides to build a city with a tower reaching to God—a culture and a religion superior to all others and normative for everyone. On their own they reach heaven and make a name for themselves. They would have no God but themselves!

One group will now seek to build a single way of life that will be seen as God's way for all peoples. Henceforth diversity will be cursed and idolatrous uniformity will be imposed. The city is symbolic of the structures and institutions that are created to protect the interest of those in control, whereas the tower is symbolic of sacralization of the structures. A way of life is created to protect the interest of those in control and a religion is formulated to make it appear as God's way for all. To question the powerful is to question God. And even the imagery of God is borrowed from the powerful. God appears as the all-powerful, the almighty, the king, the conquering hero. In this imagery, God appears as a benevolent dictator or a kindly despot. And conversely, it is only the powerful who appear to be divinelike and bearers of the *imago dei*. They alone can be beautiful like gods.

The symbol of the city and the tower are very powerful. How are great cities, palaces, monuments, and temples built? How do great empires come about? Is it not through the enslavement of the masses? It is through the heavy taxation of the people, the forced labor of the masses, and the death of many that the great structures of society come about. To this day the exploitation of the masses of the world feeds the dominant empires of the world. Thus the cities and the towers are the monuments to the enslavement, oppression, and exploitation of the masses. They are the center of impersonalism, crime, violence, anonymity, and decay. The rich live in their homes in the gardens of the countryside, while the poor stay to suffer the noise, pollution, and violence of the city.

The institutions themselves become identified with God, and the functionaries have but one goal—to serve the institution that is the source of their status and livelihood, that is a source of their life. To serve the institution appears a sharing in God's own power. Often the functionaries act as if they themselves were God. They have but one goal and that is the welfare of the institution. This happens in even the best and holiest of institutions; it is evident how this takes place even in our church institutions, which are set up to serve the people but eventually become self-serving.

It is evident that institutions are needed and are a service to humanity. We cannot live in chaos! We must have law and order to assure peace, but the question is, "In whose service do the institutions function?" Why were they set up—to hide, legitimize, and institutionalize violence or to facilitate the practice of love?[10] Even when set up with the best of intentions, to the degree that institutions and social structures become absolutized and sacralized they alienate people from themselves, from each other, and from God. They reduce people to functions and the people become servants of the system. The institutions play God, and there is no God beyond the institution, for its own monuments are its "gods" made to its own image and likeness.

Not only are people destroyed by absolutized structures, but even worse, people who live according to a different way of life are treated as inferior. The dominant group will extol its culture as the only way of life that is civilized and pleasing to God. All others have to be converted to their cultural way if they are to be saved.

In the history of religions and conquests, it is astounding and frightening to see the legitimizing role that religion has played in the conquest, subjugation, and domination of peoples. Even our own beloved Christian faith has not been immune from this role. This has certainly been the case in the conquest of the Americas by the Europeans, and it was also the case in the conquest of Asia and Africa. Christ has come not as liberator but as colonizer and slave owner. In Latin America it was a Latin European Christianity, whereas in North America it was mostly the "Wasp" Christianity, but in both cases it was a Christ who was alien to the natives and, later on, to the black slaves who were imported. In these cases Christ did not come out of Nazareth but rather out of the great capitals of the empire.[11]

The role that religion plays in the culture of the group is all important, for it is at this level of human behavior that our innermost ideas, values, judgments, and stereotypes are ultimately justified and legitimated. It is at this level that our way appears as God's way for all peoples. In the religious act, men and women create God to their own image and likeness. Thinking they adore God, they in effect are adoring themselves.

In the cities of men and women, our own humanly made monuments take the place of God while the living God becomes further and further removed from our lives. Religion is practiced, but it is more a ritual of the city with its towers and monuments than a source of communion with the God of life. In seeking the gods they have built to their own image and likeness, men and women will find themselves not only farther and farther away from God, but also more and more alienated from the God of life. The God who is infinite love and life will appear as a stranger and even as a false God. This is the sin against the spirit that will not be forgiven precisely because it will never be recognized as sin. Blindness will condemn as blasphemy the name of the true God of life. The temples of society will condemn and keep out the God of life, for such a God is the very opposite of the God of the cities and the towers; this God is the opposite of the ways of Adam, Eve, and Cain, who reign in this world order and are even worshiped in our churches.

Summary

The kingdom of death is guided and built upon the threefold inversion of God's way for humanity. God intended men and women to be responsible cultivators of creation, concerned brothers and sisters of one another, and faithful friends of God. This is the proper relationship to the world, to each other, and to God. Through the mystery of iniquity, men and women have inverted this fundamental relationship. They have become slaves of the world, enemies of each other, and antagonistic rivals of God. This inverted relationship has become the core basis of human societies and religions. It permeates every fiber of existence. It is in this way that we can say that we are born into sin and become sinful as we are formed and conditioned by the very ways of our group.

In this world order, human beings will never be able to truly achieve wholeness, harmony, and happiness, for the values they acquire from their cultures and societies will run constantly against the grain of their inner nature as created in the image of God. There will be a basic and profound emptiness, alienation, and frustration. The great tragedy is that, according to the norms, values, and goals of a sin-confused or perverted world, the more one tries to escape suffering, the more one will find oneself getting into it. It is a vicious circle because the very foundational principles of action, as created by society, are the very opposite of the principles of life as instilled in the hearts of men and women by the creator.

It is our contention that, ontologically speaking, the image of God in the human being is never totally destroyed or missing. It is this innermost *imago Dei* that causes men and women to strive for goodness and perfection. It is this image that is the very basis of the fundamental dignity of every human being. Yet it is precisely because of the confusion of the established worldviews that this quest will often lead not to a fuller life but to a destruction of life. The paradox and tragedy in sinful human society is that what the innermost desires of the heart seek they will not find, and what they desire they will not obtain. The point of conflict is that whereas the innermost desires of the human heart continue to be in conformity and in harmony with God's way of life, their concrete sociocultural and even religious formulations are almost exclusively in terms of humanity's way of death. The tension is between the ontological nature of the human person and the cultural nature as formulated by humanity itself. Further tension arises when the dominant group sees its own cultural nature as identical with the ontological nature of humanity itself and thus tries to impose its own cultural ways as the only civilizing and human way for all humanity. Once our cultural way is seen as natural, all others will be seen as inferior. This becomes all the worse when our cultural way is equated with the only true reflection of God.

It is this tension that allows goodness and development within our destructive walls. But it is likewise this tension that is at the basis of the ambiguity of all human progress and development. We build great cities and civilizations only to see them decay and, even more, become the sources of human corruption and alienation. Our skyscrapers put us close to heaven but keep God away from us. Our own monuments or temples keep us away from God and hide the mind and heart of God! They are the source of the darkness of the world and the blindness of humanity.

The Kingdom of Life

From the very beginning, God's project has been the communication of life. The life of God is itself the light of the world. But humanity's project of death and darkness, of destructiveness and confusion, has interfered. Life-bearing values have been traded for death-bearing ones to such a degree that success leads to failure, fulfillment to emptiness, peace to war, and life to death. The quest for material gain, prestige, and power shapes and conditions our institutions, our thought patterns, and even our religions. We call for justice, revolution, and reform, only to discover that the same old demons come through hidden under new slogans, ideologies, social systems and religions. Is liberation from this vicious circle possible?

The Old Testament is a monument to justice within an inherently unjust world. Justice is certainly one of the central ideas of the Old Testament. It appears as a moral virtue that leads people to the observance of God's commandments so as to receive a just return. Conduct in conformity with the law is the source of merit and prosperity.[12] The prophets call for a humanization of society, of institutions, and of human relations. They denounce the crimes of society. They call for reform and cry out against the injustices that reigned in their land. But they did not go to the very roots of injustice itself. The core values of a sinful world were not questioned. They attempt to curb and to limit the malice of sin, but sin itself is not tackled. They struggle against evil but do not go to the roots of evil.

Jesus does not call for justice. Instead, he offers a solution that will uproot and eradicate injustice from the world. He goes to the very roots of an unjust world order.

As Christians we are convinced that Jesus is the beginning of the new creation. He is the new Adam. He is the beginning of the new humanity. He is not a mere reformer or revolutionary; he is the first of a new race, of a new day of life, and indeed of a new creation.

To appreciate the fullness of the new Christian beginning, it is important to appreciate that it cannot be understood by the wisdom of this world.[13] To this world order confused by sin, God's wisdom will always be a scandal and a stumbling block. Prophets and sages will be sent to call the world to conversion, but they will be persecuted and killed (Matt. 23:24). In this world order, reformers will be tolerated, conformists will be considered good people, and the successful will be looked upon as the saints of the secular world. But the true physicians of life will be expelled and done away with.

From the very earliest preaching of the followers of Jesus, the theme of the world's rejection of God's way of life is evident:

This Jesus is the stone *rejected* by you the *builders* which has become the cornerstone. There is no salvation in anyone else. For there is no other name in the whole world given to men by which we are to be saved." [Acts 4:11–12][14]

The builders of the world order must reject the author of life because he comes to make known the hidden foundations of the ongoing and increasing injustice of the world. He will reveal the false foundation of world order and offer us a new foundation. Jesus makes his own the words of Psalm 78: "I will open my mouth in parables. I will announce what has lain hidden since the foundation of the world." What is this secret that has been hidden since the foundation of the world? That the killing of Abel—of the weaker brother—is the cornerstone and foundation of human cultures and societies. (Luke 11:50 and Matt. 23:34–36). Laws will have to be passed against murder because men and women will see the elimination of the others for their own survival and advancement as an ordinary and necessary way of life. Movements for justice will attempt to limit or lessen injustice, but they will not get to the root of injustice. When the definitive truth of life is made known, it will not be understood—it will appear as scandalous (Matt. 15:12) or as "too much" (Matt. 13:57) or as the words of a possessed bastard (John 8:48):

> Why do you not understand what I say? Is it because you cannot bear to hear my word. The father you spring from is the devil, and willingly you carry out his wishes. He brought death to man from the beginning. And never based himself on truth; the truth is not in him. Lying speech is his native tongue. He is a liar and the father of lies. [John 8:44]

> But because I deal in the truth, you give me no credence [John 8:45]

From the beginnings of cultures, societies, and religions, the death-bearing values have become the foundation and permeating spirit of life in this world. They have become the innermost norms of judgment and the unsuspected criteria of evaluation. They provide us with our ultimate priorities and are even the basis of common sense.

To know and appreciate Jesus and his way to restore life to humanity, we cannot judge according to the ways of human beings, but must seek the ways of God as revealed in Jesus himself. We cannot expect our Savior according to our human expectations, but must welcome him according to the wisdom of God who wants us to live (Matt. 16:23). It is in Jesus himself that the way of the kingdom of life will be revealed and made possible for us.

Liberating Mastery over the World

In this present world order people want to insure themselves of life by obtaining material possessions; Jesus has nothing. "The Son of

Man has nowhere to lay his head" (Matt. 8:20). Jesus is never pictured as owning anything. It is evident that he certainly enjoyed the things of this world. One of the most common characteristics of Jesus was his enjoyment of table fellowship. Yet he appears as being completely detached from the goods of this world.

He exhorts his followers to go after true riches, not the ones that can rot or be stolen, but the everlasting ones. "No one can serve two masters. He will either hate one and love the other or be attentive to one and despise the other. You cannot give yourself to God and money" (Matt. 6:24). The contemporary consumer mentality and society would certainly not be at ease with the words of Jesus: "Stop worrying, then, over the questions like, 'What are we to eat, or what are we to drink, or what are we to wear?' The unbelievers are always running after these things" (Matt. 6:31–32). The key of this section is in the words: "Seek first his kingship over you, his way of holiness, and all these things will be given you besides" (Matt. 6:33). Jesus is not against the things of this world. They are good and to be enjoyed by human beings. But he does place their use in the proper perspective. Use them and enjoy them, but do not become enslaved to them. There are more important things in this life than the possession and use of material things (Luke 16:9–15).

Jesus clearly tells us to give to the needy (Matt. 25:31–46), to share what little we have with one another so that it may be distributed among everyone in need (Matt. 4–21; 15:32–38; 6:32–44; Luke 9:10–17; John 6), to give to the other more than is required by the law, in other words not only a "just" salary but a generous one (Matt. 5:40); and even more than that, he praises the widow who has contributed, not out of her surplus, but out the very substance of her life—"has given what she could not afford" (Luke 21:1–4).

But Jesus goes even further. If you really want to be perfect, that is, if you really want to be free, then go, sell all that you have; give it to the poor, and follow Jesus on his way (Matt. 19:16–22). The more you possess, the more difficult it will be to give it up and follow Jesus on his way. Money leads to idolatry (Matt. 6:21–24). This is why it will not be easy, according to Jesus, for the rich to enter the kingdom of heaven, not because they are morally better or worse than the poor or the middle class, but because their hearts will be more in their possessions than in others or in God (Matt. 6:21).[15]

The abandonment of all their possessions is basic to the following of Jesus (Luke 12:33; 14:33; Matt. 10:21). This is the first necessary rupture with the scale of values of the present world order. It is not rational according to the present order of reason, but it is certainly liberating. The more one becomes detached from these things of the world, the more one will be able to be truly centered on God and God's way for humanity. As the first deviation entered through materialism, so will the beginning of authentic life begin by a turning away from the scale of values that makes of material possessions the all-important element of life and the measurement of life itself.

In this lifestyle Jesus lives out the life-giving relationship to the material world: use it responsibly, enjoy it, share it, have dominion over it,[16] but remain free of it. Do not let it possess you. Do not let it enslave you. Be free enough to share it with others and even to give it away totally. It is only through this core attitude that men and women will be free and thus begin the journey into authentic living.

We want to note here very clearly that we do not see poverty as blessing but as curse.[17] The lack of the basic material necessities of life, especially when people are deprived of them because of the greed of others, is a sin and a curse. But it is not the poor who are sinful! Precisely because the poor are condemned by the structural forces of society into this dehumanizing condition, they are chosen by God to be the initiators of the new creation. They are not chosen to remain as they are, but to begin the new way for all people. Furthermore, though poverty itself is a curse, mere material possession is not a blessing, but could easily be, and frequently is, a curse and a sign of sinfulness. Wealth that is obtained through the manipulation or exploitation of the weaker brothers and sisters is blood money that cries to heaven for vengeance. This wealth is the source of much evil and suffering both for the wealthy and for the sources of their wealth. It is only wealth that is obtained through one's own hard labor and simplicity of life that is truly a sign of blessing. Yet even this wealth is to be shared generously with others, for even the ability to work diligently is a gift that is to be shared (Matt. 10:8).

It should not be surprising that in the early Christian community, and in those movements throughout history that have tried to recapture the radicalness of the way of Jesus, the voluntary and joyful sharing of material possessions has been one of the prerequisites. Possession of goods possesses us. Only by dispossessing ourselves can we become free. For this dispossession to be truly liberating it must be freely chosen. Others cannot choose it for us. The Scriptures say that those who could have been rich but chose to be poor are the happy ones. My own father was this way, and he was certainly one of the most joy-filled men I have ever known. Be free enough so that you are not merely a just person, but a generous one.

The disciple does not choose poverty as if it were something good.

One chooses poverty so as to enter into solidarity with the poor of the world and, together with them, struggle to forge new ways of life that will eliminate both the curse of poverty and the curse of materialistic wealth. We dispossess ourselves freely from the spirit of possession so that the goods of this world might be more evenly distributed amongst all of God's children. It is this free and voluntary sharing of the goods of this world and of the fruits of our own labor that will truly contribute to the buildup of a new society, a new culture, and a new world vision that will be truly life-bearing for all people.

Freely chosen poverty for the sake of the kingdom is the beginning of the creative mastery that will truly humanize the world and lead all people to have not only life, but life in abundance. It restores men and women to their legitimate position as creative masters and caretakers of the earth.

Concerned Brothers and Sisters of One Another

The world often becomes enslaved and blinded by people's quest and struggle for power and prestige. We tend to measure the fundamental worth and dignity of people by their title, bloodline, position in society, civic status, color, nationality, and shape. Jesus not only possesses nothing, he becomes nothing, at least according to the standards of judgment of the world as created by sinful humanity. "He emptied himself and took the form of a slave. . . . It was thus that he humbled himself" (Phil. 2:7–8).

In becoming human, God becomes no ordinary person. He becomes a Jew. The Jewish people had been despised and dominated by the great powers of the world. Rejected by the world, they had found their dignity and reason for living in their conviction that they were God's chosen people. Yet they too lived in accordance with the categories of life of the very sinful world that oppressed them. Within their own Jewish people they had many circles of respectability and rejection. Jesus becomes not only a Jew, but a low class, impure, and scorned Galilean. He was a small-town boy from the frontier. Furthermore, he was the Son of Mary (Matt. 6:3) and even Joseph was scandalized with his beginnings (Matt. 1:19). According to the social criteria of respectability and prestige, Jesus is nothing!

Why such a beginning? Because in the very moment of becoming human, God reveals the lie of the world and the truth of God concerning the human. Every human being, no matter what the world has made of him or her, carries within the image of God and is the child of God. Every human being is of infinite worth. Whatever diminishes or destroys the fundamental dignity of the human person is a crime, a lie, and a sin. In Jesus—the nothing of the world—the glory of God begins to shine forth in its fullness.

From this nothingness Jesus began to live and proclaim his fundamental message: inviting all into the kingdom of God who is father of all—even the good and the bad alike (Matt. 5:45).

He instructs his followers not to seek attention or prestige (Matt. 6:1–4). He tells them that if they want to be great, to become like little children (Matt. 18:1–4; Luke 9:46–48) and that the true greatness of men and women is in the voluntary service of one another (Matt. 10:42). The rule of life is to be unlimited loving service, a loving service that is not limited to our family and neighbors but goes beyond even to our enemies and even to the enemies of public society.[18] We should not wait for people to come to us, but we should go out to seek the lost ones (Matt. 10:1–21) and those in need.

This loving acceptance and service of the other is not just in concrete deeds but, even more, in fundamental attitudes. Acceptance, respect, and forgiveness are the beginning. But even more than this is the evident joy that Jesus displays in being in the company of others. The joy flows from the inner recognition that you, no matter who you are, bring joy and blessing into my life. This attitude is not said in so many words, but it is certainly characteristic throughout the life of Jesus.

Jesus lives out the relationship of loving concern for others to the ultimate. Living for others is the second major component of liberation that eradicates injustice. We see others not as better or worse, superior or inferior, foreigners or citizens, but as truly brothers and sisters. We work not to outdo each other, but to develop ourselves to the best of our abilities so that together we might build a better society for everyone. We respect the uniqueness of each person, without manipulating or exploiting those who are weak. We respect and admire the gifts and talents of others, without putting them up on pedestals of superiority or stardom. We appreciate the image of God in ourselves as we appreciate it in others. This attitude gives me the freedom to be me and to allow others to be themselves and to work together for the betterment of everyone. In the kingdom, each of us will work in accordance with our talents and abilities, and each one of us will receive in accordance with our needs (Matt. 20:1–16): not jealousy but cooperation; not trying to outdo one another, but each doing the best he or she can; no longer destroyed by relationships of individualistic competition, but enlivened by the relationships of communitarian harmony; bearing one another's burdens and sharing in one another's joys. This new life is not the product of a new law but the logical outflow of a new existence of a new heart.

Faithful Children of God

In faithfulness to God's command to cultivate and take care of the land, men and women struggle to build up civilizations and ways of life. In humanity's quest for communion with the ultimate, it builds up religions and worship. This activity brings order out of the chaos by humanizing the environment. It gives to men and women a cohesive way of life that gives them a relative amount of security and tranquility. As thought evolves it allows people to discover and give meaning to reality. All of this culture-building activity is the sign of the uniqueness and greatness of human beings.

However there is a twofold tragedy. One is that cultures are built more upon the foundations of Cain than of God. The other is that they become identified with God, and to question them is to question God. To the degree that cultures become absolutized, they no longer allows human growth and development. They cease serving the people and become self-serving. Rather than humanize, they now dehumanize. They kill the human spirit, and turn people into functional robots.

Human structures are necessary for life, but they can never take the place of God. Jesus never appears as an anarchist. He does not call for the overthrow of government, society, or religion. But he does exhibit an amazing freedom from the blindness and enslavement of all humanly made structures, including religion. He is neither rebellious against Rome nor subservient to Caesar (Luke 20:25). Jesus is a faithful Jew till the very end, who in his very faithfulness to God does not hesitate to question the abuses of Judaism in a powerful way. He chastises the thinkers, leaders, and ideologues of society because they so absolutize their thought that it becomes oppressive of human beings. Their ideas and their interpretations become their gods and, in effect, keep the people from God (Matt. 15:1–9; Matt. 23:1–34). Their dogmatic ways lead people to destruction (Matt. 15:14). He does not hesitate to question even the most sacred edifice of his people —the Temple. For religion itself must be purified if it is to be a liberating service to people. Segregation and hatred of others is bad enough in itself, but it becomes catastrophic when it is carried out in the name of divine righteousness.

Because all humanly made structures have their foundations in Adam and Eve, Cain and Abel, and Babel, it will be necessary to go to their very foundations so as to liberate them from their blindness and enslaving spirit. "Every plant which my heavenly Father has not planted will be rooted up" (Matt. 15:13).

Jesus does not eliminate human structures, but he does propose a radically new foundation for all the structures of humanity. Acceptance of the absolute sovereignty of God and God's way for humanity is the only authentic foundation of human structures and civilizations. Yet this acceptance neither dehumanizes nor enslaves us, for it is not the relationship of a master to a slave, or even a teacher to a student, but that which exists between loving parents and their children. The inner essence and ultimate identity of Jesus was his intimacy with God as Parent. This was the basis of his authenticity and freedom. Yet, this intimacy did not mean doing his own will, but God's will. Even in the most difficult moments, his prayer is, "Yet not my will but yours be done" (Luke 22:44). And he introduces us to the proper relationship with God: "Our Father in heaven, hallowed be your name, your kingdom come, your will be done on earth as it is in heaven . . ." (Matt. 6:9–10).

To do the will of God, who is the author of life and who alone knows what it means to be alive, is the beginning of real life for humanity and the foundation of the new world order of peace. Obedience to God is the beginning of human freedom. Whoever refuses to listen to God, trust in God's ways, and obey God's counsels, will find him- or herself imprisoned within the confines of a very limited and limiting self-made world.

For Jesus true life is keeping the Father's commands and living in his love (John 14:31; 15:9–11). It is not the blind obedience of servants, but the trusting and liberating obedience of lovers. The followers of Jesus are invited into the life-giving relationship with God as our loving Father.

It is only the God of people who is sovereign, and it is only God's people who are sacred. Nothing else—Caesar, the Law, Tradition, or the Temple—can be so sacred that they cannot be questioned or criticized. Only one criterion is absolute: Is it of service to all people and especially to the poor, the needy, the orphan, the widow, and the stranger? For Jesus it is our response to the other in need that is absolute; everything else is secondary (Matt. 25:31–46). The basis for this concern is that in recognizing that God is truly our Parent, we equally recognize that everyone else is our brother or sister. Because God shares God's own life with men and women, whatever we do for others, especially the "nobodies" of society who are ignored by others, we do for God (Matt. 10:42). But to the degree that we ignore, enslave, exploit, and kill the other, we do it unto God.

It is not from the perspective of human cultures that we can judge people, but rather from the perspective of the fundamental worth and dignity of every person that we judge all human reality—including the human expressions of the sacred.

Men and women are not only the image of God but, even more, the children of God! They share in God's own life and are invited to participate actively and intelligently in God's historical project for humanity.[19] Jesus and God are one. He invites us—regardless of our nationality, color, class, status, reputation, or religion—to share in this one life. It does not matter what your background is or where you come from, the all-important thing is that in your life you recognize God as your Parent and seek to live out God's will in all things (Matt. 12:48–50).

It is this faithful intimacy with God as our Parent that will allow us to situate ourselves within human institutions and even work with them and through them without becoming enslaved by them. Faithfulness to God relativizes human idols and allows us to experience the joy of authentic human freedom in the midst of the enslavements of this world and its institutions. This is the freedom of the martyrs whom not even the accusations of being atheists or enemies of the state could separate from the true source of life and happiness. Intimacy with God and active participation in God's plan does not remove us from involvement in the affairs of the world, but it does allow us to participate without becoming enslaved. As Christians we are called upon to be the "artisans of a new humanity." The true greatness of men and women will be the cultivation of societies and cultures based upon human respect, concern for others, and generosity. Justice will be fundamental, but charity will impel us to go even further than the basic demands of justice. Yet in our struggles for betterment, we know that no human structures or personages, no matter how great or important they might be, can take the place of God. It is under God—the God of Jesus—that people will be able to gradually obtain their true greatness, their desired freedom, and their true fulfillment.

Because Jesus went to the very foundations of all human societies, humanity had to get rid of him. When he enters Jerusalem, "the whole city was stirred to its depths, demanding, 'Who is this?'" (Matt. 21:10). The bankers, educators, political and religious leaders are disturbed. It is the structures of a sinful humanity that are alarmed, for their life-source has been threatened. Those outside the structures—"the crowds" (Matt. 21:11)—recognize him as the prophet from Nazareth. But the powerful and the elite are stirred to their depths. They have to get rid of him. Otherwise their "sanctu-ary" (John 11:48) will be done away with. Because Jesus has ques-tioned the very foundations of all human sanctuaries and nations, he must be destroyed. The city with its temple decides to get rid of the threat. The kingdom of death strives to survive by putting to death the kingdom of life. He is taken outside the city, killed, and buried in the garden tomb.

As the foundations of the present world order of sin started in the garden with the greed of Adam and Eve (Genesis 3), so now the creation makes its definitive irruption in the garden (John 20:11–18). Sin condemned love as rabble-rousing and blasphemous, killed him, and buried him in the garden in the place where he had been cruci-fied. Out of the tomb in the garden, God raises the new man. Jesus, the faithful witness of God's way, was rejected by the builders of society but resurrected and confirmed as the Lord of creation by the God of life. The risen Lord now appears as the Gardener—the cul-tivator of the new creation. In the resurrection, God ratifies and con-firms the way of Jesus as God's way for humanity.

Mary Magdalene, who had followed him faithfully even unto the cross, who had never left him or become embarrassed by him, is the first one to see him and to go forth to proclaim the good news: "I have seen the Lord." This new couple is the beginning of the new creation of *shalom*—of a new state of being. The two earthly "rejects" are now the beginning of the new foundation. Jesus never broke the life-giving relationships with the world, with others, and with God; and Mary Magdalene never broke her relationship with Jesus. This new life-giving relationship that Jesus lived to the very end is the beginning of new life for each one of us and for the world. In him, the proper relationship has been re-established. This is the new life of the world and the basis of God's peace to reign in the world, and the world will become a peaceful garden of health and plenty (Apoc. 21:22, 22:1–5).

Conclusion

In Jesus and his followers, the kingdom of life—the reign of God—has indeed begun, but its completion is a long way off. In the present era those who are committed to generosity have to work for justice, for it is a common fact that many in the world are still committed to and guided by the underlying principles of the death-bearing world. We need laws to control the crime, violence, and injustice. Peace can only come through justice. But laws in themselves will never be suffi-cient. We must continue to work for conversions to the way of the God of life. That means a complete inversion of the values of our human societies, which for the most part continue to be structured upon the value systems of Genesis 3, 4, and 11. In the present era we are living in the midst of the multiple struggles between the kingdoms of death and the kingdom of life. As Christians following the lead of the primitive Christian communities, we know that our efforts will make a difference, even though an immediate result will not always be present or evident. Even when our lives are taken from us, we know that we resurrect and continue to live in the movements of our people. Our strength is our hope, our courage is our faith, and our life is the unlimited love that we have for others. To turn the present world order of death inside out so that it may become the kingdom of life is our mandate and our quest.

It will only be at the end of time when the historical project of God comes to completion that the cities—the symbols of humanity's efforts—will be converted into beautiful gardens—the symbol of god's gift of life to humanity. Humanity's efforts guided by God's wisdom will create new civilizations of peace—of wholeness. The cities will become beautiful gardens as a result of men and women's cooperation with God. These garden-cities are symbolic of civilizations built out of the kingdom of death.

Clear rivers of life-giving water will flow through our cities, which will be filled with trees of life that will produce fruit twelve times a year; their leaves will serve as medicine for the nations. The gates of the cities of men and women—the political and cultural frontiers between nations—will never be shut to anyone, for no person will be considered profane, unworthy, stranger, or outsider. There shall be no darkness, for the truth will be known as it really is, and there shall be no temples, monuments, or towers in the cities, for God alone will be God. There, we shall see God face to face (reflection based on Apocalypse 21 and 22).

In the end life will be the perfect and unending relationship with one another, with all of nature, and with God. In the interim we must work diligently for justice. In the end struggles for justice will no longer be necessary, for the justice of God will reign. The proper relationships will have been re-established. Humanity will have truly been rehabilitated. There will finally be peace on earth because the orderliness of all creation will be a reality. Beginning in Christ, God has placed us in the proper relationship. When what has started in Christ comes to perfection in all, life will indeed exist in its fullness— SHALOM.

NOTES

1. For an excellent presentation on the evolution of the biblical meaning of justice, consult E. Schillebeeckx, *Christ, the Experience of Jesus as Lord* (New York: Seabury, 1980), especially pages 132–54. This essay is the work of a pastor and will therefore concentrate more on the function of sin and grace in the historical and concrete life of the world in which we live.

2. For some clear examples, consult F. Houtart, "The Global Aspects of Dependence and Oppression," in V. Elizondo and N. Greinacher, eds., *Tension Between the Churches of the First World and the Third World* (New York: Seabury, 1981), pp. 3–11.

3. On the use of the term *definitive* instead of *eternal* in John 6:68, consult *El Evangelio de Juan*, translated by J. Juan Mateos and J. Barreto (Madrid: Cristiandad, 1976), p. 352.

4. For a good work on the development of culture and the interplay of biology and the environment in the formation of culture, consult J. Ruffie, *De la biologie à la culture* (Paris: Flammarion, 1978).

5. For some creative insights on the couple as the image of God, consult John Paul II's Wednesday audiences of October 31, 1979, to January 16, 1980. All were published in the *Osservatore Romano*.

6. One of the great scandals of the world continues to be that those who are today called underdeveloped and uncivilized by the dominant powers of today's world have been robbed of the great art treasures produced by their people. The monuments of the incredible achievements of the ancient civilizations of the world are found today in the great museums of New York, Berlin, Paris, London, and the Vatican, while the very peoples they were stolen from are called savage, uncivilized, culturally deprived, and backward. I wonder when Christian countries will return the great treasures of art to their legitimate owners.

7. R. Girard, *Des choses cachées depuis la Fondacion du monde* (Paris: Grossett); W. Ryan, *Blaming the Victim* (New York: Vintage Books, 1976) and M. Marty, *The Righteous Empire* (New York: Macmillan, 1970).

8. This phenomenon happened, not only in the beginnings of Latin America, but within our own times wherever occupation troops have gone in: Europe, North America, and Asia—especially in Korea and South Vietnam.

9. Whereas true love between people that really goes beyond the racial stereotypes that keep people socially apart is a beautiful thing, marriage across racial lines as an inner desire to prove oneself or because only the members of the "superior" group appear as truly beautiful and desirable is both destructive and insulting.

10. R. Burggraeve, "The Ethical Basis for a Humane Society according to Emmanuel Levinas," *Ephemerides Theologicae Lovanienses* 57 (1981); Gibson Winter, *The New Creation as Metropolis* (New York: Macmillan, 1965).

11. This was the key theme discussed at the general assembly of the Ecumenical Association of Third World Theologians meeting in New Delhi, India, in August 1981. Christ and the Church came to the continents of the Third World as justifying and even sacralizing the conquest, rape, and destruction of these peoples. Today, one of the key challenges of Christians of the Third World is to reclaim the original Jesus and the original movement of the first followers of Jesus who came from among the ranks of the poor, the marginated, the servants, the slaves, and the foreigners. For a good analysis of early Christianity, consult G. Theissen, *Le Christianisme de Jesus* (Paris: Desclee, 1968); T. Balasuriya,

Eucharist and Human Liberation (Sri Lanka: Centre for Society and Religion, 1979); L. Boff, *Eclesiogenesis* (Sanander: Sal Terrae, 1979).

12. S.v. "Justice," Léon-Dufour, *Dictionary of Biblical Theology* (New York: Desclee, 1974).

13. 1 Cor. 1:17–31; 3:1–16; Luke 10:21–22; Matt. 11:25.

14. It is my contention that the theme "rejection/builders" is key to understanding the liberating way of the Son of God who became human for our salvation. It is picked up from Ps. 118:22 and Isa. 28:16 and is used consistently in the New Testament, beginning with the earliest kerygma of the Church in Acts 4:11. It is also used in Matt. 21:42; Mark 12:10; Luke 20:17; Rom. 9:33; 1 Peter 2:7. This whole theme of the world's rejection is also picked up by John's Gospel and is especially brought out in John 1:11 and 15:18–16:4.

15. Consult also the Epistle of James.

16. The miracles of Jesus were signs of the kingdom. Many of the advances of modern technology in the fields of housing, food, and medicine can certainly be seen as signs of the kingdom, especially when the advances of science are used in the service of people and not against them. The daily achievements that take place in our hospitals and on our farms produce effects that surpass the miracles of Jesus. The question is: "In whose favor are they used?"

17. For some excellent clarifications of the notion of material poverty as a curse, consult the final document of the Third General Conference of the Episcopacy of Latin America, generally referred to as "Puebla," especially the paragraphs numbered 1154–1160, 30, 64–70.

18. It is not infrequent that upon closer analysis, the ones who appear to be the enemies of "law and order" are in effect the defenseless victims of those in control.

19. *Dei verbum* of Vatican II, no. 2; Eph. 1:3–10.

QUESTIONS FOR REFLECTION AND DISCUSSION

1. What is the biblical foundation for human responsibility for the world?

2. Can there be a just war in our time?

3. What differences exist between the biblical notion of justice discussed in this essay and the idea of justice in the U.S. Constitution?

4. In what sense is companionship the fulfillment of humanity?

5. How can we reconcile the prevalence and strength of the "kingdom of Death" in human history with the vision of humanity as *imago Dei?*

II

EDUCATIONAL

ISSUES

5. Religious Education for Justice by Educating Justly

THOMAS H. GROOME

IN MANY WAYS the title is a summary of what I want to say: that religious education must educate for justice and that such educating must be done justly. I will begin by identifying my own social/political context and the perspectives from which I speak. I will then attempt to clarify how I understand the word *justice*, or at least how I am using it here. I will lay out two basic theses, attempt to substantiate them, and conclude with some pedogogical principles that might enable us to educate for justice by educating justly.

My Context and Perspectives

I come to this topic as a white male, but one who has struggled for some time now to journey faithfully toward an inclusive consciousness that opposes social discrimination of any kind.

I come to it as a middle-class American, a citizen of the richest and most consumer-oriented society in the world, but an American who is convinced that our credo of liberty and justice "for all" does not mean for all Americans alone but for our whole human family, an American convinced that the struggles for justice and freedom in the Third and Fourth Worlds demand a revolution in values and lifestyle in our First World.

I come to the topic as a confessing Christian, but one who is deeply convinced that Christianity must show itself to be capable of empowering personal and social transformation if it is to be worth my life investment and, I might add, if it is to be faithful to its own "center."

I come to the topic as a religious educator, but one convinced that the process of religious education must promote a socially critical consciousness that in turn empowers emancipatory action toward the end of humanization and mutuality for all God's people.

As a religious educator I work in these contexts and in the historical context of a Christian faith community. For this reason, I will not deal with the mandate of all education to educate justly and for justice, although that indeed is my conviction. I will speak instead from and about my own particularity and praxis as a Christian religious educator. In addition, my understanding of social justice is shaped, in large part, by the trajectory of development that is evident in the corpus of Roman Catholic social teaching since *Rerum novarum* of 1891.[1]

A Working Definition of Justice

The Catholic understanding of justice arises from a dual commitment to the dignity of the *individual* human person and to the *social* context of human existence in which that dignity finds expression. Because we are created in the image and likeness of God (the *imago Dei* tenet has been a grounding principle of social teachings in the Christian church since the Alexandrian School of the third century)[2] each person has certain inalienable rights that are his or hers by "copyright" and not by the generosity of any social system. On the other hand, these rights are always exercised in a social context and therein must be both promoted and regulated to ensure the greatest good for all members of the society. Each society or social grouping in turn must exercise its rights in a way that respects and promotes, not only the rights of its own members, but the rights of people in other societies as well.

In light of the individual and social groundings of human rights the promotion of these rights requires three constitutive expressions or dimensions of justice, namely *commutative, distributive*, and *social* justice. These dimensions are constitutive of justice in that each one is essential to the realization of justice for all in an historical context. David Hollenbach has offered insightful and succinct descriptions of each expression of justice, and his position will serve us well here.

Hollenbach writes, "Commutative justice is concerned with the relationships which bind individual to individual in the sphere of private transactions."[3] In other words, commutative justice is the guarantee of equal dignity and rights for individuals in their one-on-one relationships. Because those human rights are always exercised in the context of society, that society, if established for the common good of all, has a responsibility to promote and guarantee the equal rights of its own members, without violating the rights of people in other societies. The society must see to it that access to common rights is distributed equally to all. Thus, "distributive justice determines how public social goods are to be allocated to individuals or groups" so as "to ensure that the rights of all are guaranteed in social, economic, political and cultural interaction."[4]

As the whole society has duties to the individuals within it, conversely, the individual members have duties to the whole society. The latter is the dimension of social justice. "Social justice specifies how the activities of individuals and groups are to be aggregated so that they converge to create the social good."[5] Or to state that another way, "social justice is the measure which orders personal activities in a way which is suitable for the production and protection of the common good."[6]

As these three dimensions of justice find expression in historical reality, there is also, from the perspective of Christian faith and Catholic social teaching, a guiding spirit that should empower and pervade the doing of justice if minimalism and legalism are to be avoided. This is the spirit of universal love that is required of us by the biblical mandate to love God and our neighbor, with neighbor knowing no bounds—to love especially the poor, the downtrodden, and those to whom justice is denied. There has been a growing awareness in Christian social teaching that living justly and for justice must be grounded in *agape* love as exemplified in the life and preaching of Jesus.

In the *Summa Theologica*, Thomas Aquinas insisted that love and justice co-exist in the same unity as matter and form; in other words, authentic love and true justice cannot exist apart from each other. We have often forgotten Aquinas's insight. We have managed to separate the two of them, thus privatizing Christianity and reducing love to a one-on-one affair with little or no social responsibility. Contemporary Catholic social ethics, informed by social analysis, is convinced that the Great Commandment can only be lived historically as the struggle for justice—distributive, commutative, and social.

Based on these reflections, I offer the following definition of justice from a Christian faith perspective: Justice is doing the truth in love. The "truth" is that there are certain inalienable rights and duties that individuals have with and to each other (commutative justice), that the society has to its members (distributive justice), that the members have to society (social justice); and these rights and duties must be *done* (not just made into ideas for reflection) with the gospel spirit of *agape*—unconditional love for others as for ourselves.

Two Theses

I propose two closely related theses: (1) that *all* Christian religious education regardless of context or curriculum must educate for justice, and (2) that such religious education for justice requires that we educate justly. In laying out the following rationale for my theses I am not implying that only people of Christian faith can be committed to the struggle for justice. On the contrary, the established Christian churches of this country are often poor fellow travelers in the quest for justice. People from other ideological frameworks have seemed at least as much, if not more, committed to justice than confessing Christians. But I *am* claiming that if confessing Christians take the center of our faith tradition seriously then that will indeed place upon us the mandate to educate for justice, for doing the truth in love.

Scriptural/Theological Rationale

The Christian faith community must educate for justice and do so justly because the central theme in the preaching and life of Jesus was the reign of God. As long as the symbol of God's Kingdom remains central to how we understand lived Christian faith, then the quest for justice can never again become peripheral to, or merely one aspect among many others in, what it means to be Christian or to sponsor others to so live.

Contemporary Scripture scholars and theologians are agreed that the central theme in the preaching and life of Jesus Christ was the Kingdom of God.[7] In the Hebrew Scriptures, the symbol of God's Kingdom expresses two convictions that are rooted deeply in Hebrew consciousness. It expresses the *effective present rule and sovereignty* of God in the world as its creator and sustainer, and it refers to *the final completion of creation* at the "end time" when God's will for creation will be achieved perfectly. Because of God's present activity within history on behalf of God's reign, the Hebrews believe that the Kingdom is already happening in our time and will come surely to final completion at the "end time."

Since it is happening now through God's activity and will come to completion at the "end time" by the power of God's grace, the Hebrews believe that the Kingdom is always the gift of God. But because they believe that God has entered into a covenant with them, they are convinced that as God's people they must live now according to God's will for creation. Central to this will of God for creation is the realization of the values of peace and justice. Thus, their covenant binds them to live with those values now in human time even as they await the completion of the Kingdom of Shalom in God's time.

In his preaching and living for the reign of God, Jesus was in continuity with his Hebrew roots. For him too, the Kingdom is a dynamic and concrete reality that points to God's saving action in the midst of history to bring about the complete realization of God's will for all creation. For Jesus also the Kingdom is both "already" and "not yet." He goes beyond his Hebrew tradition, however, in at least one significant way. *He considers the Kingdom to have already and definitely arrived and points to his own person, his work and ministry, as its effective agent.* In other words, Jesus understood himself to be God's definitive act in history on behalf of the Kingdom. As such, the Kingdom is, as always, God's gift. It is not something that can be brought about by human effort alone. But as it placed a mandate to live according to its values on the Hebrews, so Jesus made it clear that the gift of the kingdom in him demands a response now within this historical time. We must live now according to God's will. That will becomes a law for us that Jesus summarized as the radical law of love. His preaching of the law of the Kingdom is radical in that it is not only a law to love God *and* one's neighbor, but a law to love God *by* loving one's neighbor as oneself, with "neighbor" knowing no limits.

Although the Kingdom was the central theme in the preaching and life of Jesus, its centrality was not as evident in the preaching of the first Christian community and less so over the centuries since then. The first Christians began to preach Jesus as Lord and Savior. Implied in that *kerygma* was the preaching of what Jesus preached—the Kingdom—but it was more often left implicit than made explicit. When the Kingdom was preached, it was presented typically in a manner that overlooked the historical character and alreadyness of the Kingdom within history. It was preached exclusively as an otherworldly reality for after death, thus overlooking Jesus' insistence that the Kingdom is to be "already" even as it is "not yet."

Both the Kingdom's loss of centrality and its loss of historicity have been challenged, however, in our time. Beginning some two hundred years ago, there has gradually emerged a new awareness that (1) the Kingdom must be preached as the central theme of the gospel of Jesus, whom Christians accept as Lord and Savior, and (2) that the Kingdom is not just for later but is to begin and to be responded to within our historical time. In other words, there is a newfound awareness that the Kingdom as preached by Jesus places on us the mandate to live by its values now, even as we move toward its completion at the end time.

In one sense, we can say that by our historical activity we are to be co-creators with God of the final Kingdom. This does not mean that we are equal partners in bringing it about. The Kingdom is here and will come to completion by God's grace. But as God works out the

Kingdom within human history, God has chosen to work through the human activity that constitutes this history of ours. Thus, our human response to God's will for the Kingdom is not superfluous or inconsequential to its realization. In the mystery of the partnership into which God has entered with us, what we do and how we live "make a difference" for the completion of God's reign. Vatican II, in its *Constitution on the Church in the Modern World*, described our task well when it said that human effort is to "make ready the materials" of the Kingdom (no. 38) and that the "fruits" of our efforts will endure in the final Kingdom (no. 39).[8]

This recentalizing of the Kingdom of God in Christian consciousness and the awareness of the historical responsibility that the Kingdom places on us have far-reaching consequences for how and why we do Christian religious education. The symbol of the Kingdom has not been missing from our enterprise in the past, but traditionally Christian religious education has favored Matthew's phrase, "the Kingdom of Heaven." (Matthew was a good Jew and, not wanting to use the name of God, used "Heaven" as a synonym.) As a result the symbol was presented as the task of saving our souls for later on in Heaven. In fact, "the salvation of souls" was often posed as the *raison d'être* of Christian education. But without newfound awareness that the Kingdom of God (the preferred term of Mark and Luke, and of John when he refers to the Kingdom) does not point only to an extrahistorical reality but has already begun and is to be co-created by God's grace and human activity within history, Christian religious education takes on an urgent intrahistorical purpose as well as an extrahistorical one. The task of Christian religious education is to sponsor people to live now with and for the values of God's Kingdom within our historical time and thus participate, by God's grace, in the coming of God's reign.

Ultimately, the mandate that the Kingdom places upon us within history is to "do the truth in love." In other words, if Christian religious education makes the Kingdom of God as preached by Jesus Christ its central theme, then it must educate for justice. In addition, how the enterprise is carried on must itself stand critiqued under the mandate of the Kingdom. Christian religious education must not only educate for justice but must do so justly. If an unjust educational process is used to educate for justice, it is likely to defeat its own purpose. In education for justice, the purpose and the process must be at one.

Pedagogical/Political Rationale

Because the ultimate purpose of Christian religious education is to lead people out (*e-ducere*) toward the reign of God, it must educate justly and for justice. But inherent in the very nature of the pedagogical act itself we find another compelling reason why Christian religious education must make educating justly and for justice the central and constitutive element of the whole enterprise.

I understand the act of educating as "a political activity with pilgrims in time that deliberately and intentionally attends with people to our present, to the past heritage it embodies, and to the future possibility it holds for the total person and society."[9]

A political act is any deliberate and structured intervention in people's lives that attempts to influence how they live their lives in society. Since education is always a historical activity that is carried on by some social group in order to influence how people live their lives in society, it is eminently political. By what we teach or fail to teach, and by how we teach it, education has far-reaching social/political consequences. Education is never politically neutral. By the very nature of the activity, education cannot be a "private" or "objective" enterprise that is "value free." It is a public and social activity that is always value laden. Education can pretend to be nonpolitical by attempting to take an "objective" stance toward the present social realities within which it takes place. But then it has the inevitable consequence of fitting people into those social realities as they presently exist. As such, it is practicing politics, albeit the politics of maintenance and silence. Education of any kind can also prepare people to participate critically and creatively in history for its transformation. And then it is being no less and no more political than if it practiced the politics of silence.

Christian religious educators may be tempted to agree that general education is indeed political but that religious education is not, that our enterprise deals only with the spiritual life and as such is apolitical. Such a position falls into the false (although time-honored) dichotomy often made between religion and life, between the individual and the citizen, between salvation history and human history. That our enterprise, too, has political consequences can be seen most obviously in the context of our curriculum decisions.

The curriculum question can be posed as follows: What stories, traditions, values, myths, practices, and so on will we make accessible to learners in the present and how and to what end will we make them available? Like other educators, religious eductors can choose a version of our Story and Vision that will help to legitimate and maintain the present as it is, or we can choose a version that will recreate our present toward what it ought to be but is not yet. A look at some of the curriculum options regarding the major themes of our Christian faith tradition may help to clarify my point here.

When we present an understanding of *Christian existence*, we can call people to live by the values of the Kingdom within history or we can present Christian existence exclusively as a quest for the salvation of one's own soul outside of history, thus allowing people to be oblivious to their responsibilities for the Kingdom in the world.

God can be presented as an almighty, removed, and all-male God or as an inclusive God who is with us to call us to mutuality and relationship with each other. *Sin* can be presented only as a private and personal affair between the individual and God, or it can also be presented as an injury to the social well-being that promotes and perpetuates itself by becoming congealed in sinful social structures. *Repentence*, too, can be presented as a private matter or as the call to *metanoia*—transformation that is both personal and social.

Our *Christology* can be that of a "good old plastic Jesus" who was "nice" and saved us by "coming down," or we can present the radical Word of the historical Jesus who lived, died, and rose up to free us and demanded a response from us of living with and for freedom within our historical setting.

The *sacraments* can be presented as automatic channels of God's grace for our own sanctification alone, or they can be presented as mediations of God's saving activity that empower us to live for others and for the world. The *Scriptures* can be presented with an exclusive emphasis on the "kingly trajectory" in which we find consolation and legitimation, or we can also include the "prophetic trajectory" in which we will find confrontation and critique of ourselves and of our social structures.[10] We can present the *Church* as a sectarian salvation club for getting souls to heaven or as a universal sacrament of God's Kingdom in Jesus that is to effect what it signifies—the coming of God's reign in the midst of history.

The examples could go on, and similar questions could be raised regarding any theme or dimension of our faith Story. Nor can we assume that we have always made our curriculum choices out of an emancipatory interest, in a way that enables people to do the truth in love. Paul Surlis contends that in fact we typically do the contrary. Writing about the political nature of religious education in America, Surlis says:

> To uphold and legitimate existing social and political institutions is a massive contribution which religion makes to the existing state of affairs. More-

over, in focusing attention on personal sin and sinfulness and on the practice of inter-personal love, religion loses its counter-cultural, prophetic or
critical stance vis-à-vis public values and policies. Privatized religion is not
non-political. It is political in that it supports the way things are.[11]

There are at least three important implications that flow from this
reflection on curriculum. First, whatever curriculum choices we make
in religious education will have political/social implications for ourselves and for the lives of the people we educate. Second, the diversity
of examples just cited should remind us that education for justice
cannot be merely one isolated theme among many others in the content and activity of Christian religious education. Justice is not a "separate" topic, and education for justice cannot be treated, as is often
the case, as merely one elective among many in our curriculum.

In *Justice in the World* the second general assembly of the Synod of
Bishops (1971) declared:

> Action on behalf of justice and participation in the transformation of the
> world fully appear to us as a constitutive dimension of the preaching of the
> Gospel, or, in other words, of the Church's mission for the redemption of
> the human race and its liberation from every oppressive situation.[12]

If justice is a "constitutive" dimension of the gospel, then every aspect of our gospel, faith that we teach must make present the mandate
of justice. Whether we are teaching Christology or ecclesiology,
theodicy or sacraments, the call to justice must be present in how and
what we teach; otherwise we are not teaching the Christian gospel.
Justice must be a constitutive dimension in every aspect of our curriculum.

Third, since education is, by its nature, a social/political activity,
then education for justice must be done by a political act that is itself
just. This third implication sounds even more compelling when we
state it in Freirean terms. A "banking method" of educating for
justice defeats its own purpose because it is unjust.[13] An educational
praxis that robs people of their own word and deposits already formulated information in passive receptacles (even though it may be
"justice information") is inherently unjust and is most likely to promote further injustice. In other words, to educate for justice, Christian religious education must educate justly.

Educating Justly for Justice: Some General Principles

In light of and in response to the foregoing reflections on educating
justly for justice, I offer the following principles for the praxis of
Christian religious education.

General Principles

1. The educational process must invite people to express their own word, to name their own reality. If only the teacher does the naming, then the participants are brought to the teacher's "knowing" rather than to their own. Such a banking process is inherently unjust and is not likely to bring people to decision and action to reshape their social reality. To fulfill this principle of naming, the educational process must be one of dialogue and mutuality between all of the participants in the learning context: students with teacher, teacher with students, and students with each other. It cannot be a situation in which the teacher acts "over" the students or "for" the students. Instead, there must be a group of people who are "with" each other in dialogue as co-learners.

2. Having named reality, the participants must be brought to critically reflect upon what they have named. Without critical reflection, reality as it appears to be is taken as a given and is likely to be accepted fatalistically instead of re-created toward the values of the Kingdom.

Critical reflection invites the activities of critical reason, analytical memory, and creative imagination. With critical reason people can "decode" (Freire's word) reality that comes to them coded. With critical reason they can move beyond the appearances of reality and distinguish between what is and what ought to be. Analytical memory invites people to uncover the genesis of their own social activity, to see the constitutive interests, assumptions, and ideologies that undergird present praxis. Creative imagination invites people to create toward an alternative future, rather than allowing the future to be determined by what is "given" in the present.

From such critical reflection on what is named or expressed as "present reality," the participants can come to critical consciousness (what Freire calls conscientization) that will find expression in action for justice even as it arises from present praxis.

3. In the context of Christian religious education for justice done justly, not only must the "knowing" of the participants (in the praxis sense of knowing) be attended to, but the "knowing" that comes to us from the "faith handed down" through the broader Christian community must also be made accessible to the learning group. To represent this faith of the community I use the metaphors of the Christian Story and Vision.[14]

The faith of the Christian community is the Story of how God has been with our people and how our people have responded to God's activity and intensions. Those intentions are the Vison that arises from the Story to call us forward to God's reign. As such, the Story and Vision both console and confront us; they offer the gift of God's Kingdom already and the sure promise of its fulfillment even as they demand that we live within our time with the values of God's reign.

In making accessible the Story and Vision of the broader Christian community, the educator must be aware of the social/political implications of the choices he or she makes in selecting what to make present and with what emphasis. The examples of different curriculum choices that I mentioned above are relevant here. The guiding principles in all curriculum decision for Christian religious education are (a) that the Word of Scripture is a Word of justice, and (b) that the holiness of God to which we are called (the Kingdom) is the justice of God. In light of these principles, whatever is made accessible from our Scripture and tradition must be likely to promote and empower the quest for justice. If our curriculum does not promote justice then it is unfaithful to the "faith handed down."

4. The Christian Story and Vision that call people to a faith that does justice must not be imposed upon people's lives as an ideology from outside of lived experience nor as a final word that robs them of their own word. The Story and Vision must be made accessible in a way that invites people to personally appropriate them to their own lives and situations. This fourth principle means, then, that the educational process must promote a dialectic between what the participants have named and reflected upon (their own stories and visions) and what is made accessible as the faith of the broader Christian community. In order words, what the participants already "know" and the version of the Story/Vision made accessible to them must be placed in dialogue and dialectic with each other. In this way the stories/visions and the Story/Vision can become mutual sources of truth, correction, and creativity for each other. Without such dialogue and dialectic, the word of the participants is silenced and the word of the educator becomes a hardened and unquestioned ideology that is not likely to promote justice.

5. Justice, from a Christian perspective, is realized when the truth is done in love. Justice is not achieved by simply *knowing about* the truth or love, but by *doing* the one in the other. In other words, if Christian religious education is to promote justice, then it must invite people to decision, action, and commitment on behalf of justice and not simply to a body of new ideas. Such an invitation to praxis must be a deliberate and intentional part of the educational process and not merely implied, assumed, or left to chance.

This "invitation to decision" principle arises from the conviction that education for justice done justly must arise from historical praxis, be informed and empowered by the faith of the Christian community, and return to historical praxis again. In light of this, not only should the educational process invite decision, but where possible and appropriate (according to the particular topic of the curriculum) the educational enterprise should provide opportunities for overt historical activity that will be a doing of the truth in love.

Basic Principles

I call these last two principles basic because they undergird the general principles already outlined; they refer to the attitude that the religious educator for justice done justly must bring to the task.

First, "elitism" of any kind must be avoided at all costs if the educator is to be with the students as co-learners in a relationship of dialogue and mutuality. There is a certain kind of self-righteousness and "better-than-thou" attitude that can creep into the mentality of educators committed to justice. When Jesus said, "Let the one among you who has not sinned be the first to cast a stone at her" (John 8:8) he was attempting to show, among other things, the democratic nature of sin. None of us is without sins of injustice. Thus, self-righteousness and elitism are inappropriate and foreign to the enterprise of education for justice. (They are, in fact, unjust.) As we attempt to sponsor people to do the truth in love we must do so in humility and with an awareness of our own complicity in injustice.

Second, religious education for justice must avoid promoting a debilitating kind of guilt that leaves people powerless instead of empowered to act. Over our history, Christian religious education has often had the consequence of causing such debilitating guilt. We must learn from our past mistakes. There is a kind of healthy guilt that all of us should have about the injustices in our world; it must be a guilt that empowers to action and not one that overpowers into paralysis and inactivity. Two caveats may help to avoid promoting such paralyzing guilt.

First, the critical analysis of reality that is carried on in the religious educational process must not be unduly psychological but must be done from a sociological perspective as well. Too much psychologizing gives the impression that fault and blame belong to the individual as individual. The end result of such psychologizing can be to blame the victim. Thus, there is an absolute need for a sociological analysis that raises up and critiques the social and political structures that mediate injustice. But sociological analysis must not be allowed to go to the other extreme of blaming the generic "them" for all injustice in society. This would only allow the participants in the learning process to renege on their personal responsibilities. The reality of injustice and the mandate to promote justice must be reflected upon from both psychological and sociological perspectives, because the sources of injustice are both personal and social, and our sins of injustice are both personal and social.

A second caveat, if debilitating guilt and historical paralysis are to be avoided, is not to presume that the work of justice is either a human task alone or the work of God alone. In the context of working for justice there are two bad heresies to be avoided. One is the Catholic heresy of "good works." The other is the Protestant heresy of "cheap grace." The first is Pelagianism revisited and will lead to debilitating guilt when we see how far short our human efforts fall. The second accepts the givenness of sin with fatalism and leaves its redress entirely to God.

In the mystery of the covenant that God has entered into with us, the Kingdom and its presence/coming is indeed the gift of God. But God's grace works typically through human agency, and we have the obligation of being responsible instruments of God's activity. Unless we remember that there are two parties to the covenant, we will fall into either debilitating guilt or historical irresponsibility.

Conclusion

To do the truth in love is the historical mandate placed upon us by the preaching of Jesus, whose central theme was the Kingdom of God. In Christian religious education justice must be a constitutive element of all our curriculum and of all our educational processes as well. No aspect, topic, or activity in Christian religious education can be free of the Kingdom's mandate. We must educate for justice and do so justly.

NOTES

1. See *Rerum novarum*, translated, in Etienne Gilson, ed., *The Church Speaks to the Modern World: The Social Teachings of Leo XIII* (Garden City, N.Y.: Doubleday Image, 1954).
2. See Walter Burghardt, "Free Like God: Recapturing an Ancient Anthropology," *Theology Digest* 26:4 (Winter 1978), pp. 343–64.
3. David Hollenbach, *Claims in Conflict: Retrieving and Renewing the Catholic Human Rights Tradition* (New York: Paulist Press, 1979), p. 145.
4. Ibid., pp. 245 and 151.
5. Ibid., p. 145.
6. Ibid., p. 152.

7. For a more complete statement on the centrality of the Kingdom of God to our understanding of Christian faith, see Thomas H. Groome, *Christian Religious Education: Sharing Our Story and Vision* (San Francisco: Harper & Row, 1980), especially chapter 3.

8. Walter M. Abbott, ed., *The Documents of Vatican II* (New York: America Press, 1966), pp. 235–38.

9. See Groome, p. 21.

10. I take the terms *kingly* and *prophetic trajectory* from Walter M. Brueggemann. See *The Prophetic Imagination* (Philadelphia: Fortress Press, 1978).

11. Paul J. Surlis, "Youth Ministers and the Politicization of Youth," *The Living Light* 18:3 (Fall 1981), p. 254.

12. Synod of Bishops, Second General Assembly (1971), "Justice in the World," in *The Gospel of Peace and Justice*, Joseph Gremillian, ed. (Maryknoll, N.Y., Orbis Books, 1976), p. 514.

13. See Paulo Freire, *Pedagogy of the Oppressed* (New York: Seabury Press, 1970), pp. 57 ff.

14. See Groome, chapter 9, for a more detailed statement on the metaphors of Story and Vision.

QUESTIONS FOR REFLECTION AND DISCUSSION

1. How does the Kingdom of God function to move religious education in a more social and ethical direction?

2. What is the full meaning of education for justice?

3. What do you think is the role of guilt in education for justice? Is there any positive feature to inducement of such feelings?

4. What is the relationship between education for justice and educating justly?

5. What is the concrete value for an educator for justice in acknowledging that we are aided by God's grace in this enterprise?

6. Justice, Peace, and the Pedagogy of Grass Roots Christian Community

MAURICE L. MONETTE, O.M.I.

TO APPROACH basic Christian communities as if these were some new type of education for justice or to dismiss them as some quaint phenomenon appropriate only in the Third World would be to misunderstand their profoundly radical nature. Basic Christian communities are in fact *the* vehicle for a new pastoral response to recent major developments in global politics, economics, and culture. These communities, moreover, represent a new way of conceiving social justice education.

It is the purpose of this article to explore the radical significance of basic Christian communities for justice education in the United States. This radical impact can most clearly be seen in the light of a brief analysis of recent U.S. social reality and in contrast with what we will call "liberal" justice education.

Our discussion will focus mainly on the Catholic ecclesiastical context, since it is that context in which the pivotal *communidades de base* of Latin America are emerging and the context with which this author is most familiar.

The United States: A Social Analysis

That the social, political, cultural, and economic reality of the United States has changed since the late sixties is not news to those of us who have lived through it all. The profound nature of that change, however, is brought home to us in analyses like that in Joe Holland and Peter Henriot's *Social Analysis: Linking Faith and Justice.*

Henriot and Holland divide the history of industrial capitalism into three stages: laissez-faire, developing during the nineteenth century; social welfare, from 1900 to 1968; and national security, from 1968 to the present. It is their thesis "that our present social context represents a third stage of industrial capitalism and that this stage is fundamentally different than the second stage during which most of us grew up.[1] New pastoral strategies are needed in response.

The dominant feature of our economic life, the authors tell us, is now the transnational corporation and the transnational bank. Transnationals have increased control over national economies and, because of geographical and industrial diversification, over national workers' movements as well.[2] The deep structures of capitalism, namely capital and technology, have thus undergone fundamental change: capital has become less national and increasingly transnational, and technology, less balanced in terms of capital and labor and more capital intensive (using less labor in relation to capital). In consequence life in the United States will be different: *Economically*, a condition of permanent inflation will continue to cause structural unemployment,[3] disintegration of strong unions, breakdown of the alliance between management and labor, and downward mobility for the once prosperous majority of the population. *Politically*, social welfare considerations will yield to national security imperatives. The domestic scene, in other words, is being streamlined for reasons of international competition. The state is becoming more authoritarian and less regulatory than in former days. *Culturally*, our preoccupation with national security will continue to shift our focus from progress and abundance to austerity and lowered expectations. Our nation's understanding of freedom as opportunity for all is giving way to that of freedom as security for the profitable investments of the few.

If this analysis is accurate, the new stage of capitalism does not auger a bright future. Especially hard hit will be the already marginalized, the middle class, and the labor unions. Internationally, the effect will be disastrous on Third World countries, especially given their lack of a social welfare base to cushion the impact of the national security state.

Advanced Capitalism and the Church

How has the Catholic Church responded to the recent stages of capitalism?[4] Since Leo XIII the Church's response to liberal capitalism has consisted in adapting the traditional religious institution to secular democracy and capitalism. The Church, in other words, has liberalized itself in order to conquer liberalism for Christ. Founded on the principle of the separation of church and state, this pastoral strategy has thoroughly immersed the Church in the liberal world by way of parallel social institutions (e.g., hospitals, credit unions, schools). The Second Vatican Council, with its documents on the Church in the modern world and on religious freedom, has consolidated the gains of this strategy. Vatican II, however, has been more than a summit for the adaptive stance; it has become the source of a new pastoral stance toward national security industrial capitalism. It is evident in our previous analysis of this advanced capitalism that there are desirable limits to the Church's adaptive stance. If the Church is to be faithful to its story and vision, it cannot support the state that systematically encourages widespread marginalization and violates basic human rights in the name of profit and security for the few. These problems with the new stage of capitalism have warranted a shift in the response of the Church. Its previous tasks of preserving tradition and helping people through liberal change are giving way to the new task of transforming society. In the name of justice, the Church's new role is to call for the transformation of technology and capital to serve basic human needs and fundamental human rights on local as well as global levels.

The main lines of this new strategy are already emerging. The initiative for change, however, is not coming exclusively from religious professionals and bishops as in earlier decades or from the middle classes in Europe or the United States. The initiative is arising from those who have much at stake in the search for a more just society: the poor, the laity, and the peoples of Third World countries.[5]

It is within the context of this new pastoral thrust that we can, I believe, speak most accurately about the significance of basic Christian communities. These small vibrant communities of and for the poor are emerging as the main vehicle for the transformative pastoral strategy. Informed by biblical spirituality, these spontaneous communities are assuming the mission, not of Christ as King as in previous stages, but of Christ as Prophet and Servant.

Justice Communities: An International Response

The number of *communidades* in Latin America is staggering. There are fifty thousand in Brazil alone. They are arising from within a situation of social and political oppression perpetuated by military dictatorships attempting to achieve rapid industrial growth. Marginalized and voiceless, the poor are seeking the protection of an institution in which they can find the courage, strength, and hope needed to build a better future. Its own liberty curtailed by laws of national security, the Church is nevertheless shaping itself according to the needs of the poor. It is becoming the haven of the oppressed.

These *communidades* defy definition inasmuch as they differ greatly in their structure, their degree of cohesion, and their aims. One observer of the scene has discerned three categories of *communidades*, or three stages in their development:

1. Communities of prayer and gospel-sharing. These are communities that are concerned, especially in their early days, only with the formation of religious groups and the strengthening of ecclesial and sacramental life.
2. Communities of mutual aid. These are communities that in addition devote themselves to certain social tasks—to charitable action, to mutual aid within the neighborhood—and begin to think about improving or building collective facilities like dispensaries or primary schools.
3. Communities that change society. These are communities that go a step further along the road to political awareness and begin to demand social reforms.[6]

How are *communidades* formed? It appears that generally *communidades* proliferate where there is support from priests and bishops. Often they are born when a pastoral worker gathers people to reflect on the gospel. Participants come to realize that they are not merely part of some ecclesial structure, but that they themselves *are* the Church. Leaders emerge as servants from within the group. Together these victims of injustice critically reflect on their plight in the light of the gospel and seek appropriate active response. The *communidades* were born in the early sixties during the severe shortage of priests. Now, they are re-creating, and not merely improving, the very institution that gave them birth.

Church people in the United States are increasingly curious about the Third World phenomenon of *communidades de base*.[7] Perhaps this curiosity stems from a deep yearning for more intense communal life, perhaps from a growing identification with the plight of the poor, perhaps from a glimmer of hope that the Church can be more than a noncritical sidekick of the political and economic powers that be. Whatever the case, these communities are not foreign to our own soil. They exist in the First World as well as in the Third.

In countries like the United States, we cannot generally claim to be victims of great social and political oppression. Our social life is not constrained by military dictatorship; our channels of social mobility are rather open; our politics are democratic. There are, however, members of our society who are indeed victims. An increasing number of them are members of our church.[8] Their cries are as urgent and desperate as the cries of the victims in the Third World. It is in response to these cries and to the structures that perpetuate suffering that communities of justice have also arisen in our First World countries.

Christians are organizing around a variety of justice issues: poverty, unemployment, workers' rights, world hunger, prison reform, womens' rights, human rights, disarmament, nuclear energy, and others. Two types of communities seem to be forming. One researcher has categorized these as "popular" and "progressive":

1. Popular communities are characteristically composed of the exploited and marginalized people in our society. These are organized by the poor to advance their own struggle for justice. Leadership stems from the group, although clergy and religious professionals often provide support and assistance. In most cases the community life of these groups involves prayer, liturgy, or gospel reflection. Their link with the institutional Church is often unclear. Sometimes the Church provides moral and material support, sometimes resistance and negative reaction.

2. Progressive communities, on the other hand, are composed of Christians who have become increasingly aware of social and economic injustices at home and abroad. While notably different in terms of issues, analysis, and style, these groups are characterized by their engagement in and support for the struggles of exploited and marginalized people. They focus on education and action designed to increase public awareness and to generate pressure to change policies. Gospel reflection and liturgical events are integrated into their community life. Many such groups receive moral and financial support from the institutional Church, at the national if not the diocesan and regional levels.[9]

The Educative Justice Community

Basic communities are not some new type of justice education. They are primarily communities, communities of the poor and for the poor engaged in the struggle for justice. They are "educative" but not "educational": their primary purpose is not education. The rise of basic communities represents, I believe, a major shift in our understanding of religious education and the Church's mission of education. The diagram (Table 1) illustrates in broad strokes this shift from what we will call a "liberal" model to a "radical" model. Both models have co-existed in the United States since the early seventies. The liberal model reached its peak in the late sixties. The radical model is in ascendance, but confined to small sectors of the Christian population.

Liberal education is in essence a renewal venture.[10] The Second Vatican Council stirred a wave of change that left Catholics breathlessly in need of catching up. Education has helped them to cope with the modernization of their Church. It has done so through classes in the theology of the Council and sacramental preparation programs for parents and training programs for those assuming the new lay liturgical roles. Through education, it is hoped that members will adapt to a Church that is in turn adapting itself to a modern world. There remain, of course, those who resist adaptation and use education mainly to defend and preserve the ways that belong to more reactionary times.

In the context of this adaptive stance, the immediate purpose of liberal education has been to nurture faith in such a way that it frees one's humanity, self-actualizes the Christian as a person and promotes growth and self-fulfillment. This purpose has often been contrasted with indoctrination that regiments individuals and stifles pluralism in the name of a "higher" good. The liberal model assumes that growth in faith can and should occur within the renewed structures of the Church.

Methodologically, liberal education is characterized by diversity. On one hand it has preferred a transmission approach not unlike that of the Baltimore Catechism. The difference is in the content, that is, the theology of Vatican II. Despite the arguments of the liberal theorists, the lecture method continues to be the most popular method of instruction.

Table 1. Comparison of Liberal and Radical Models of Education

	Liberal Education	Radical Education
Social stance	adaptive	transformative
Context	programs	communities
Purpose	faith that frees; pluralism	faith that does justice; interdependence
Method	both transmission and experiential exercises	praxis
Alliance	middle class	the poor
Initiative	clergy and professionals	laity

On the other hand, however, liberal education has pioneered various "experiential" approaches more in keeping with the purpose of nurturing personal faith. Games and discussion techniques have been used to set up the lesson at the beginning and to debrief or integrate the lesson at the end. These methods gained popularity in the early seventies when the content of liberal education shifted from theology to spirituality.

The beneficiaries and initiators of this renewal venture have been middle-class Christians. They can afford to attract and to hire the clergy and religious professionals needed to conduct the enterprise. Liberal religious education, unlike traditional education, has placed theology at the disposal not only of a privileged clerical caste but of the average Christian as well.

Within the liberal camp social justice education has not been popular. Displaced by the quest for personal growth, justice concerns have been given the backseat and have even been thrown out the window. The literature of self-fulfillment itself is addressed almost exclusively to the middle and upper classes. When justice *is* a topic of liberal education it is usually understood in terms of helping the poor to rise to higher (read, "middle-class") standards and conform to established institutions.

Whereas liberal education seeks the renewal of present Church structures through conversion of heart, radical education seeks their transformation through community action. It is characteristic of the liberal to assume the validity of the basic parish and diocesan structures and to assume the importance of the Church's efforts to adapt to social welfare industrial capitalist society. The liberal's efforts are directed at problems within these systems. The radical, on the other hand, assumes a critical posture toward the present institutions and seeks change of a systemic nature. Problem solving is replaced by paradigm shifting.

Faith is the immediate purpose of both liberal and radical education. Radical education, however, explicitly promotes faith's sociological and political dimensions. The transformation of social systems requires more than a psychological trust in a God who care for me, and even more than a psychosociological trust in a God who cares for others through me. Structural transformation is possible when people of faith become aware that suffering has sociological causes, that groups or classes within society exploit and marginalize others, and that these patterns of oppression are blasphemous in the light of the gospel. With the gift of faith in a just God, the faithful can oppose such oppression through community action and political struggle. Radical education fosters a faith that makes such interdependence possible.

The faith that does justice requires a stronger communal base than a national movement or a parish training program can provide. The numerically large parish cannot be more than what sociology calls an "association" of people. It is not a "community" in which people know each other by name, share a common mission, and accept and protect each other. Efforts to make it such lead to frustration and burnout. Communal relationships are not presupposed by radical education, they are created. Radical education is possible in small cells of people who conceive of themselves *as Church*, not merely as an interest group. As Church they worship, care for each other, scrutinize their reality in the light of God's Word, and link their efforts with those of other communities and organizations. Such groups are intent upon transforming the structures of the Church itself.

Radical education within these communities is a process in which people critically reflect upon their reality in the light of God's Word and seek an appropriate response. The process is rooted in the biblical sciences and is modeled on Paulo Freire's pedagogy of the oppressed.[11] This methodology avoids the fragmentation common in liberal education. It does not divorce one's reality from the study and preaching of the gospel, instruction concerning the social encyclicals, social analysis, and action on behalf of justice. The point of departure is one's situation in the world, which in turn is subjected to social analysis and theological analysis. A detailed presentation of one such method can be found in Groome's *Christian Religious Education* and also in his article in this volume.[12]

In this radical mode, education belongs to the exploited and marginalized people of society and their advocates. Radical education is useless to those who recline comfortably in the arms of a given social or ecclesiastical system. People don't willingly seek to change a system that feeds them and their friends. Because radical education does not assume the validity of that system, it alone can be truly responsive to the cries of those who are structurally alienated. Neither is this education some type of welfare or material aid. It is self-empowerment and mutal empowerment in hope that God's kingdom will indeed come. The justice community is not to be construed as something for everyone.[13] It requires a commitment that is profound and urgent.

These communities and the education that takes place within them are not the product of religious professionals. By their very nature they arise spontaneously from among the folk. Clergy and religious professionals can create a climate favorable for their birth and can support them while they mature, but they cannot require them to exist, nor can they impose leadership from without. From an educational perspective, these communities blur the lines of distinction between the leaders and the led, between the educators and the educatees. Educators are sometimes educated and educatees sometimes educate.

The two models we have presented are, of course, theoretical. Their purpose is to highlight the difference between two ways of conceiving education for justice, ways that correspond to our previous analysis of social reality. In practice justice education is usually a blend of both models. We should therefore conceive of our educational efforts in terms of a continuum with one model at each pole.

It is not the purpose of these models to downplay liberal education for justice in order to advocate radical education. Each has its place at a given time and in a given context. It is the opinion of this writer, however, that the social context of the United States is shifting so as to warrant a more radical stance among Christians. Justice communities are emerging on the international scene as *the* vehicle of a radical pastoral strategy. They may not, of course, be *the only* vehicle available. Perhaps articles like this one can stimulate Christians to reflect more critically upon, and to assume more and more Christ-like stances toward, our social reality. Perhaps such articles can also encourage already existing justice communities to identify themselves and network with each other for more critical discernment of their calling.

Conclusion

It does not seem accidental to me that the Christian concern for social justice and our contemporary quest for human community should intersect at this time in history. Whenever I mention basic Christian communities, someone is bound to protest that we in the United States are too individualistic and too hedonistic to sustain these communities. Our individualism and our hedonism do not need documentary support, but neither does our sense of isolation and our quest for community. Sociological literature is replete with evidence of the breakdown of traditional communities, families, neighborhoods, ethnic groups, and churches. We are not comfortable with this breakdown. During this century, the Western world has seen an unprecedented search for community. Industrialized as we are, we remain social beings, beings with fundamental needs that require fulfillment through a social context. We need to belong, to be accepted, to participate, to share common values, to be protected and identified. These fundamental needs are the fabric of communal ties.

Individualism, I agree, is indeed a hindrance to the emergence of Christian communities; but at the same time, the isolation that it occasions is a powerful catalyst for their expansion. Historically, in the United States, there is an unprecedented urgency for our community-building efforts. As Robert Nisbet and others have pointed out,[14] this contemporary quest for community co-exists with an extraordinary expansion of the power and function of democratic states. This is a fateful combination. Should there occur a major crisis of scarce and unequally distributed food, fuel, or other resource, there would be no moral community to serve as a basis for a consenual solution to the crisis. In the absence of communal commitment to shared values and acceptable authorities and a willingness on the part of individuals to sacrifice for the sake of the common good,[15] authoritarian government would surely intervene, perhaps at the expense of our freedom. The possiblity of such intervention is quite evident if one accepts our previous analysis of national security state industrial capitalism. If we refuse to attend communally to the justice issues that impinge upon our lives, these issues will, for the sake of survival, have to be ruled on by some authority external to a moral community.

Christian communities for justice are providing us with an antidote to individualism and powerlessness.[16] Justice education per se can provide us knowledge; but Christian communities for justice can perhaps provide that credible base we need for the renunciation demanded by a faith that does justice.

NOTES

1. Peter Henriot and Joe Holland, *Social Analysis: Linking Faith and Justice* (Washington, D.C.: Center of Concern, 1980), p. 29.
2. In the social welfare stage, capital was becoming national in its sphere of movement and influence; technology was moving into a capital/labor balance. These shifts gave birth to national labor unions, social welfare legislation (social security, minimum wage, unemployment compensation, etc.), and the consumer society we inherit today.
3. This phenomenon means plant closings and capital flight in the First World and lack of urban labor for the masses of peasants displaced from the agricultural sector in the Third. A permanent underclass is being created that will never enter the mainstream of productive life in contemporary society (ibid., p. 35).
4. The analysis that follows is based on that of Henriot and Holland.
5. See Walbert Buhlmann's *The Coming of the Third Church* (Maryknoll, N.Y.: Orbis Press, 1978).
6. Gottfried Deelen, "The Church on Its Way to the People: Basic Christian Communities in Brazil," *Cross Currents*, Winter 1980–81, pp. 385–408.
7. For an up-to-date discussion of basic Christian communities in the Third World,

see *The Challenge of Basic Christian Communities*, edited by S. Torres and J. Eagleson (Maryknoll, N.Y.: Orbis Press, 1981).

8. Hispanics already constitute one third of the U.S. Catholic population. They as a group are very poor: 21.4 percent of all Hispanic families are below the poverty level (as compared to 9.3 percent of the total U.S. population). Puerto Ricans are the poorest families in the country: 38.9 percent are below poverty level; they are poorer than blacks or Native Americans. Hispanics will be the dominant influence in the Church during the next century. See Joseph Fitzpatrick's "The People" in *The Context of Our Ministries: Working Papers* by the Jesuit Conference, Washington, D.C., pp. 27–29.

9. Tony Clarke, "Communities for Justice," *The Ecumenist* 19:2 (January–February 1981), pp. 17–25.

10. The liberal model takes its name from its immediate purpose, which is to free the individual to live the faith in the context of the modern world, more specifically, capitalism in its second stage.

11. Paulo Freire, *Pedagogy of the Oppressed* (New York: Seabury, 1970).

12. Thomas H. Groome, *Christian Religious Education* (San Francisco: Harper & Row, 1980).

13. Justice communities may appeal to the many young people who have rejected membership in the mainline churches that are most identified with the American Dream. See Carl S. Dudley's *Where Have All Our People Gone?* (New York: Pilgrim Press, 1979), especially chapter 2.

14. For a more adequate discussion of this problem see Philip Murnion's "Community/Criterion for a Justice Ministry," in *Origins* 4:28 (January 2, 1975), pp. 433–41.

15. For a discussion of the kind of sacrifice demanded today by the common good see Marie Augusta Neal's *A Socio-Theology of Letting Go* (New York: Paulist Press, 1974).

16. Powerlessness is discussed in terms of a structural lag between the development of our social institutions and the rapid evolution of global interdependencies in Gerald and Patricia Mische's *Toward a Human World Order* (New York: Paulist Press, 1977).

QUESTIONS FOR REFLECTION AND DISCUSSION

1. How do you conceive the mission of the Church given the social and political reality of the United States today?

2. Evaluate whether your educational efforts are directed toward adaptation or toward transformation of ecclesial and societal structures?

3. Do you yourself feel powerless and helpless? Would participation in some type of grass roots Christian community meet your needs?

4. What does the distinction, made in this essay, between the "educative" and the educational" mean to you?

5. In what ways are capitalist and gospel values in tension or contradictory?

7. A Word About Teaching Justly

MARY C. BOYS

> Words strain,
> Crack and sometimes break, under the burden,
> Under the tension, slip, slide, perish,
> Decay with imprecision, will not stay in place,
> Will not stay still.
>
> T. S. ELIOT, "Burnt Norton"

WE TEND TO mistrust words, preferring instead to see deeds. Talk is too easily "idle" or "cheap," words too often "empty." Smooth-talking salespeople, pretentious preachers, glib analysts, and vacuous-sounding politicians all make us wary. Moreover, who among us cannot remember a time when, like Peter, we betrayed ourselves by our speech (Mark 14:70)?

Perhaps our caution is instinctive because we know the power of words. The message of forgiveness, the pledge of fidelity, and the testimony of the martyr all bring new life; such honorable words remind us of occasions when our speech expressed that which lay deepest within. We resent "mere rhetoric" because it manipulates, thereby emptying speech of significance. We respect eloquence born out of struggle, commitment, and passion because such language expresses the fragile strength of the human spirit.

And so we return again and again to the Scriptures, to poetry, to those classics that nourish and challenge and convince us. We hear in them not fashionable words—slogans and banners—but the language of transformation. We see in their images not mirrors of ourselves, but new lenses by which to look at reality and to correct the distortions of our excessive self-preoccupation. In short, we depend upon words to revivify us.

Why then, it might be asked, does a tradition that has such powerful words about justice have such little impact? Why do the people who embody that tradition feel so far removed from these words? Why are these words so lacking in power to transform and bring new life?[1]

These questions provide the point of departure for this essay. Many subsequent directions are possible, but I intend to explore just one in particular: the contribution of education, especially teaching, to a "faith that does justice."[2] My thesis is simple: *If the Church is to come to a more profound understanding of its relation to the political and social order, then it must place a priority on education rather than on proclamation.* I will develop this argument by (1) analyzing the distinction between ecclesial proclamation and a church that educates and (2) proposing ways in which the Church might "teach as Jesus did." I have no illusions that this twofold exploration will provide final answers or even less hazardous routes to the promised land; my hope is that, linked with the other essays in this volume, it may provide a stimulating word to those committed to doing what the Lord requires: to do justice and to love kindness and to walk humbly with your God (Mic. 6:8).

Proclamation and Education

Church people have long been suspect because of their propensity for pomposity. When Jesus instructed his (Jewish) disciples, "And in praying do not heap up empty phrases as the Gentiles do; for they think that they will be heard for their many words" (Matt. 6:7), he delivered a rebuke that the gentile church has often, ironically, failed to heed. To transfer his advice to another time and context: "And in acting justly, neither manufacture slogans nor multiply words as the bureaucrats do; for they think that they will be heard for their many words." Church bureaucrats need not absorb the full share of the blame, lest others of us thereby exempt ourselves. The point, however, is that our fascination for official statements and documentation can all too readily be mistaken for the enactment of justice.

The legitimacy of a development of a body of ecclesial teachings is, of course, not at issue. Because the Church has been entrusted with certain responsibilities—forming community, making known God's Word, serving God's people, ministering to God's judgment, and manifesting its own sacramentality—it has consistently been obliged to articulate the sources, understandings, and practices of its various ministries.[3] Particularly because the ministry of the Word has had priority,[4] the Church has from its inception placed great importance on preaching, teaching, and formulations. Thus it came to possess creeds and other dogmas, doctrines and other expressions of ecclesial concern. The creedal and dogmatic formulations, in particular, were born out of intense argument and controversy. Unfortunately, the critical context out of which they were fashioned has seldom been taught; thus, the teachings tend to be presented as absolutized propositions rather than as theological judgments of a particular time and perspective.

But the problems with regard to issues of justice is not so much that the ecclesial statements have been dehistoricized as that they have yet to become *words that make a difference*. Consider, for example, how frequently people have quoted to them the clarion call of the 1971 Synod of Bishops: "Action on behalf of justice and participation in the transformation of the world fully appear to us as a constitutive dimension of the preaching of the Gospel, or, in other words, of the Church's mission for the redemption of the human race and its liberation from every oppressive situation."[5] Especially in the United States, with its tradition of separation of church and state, this statement demands careful analysis and reflection. It borders on the irresponsible to cite it continually without any sustained development of why the Church, by virtue of its nature and mission, is necessarily involved in the political order.[6] To expect "hearers of the Word," many of whom were nurtured in more private ways of piety, to absorb the meaning and implications of the synodal statement in a ten-minute homily reflects both pastoral naiveté and educational ignorance.

Here, it seems to me, is manifest the most basic and troubling issue: until the Church's changed self-understanding is grasped and in some fashion appropriated by its people, statements on issues of justice will be "mere rhetoric," declarations proclaimed from afar (Rome or the chancery) with little impact. Even more serious is a situation I observe with increasing frequency: the anger of many life-long, dedicated church people about official ecclesial involvement at what might be termed the "strategic" level of political life and their subsequent bitterness toward the Church. As a case in point, consider the reaction to the Roman Catholic Archbishop of Seattle, Raymond G. Hunthausen, when he proposed that Christians might consider withholding 50 percent of their income taxes "in nonviolent resistance to nuclear murder and suicide."[7] The reaction could be heard nationwide.[8] Many were convinced that the archbishop was being disobedient to the pope, because the latter had decreed that priests should stay out of politics. One would naturally expect those on the far right of the ideological spectrum to respond negatively to the proposal, but the potentially more divisive reaction comes from moderates who see no connection between the Church and the political order. Of course, they maintain, the Church should promote peace and justice, but it has neither the right nor the responsibility to protest specific armament programs (such as the MX missile system), domestic programs (e.g., welfare cuts), or foreign policy (e.g., U.S. involvement in El Salvador). Hunthausen himself avers to such thinking:

> I would like to clarify a few points about which some seem to be misinformed. First of all, as the bishop of this diocese I have not only the right but the duty to speak out on the concrete issues of the day as they affect the values of the Gospel tradition. It is not enough for a bishop to utter general principles: he must also take the risk of applying them in the best way he knows how to the actual life situations he and his people must face. He may not keep a so-called "prudent silence" in the face of great moral evils; nor may he expect the pope to do the task for him. The reason for this is that concrete situations vary from place to place. . . .
>
> Secondly, I strongly reject the notion that because the episcopal office is a religious office a bishop may not speak out on issues that involve the political realm. There are some who mistakenly think that Pope John Paul has forbidden church leaders to speak out. This is false; and it is also dangerous. . . . To think that I and other bishops have no right to speak out on social and political issues that touch the welfare of persons is to reduce the role of the bishop and of Christianity to the realm of individual morality.[9]

But Hunthausen's response will not assuage the anger of many who find his thinking too foreign to their own formation. Indeed, there are no easy answers. We are a church only recently able to permit pluralism, and the differences among us are vast, perhaps impossible to reconcile. The problems at stake are terribly complex, always defying simplistic solutions and usually only partially resolvable. Furthermore, once the language of peace and human rights is taken seriously, the complicity of us all in sinful structures of war/defense and oppression is painfully evident.

A pluralistic church cannot achieve total consensus, and it seems inevitable that disagreement on the strategic level will continue; indeed, such differences may be a sign of maturity and may contribute to more informed opinions and positions. But until the Church begins to grapple more openly and deliberately with what it means when it says that action on behalf of justice is "constitutive" of the preaching of the gospel, it will continue to find its members divided and angry.[10] In sum, what the Church needs is to place less emphasis on proclamation in order to stress education.

What I am proposing is a rechanneling of energies and resources so that the insights presently embedded in documents might instead take root in people. I understand education to involve a long-term commitment: It requires intentional, sustained, and systematic efforts to make knowledge accessible; to reconstruct experience, attitudes, and skills; to examine implications; and to develop new visions. Education is the ministry of a pilgrim church that respects the time and freedom its members need in order to make their own connections between the gospel and the transformation of the world. Education is infinitely more complex and fraught with ambiguity, diversity, and slowness than are proclamation and indoctrination. *Ultimately, however, it is the only just way of promoting justice;* a Church that proclaims justice as constitutive of its gospel must do justice to its members.

Norman Brown aptly captures the essence of the distinction between proclamation and education when he quotes Heraclitus: "to teach is not to tell, not to tell."[11] Teaching is a "moral craft," that is, it rests on the recognition that something of value is being passed on by someone with profound respect for the other.[12] Teaching certainly involves conveying information, but it encompasses far more than transmitting data. Thomas Greene speaks of the "activities" of teaching as activities of *deliberation* and *inquiry,* such as knowing, believing, thinking, learning, explaining, judging, wondering, defining, and demonstrating. Collectively, these activities suggest a process whereby "people might test their capacity to face the truth and enhance their ability to change their minds"; their change of mind may happen not only "in respect to what they believe but also in respect to what they decide to do."[13]

I have found it helpful to think of teaching primarily as "providing access." Negatively, this means staying out of the way, not preventing others from entering into other perspectives on reality. Positively, I see it as inviting others to enter into new understandings, setting up conceptual frameworks to provide order, introducing people to varied viewpoints, showing them why and how classic understandings developed, inviting them to dialogue with voices very different from their own, suggesting possible implications, and encouraging appropriation according to their own readiness and ability. Teaching demands ability to present material with coherence and logic; even more, it involves the art of asking the right questions.

To provide access to the Church's tradition of education for justice entails *at minimum* these understandings: (1) recognition of the linkage of the relationship between the lordship of God and of Jesus with social systems; (2) re-mediation of understandings of the gospel that were obscured by excessively individualistic interpretation; (3) demonstration of the shift in the Church's self-understanding between

Vatican I and Vatican II; (4) dialogue with voices from the Third World; (5) analysis of the effects of industrialization and technology on the world order; (6) reflection on the relationship between Christianity and culture. Obviously, explanation is not the sole nor necessarily the superior means of access to these understandings. Field trips, films, reading, discussion, role-playing, and simulation games are all supplements or alternatives to lecturing. The teacher's role is to structure situations and to provide resources by which people might come to claim information, concepts, and attitudes. Teaching is not as simple or as quick as delivering a pronouncement; it calls for deep understanding and artful skills by which others can enter imaginatively into the issues and questions. It differs sharply from indoctrination, in which the instructor determines the entire agenda,[14] and also from advocacy, in which the leader rallies others to a cause. On occasion the teacher may properly function as an advocate, but the full range of the activities of teaching transcends this one dimension of working for justice.

To summarize thus far: If the Church's statements in regard to justice are to be more than "mere rhetoric," and if the Church is to make action on behalf of justice truly "constitutive" of the preaching of the gospel, then it must attend to its responsibility to educate. If the Church is to be teacher, then it must do more than simply tell; it must devote time and resources (both human and material) to providing people with access to its traditions.

Teaching, furthermore, properly belongs to a pilgrim church. A church that has already arrived at conclusions has no need to teach; it merely transmits the answers by indoctrination. A pilgrim church must listen and observe on its journey. Its conversation while on the way is called theology;[15] teaching keeps theology alive and moving. And precisely because Jesus was known as teacher,[16] it is pertinent to ask, "What would it be like 'to teach as Jesus did' "?

What Would It Be Like "To Teach as Jesus Did"?

In 1972 the Catholic bishops of the United States issued a pastoral letter, *To Teach as Jesus Did.*[17] Declaring that education is one of the most important ways the Church fulfills its commitment to the dignity of persons and to the building of community, the bishops derived a new priority from this long-standing conviction: The continuing education of adults should henceforth be seen not at the periphery but at the center of the Church's educational mission. Moreover, they continued, programs for adults should be characterized by self-direction, dialogue, and mutual responsibility.[18] Their pastoral letter identified three interrelated dimensions of religious education—message, community, and service (which the cognoscenti utilized in the original Greek as *kērygma, koinōnia,* and *diakōnia*)—and these terms became key for structuring and evaluating many programs. But, whatever else the impact of the document,[19] it contained a curious omission: Despite its title, no attention was devoted to how Jesus actually did teach, and what, therefore, this might mean for the Christian community.

The question of how Jesus taught is more complex than it might first appear. Because the Gospels are not transcripts of the life of Jesus but theological presentations of his mission and ministry to specific communities in the latter third of the first century, they actually provide a sort of "double-layer": Jesus as teacher and the evangelist as teacher. The second layer, however, is visible only when one takes a closer look; the evangelists teach about Jesus' teaching by means of selection, wording, and arrangement. There is no infallible guide to teasing apart these two layers; even the so-called criterion of dissimilarity (only when a word or deed of Jesus diverges from that of rabbinic teachings or of the primitive church can one authenticate it as originating from the "historical" Jesus rather than from the creativity of the evangelist) is of limited usefulness, because it cannot sufficiently account for the deep continuity the Jewish Jesus would surely have had with his own tradition.[20]

Distinguishing between their own presentations and the precise words of Jesus was not the interest of the evangelists; on the contrary, much of their teaching happens by means of the rich diversity in the way they place and report the sayings of Jesus. Often, differing details provide clues to each evangelist's theological intent. One needs only to look at the Lord's Prayer to see how the Gospel writers adapted Jesus' teachings.

Matt. 6:9–15:	Luke 11:2–4:
"Pray then like this:	And he said to them, "When you pray, say:
Our Father who art in heaven,	'Father,
Hallowed be thy name.	Hallowed be thy name.
Thy kingdom come,	Thy kingdom come.
Thy will be done,	
On earth as it is in heaven.	
Give us this day our daily bread;	Give us each day our daily bread;
And forgive us our debts,	And forgive us our sins,
As we also have forgiven our debtors	for we ourselves forgive every one who is indebted to us;

And lead us not into temptation,   And lead us not into temptation.' "
But deliver us from evil.
For if you forgive men their trespasses, your heavenly Father also
will forgive you; But if you do
not forgive men their trespasses,
neither will your Father forgive
your trespasses."

Luke's version—most likely closer to the original—is completely subsumed within Matthew's fuller version. The two evangelists set this prayer of Jesus in different contexts. Luke places it within the larger structure of Jesus' final journey to Jerusalem (9:51–19:27), a section in which he has much of his special material (i.e., uniquely Lukan). Matthew, on the other hand, situates the Lord's Prayer within the context of the Sermon on the Mount (chaps. 5–7). Both use it as a paradigm of prayer, but each stresses different aspects. Luke initially shows Jesus at prayer, then describes him answering the disciples' request that they be taught to pray. Of obvious importance is the attitude with which they should pray; the concluding instructions framing the Lord's Prayer entreat the disciples to be as *persistent* as the one who disturbs a friend at midnight to borrow three loaves of bread (11:5–8) and to be as *trusting* in their petitions as a son who knows his father will not answer his request for a fish with a serpent or for an egg with a scorpion. Matthew, too, has this teaching on attitudes (7:7–11; note, however, the difference in detail: the son's request for *bread* will not be met with a *stone*), but not in the immediate context of the Lord's Prayer.

Matthew seems instead to be stressing two elements. First of all, prayer should not be done to gain the admiration of others nor should it be a heap of empty phrases. The Lord's Prayer is for Matthew the word of fullness, the language of transformation, which for his community especially concerns forgiveness. Jesus prays, "And forgive us our debts, as we also have forgiven our debtors"; that is, forgive us to the extent we forgive others. His concluding instruction reiterates this: "For if you forgive people their trespasses, your heavenly Father also will forgive you; but if you do not forgive people their trespasses, neither will your Father forgive your trespasses" (6:14). For Matthew, the Lord's Prayer is the word that makes a difference in a divided community.[21] Perhaps because Luke has so many other powerful words on forgiveness in his special section (especially in chapter 15, where Jesus tells the parables of the lost sheep, the lost coin, and the lost son), he does not have the same need to teach the Lord's Prayer in a manner that stresses forgiveness.

Obviously, this is not the occasion for extended exegesis of the Lord's Prayer. But I think it is extremely useful to reflect on the *careful freedom* with which the evangelists taught the words of Jesus. They did not freeze them so that succeeding generations would need to form antiquarian societies whose sole purpose would be in verifying his exact words; on the contrary, the evangelists took the words of Jesus so seriously that they passed them on in ways that would make a difference in their own particular situations. The Lord's Prayer was too precious to etch in stone; it was meant to be prayed in community, to be adapted to needs, and to serve as an "outline" for prayer, as Origen put it.[22]

Consequently, we cannot be certain of the *ipsissima verba* by which Jesus taught—the evangelists simply had no interest in preserving and transmitting this information in the "exact" fashion our modern historical consciousness might desire. But at least three major assertions about Jesus' teaching can be made with virtual certainty: (1) Jesus taught with authority; (2) Jesus taught primarily about the Kingdom of God; and (3) Jesus characteristically taught in parables. To focus on the third aspect is also to see more clearly the other two; in addition, some reflection on Jesus as God's parable will lead directly to implications for educating for justice.

We frequently speak of Jesus "announcing" the arrival of the Kingdom of God; without denying that preaching and proclamation were part of his ministry, I would, however, suggest that teaching in deed and in word were more typical of the way Jesus presented God's saving action. He taught about the *inclusiveness* of God's Kingdom by associating with the despised members of his society—tax collectors, the unclean, sinners. Particularly scandalous was his table fellowship with these socioreligious outcasts. He taught about God's *boundless mercy* by forgiving sins, thus leaving himself open to the charge of blasphemy. But in a special way, Jesus taught about God's salvation in parables. Jesus himself is God's parable; his parables are a linguistic incarnation.[23]

J. Dominic Crossan helpfully categorizes the parables in three modes: those emphasizing the *advent* of the Kingdom as a gift of God, those *reversing* the hearer's world, and those empowering hearers to *action*.[24] Because the parables of reversal are so striking in their challenge to accepted human judgments ("What, in other words, if God does not play the game by our rules?"), let us look briefly at one, the parable of the Good Samaritan.[25]

Initially, we are at a disadvantage when we hear this familiar parable. Luke frames it as a story of example ("Who is my neighbor? . . .")

"Go and do likewise"), and so we hear it primarily as an injunction for ourselves to be "Good Samaritans." But, if one sifts through the levels of the parable, another, far more striking meaning emerges. The original hearers of the story were Jewish. Jews and Samaritans hated each other and had no basis for mutual relations (see John 4: 9).[26] Their enmity had flared in recent memory; in the second century B.C.E., the Samaritans had aided the Syrians against the Jews; in 128 B.C.E., the Jews retaliated by burning the Samaritan temple on Mount Gerizim. The Samaritan refusal to worship at Jerusalem constantly rankled the Jews of Jesus' day; in short, to them there was no such phenomenon as a "good" Samaritan. The juxtaposition of "good" with "Samaritan" was linguistically outrageous and offensive! So when Jesus told of the man beaten and robbed on his way from Jerusalem to Jericho (a treacherous road, frequently the scene of such crimes) who was ignored by both priest and Levite (an anticlerical point) but aided generously, far beyond the call of duty, by the Samaritan, his hearers must have been furious. Their way of dealing with reality was shattered. Samaritans, they all knew, didn't act that way; as Crossan puts it: "When good (clerics) and bad (Samaritan) become, respectively, bad and good, a world is being challenged and we are faced with polar reversal."[27]

The historical information regarding Jewish-Samaritan relationships is obviously crucial to catching the reversal of Jesus' parable. But we will not feel the reversal until we retell it in light of our own construction of reality.

In order that we might ourselves feel the reversal of this parable, let me attempt some contemporary renditions. My retelling is governed by the principle of "dynamic analogy,"[28] that is, finding the equivalences in our lives of the situations Jesus called into question in the first century. Thus I need to examine the "good" and "bad" of my world. I caution the reader that my attempt in no way is meant to be offensive to the characters named; the offense is directed at *my* categories, *my* way of discovering that God may not play according to my rules.

Lech Walesa is on his way from Gdansk to Warsaw when thugs set upon him. Pope John Paul II passes him by, as does Msgr. George Higgins, but Yuri Andropov stops, cares for his wounds, and takes him to a *dacha* for recuperation. Daniel Berrigan is on his way from New York to Washington, D.C., when he is attacked. Maryknoll's President Melinda Roper passes him by; so also do Archbishop Hunthausen and Fr. Bryan Hehir, but Secretary of State Alexander Haig and United Nations Ambassador Jeane Kirkpatrick, journeying together to testify for increased armaments, stop to take care of him, even postponing their congressional hearing until Berrigan is well on the road to recovery. Archbishop Helder Camara is en route from Recife to São Paulo when he is wounded. Cardinal Aloisio Lorscheider passes him by, as do Fernando and Ernesto Cardenal visiting from Nicaragua, but another Nicaraguan visitor, Anastasio Somoza, tends to him. Menachem Begin is on his way from Jerusalem to Cairo when attacked. Moshe Dayan goes on, as does Jerusalem's chief rabbi. But Yaser Arafat tends gently to him. Eleanor Smeal, while traveling to an E.R.A. rally, is violently beaten. Sr. Theresa Kane and Alan Alda hurry on to the meeting, but Phyllis Schafly, in town with Rev. Jerry Falwell for a counterrally, rushes to her side to offer succor and consolation. Andrew Young, returning to Atlanta, is pulled off the road, robbed, and beaten. Jimmy Carter and Coretta Scott King pass him by, but a local "redneck," known to be sympathetic to the Ku Klux Klan, saves his life. Members of the Irish peace movement are attacked while on tour in the United States. Senator Edward Kennedy and Speaker Thomas P. (Tip) O'Neill cannot be contacted, but Rev. Ian Paisley and Prime Minister Margaret Thatcher rush over from Ireland and England to attend to their needs.

Even as I suggest these possible ways of retelling the parable of the "Good Samaritan" I find myself apprehensive that my choice of characters is too specific, too offensive to commit to writing—perhaps even potentially libelous. Of course, I don't for a minute think that Haig would actually stop—no, not in my world. My way of apprehending the parable is threatening my construction of reality, too close to my secure perspective, too capable of reversing my categories. I begin to understand that the Jesus who told parables was not simply a preacher spinning homely little tales; the Jesus who told parables was the teacher put to death because his stories hit too close to home. Jesus incarnated truth in a manner no one anxious to preserve his or her life would dare to risk.

Much, much more deserves to be explored about these parables that judge us in their advent, reversal, and summons to action. We are fortunate that research on parables is currently one of the richest areas of New Testament scholarship, and if my essay serves to encourage readers to avail themselves of the abundant material, I will have partially achieved my goal. But, to attend more specifically to the topic at hand, what might it mean "to teach as Jesus did"?

At least two general implications might be fruitfully explored. The first involves teaching as an <u>invitation to imaginative participation</u>.

The words of Jesus were not intended to be transmitted from generation to generation solely for the sake of preservation but especially for the intent of transformation. When teaching the Gospels, the teacher needs the interpretative skills to be able to involve participants in the advent, reversal, and action. In order to do so, teachers need to employ the principle of "dynamic analogy," which requires knowledge not only of the historical context of the Scriptures, but also of contemporary context.[29] Knowledge of the *Sitz im Leben* is necessary but not sufficient; teachers need to be able to stimulate the imagination so that hearers of the Word will catch and feel its power in the present so that the future will be different. Dynamic analogy means confronting the text in such a way that the hearer asks, "With whom do I identify?" "What in my world is being questioned and why?" "How is God still doing this?" George Montague suggests that teaching is as important to the Scripture scholar as a road test is to an automobile engineer because it can provide a "heuristic rebound."[30] I suspect that only this sort of entrance into the world of the gospel will reveal to us how action on behalf of justice is constitutive.

Of paramount importance in developing imagination is the ability to pose the right questions. To teach as Jesus did means to refuse to limit ourselves to questions such as: "Did it happen precisely as described?" "Were there really two different occasions on which Jesus multiplied loaves and fishes?" "Were there actually magi?" Questions of this sort are inevitable, given the concern for historicity that has reigned supreme since the nineteenth century. But we must be more disciplined in our questioning of the text so that we ask questions about ultimacy and meaning; only when we pose questions of this sort will we let ourselves in turn be questioned by the text: *Preoccupation with superficial inquiries can be a way of avoiding a more painful interrogation.* We can too easily fall prey to what a colleague terms "bucket question," that is, questions that totally avoid the point.[31] The model of this is the Samaritan woman's response to Jesus, "If you knew . . . who it is that is saying to you, 'Give me a drink,' you would have asked him, and he would have given you living water." "Sir, you have no bucket, and the well is deep. Where do you get that living water?" The Samaritan woman, like Nicodemus, is so literalistic in her questioning that she misses Jesus' offer.

The second implication that may be drawn from the way Jesus taught involves freedom. Jesus surprised, challenged, and confronted his followers, but he always did so in ways that respected their freedom. Perhaps one of the most significant dimensions of parable telling is that it allows hearers to come to understanding in their own good time. Jesus was no revivalist, demanding instant confessions from his followers according to established formulas; instead, he taught by prophetic action and by parables—however upsetting his message, his hearers were responsible to appropriate it for themselves. It is not unlikely that when Jesus told parables, many walked home wondering just what he was saying, "Who is he?" "What if . . ." "Who could believe God is like he suggests?" Part of the authority with which Jesus taught lay in his ability to ask the right questions.

Not many of us have the genius to be able to speak in parables to the same degree as Jesus. Nevertheless, we can deepen our own grasp of the parables and, using the principle of dynamic analogy, suggest and invite possible ways of retelling. We might also beneficially utilize narrative, both fiction and nonfiction, to stimulate people's imaginative powers. For example, those committed to education for justice might fruitfully incorporate biography and autobiography as a means of sharing how others have struggled to make the gospel "constitutive." But when biography or autobiography are used, it is important to pay close attention to the detail of lives, lest by superficial observation we miss the ordinariness of the struggles—a form of idolatry all too tempting for the contemporary Christian. By cloaking the difficulties of their lives and times with our pietisms, we obscure ways we might allow them to pose questions to us.

In the *Sayings of the Fathers* (*Pirke Aboth* 3.2), Rabbi Hanina ben Dosa says, "Anyone whose deeds exceed his wisdom, his wisdom shall endure; anyone whose wisdom exceeds his deeds, his wisdom shall not endure." The wisdom of Jesus, particularly as embodied in parables, exists as a challenge to a church that finds it easier to proclaim than to teach. When the Church takes seriously Jesus as teacher, its words will have authority to transform and revivify.

NOTES

1. In this essay I am focusing particularly on the traditions of Roman Catholicism. For an especially useful anthology of its "words about justice," see Joseph Gremillion, ed., *The Gospel of Peace and Justice* (Maryknoll, N.Y.: Orbis Books, 1976). My special attention to Roman Catholicism is in no way intended to imply that other religious traditions do not have equally powerful words about justice. Likewise, when I use the term *church*, I recognize that the term extends beyond the boundaries of Catholicism.

2. See John C. Haughey, ed., *The Faith That Does Justice* (New York: Paulist Press, 1977).

3. See Bernard J. Cooke, *Ministry to Word and Sacraments* (Philadelphia: Fortress Press, 1976).

4. See Sandra M. Schneiders, "The Ministry of the Word and Contemporary Catholic Education," in Mary C. Boys, ed., *Ministry and Education in Conversation* (Winona, Minn.: Saint Mary's Press, 1981), pp. 15–44.

5. "Justice in the World," in Gremillion, p. 514.

6. "The Church's involvement in the social and political orders is justified on the basis of the social and institutional character of sin itself. Since the Church is called to combat sin of every kind, the Church has responsibility in all areas where sin appears. More positively, the Church is called to uphold and practice virtue. Justice is one of the cardinal, or 'hinge,' virtues (along with prudence, fortitude, and temperance), and social justice is one of the principal kinds of justice (alongside commutative, distributive, and legal justice). Therefore, the Church's commitment to, and involvement in, the struggle for social justice, peace and human rights is an essential or 'constitutive,' part of its mission" (Richard P. McBrien, *Catholicism*, vol. 2 [Minneapolis: Winston], p. 720).

7. Raymond G. Hunthausen, "Faith and Disarmament," speech delivered to Pacific Northwest Synod for the Lutheran Church in America at Pacific Lutheran University in Tacoma, 12 June 1981. Available in *Origins* 11 (2 July 1981), pp. 110–12. I recognize that the proposal about withholding taxes is a secondary aspect of the archbishop's comments, and that his principal point was to challenge members of the Christian community to reflect prayerfully on nuclear arms buildup.

8. See James M. Wall, "A Catholic Antinuclear Protest," *The Christian Century* 98 (14 October 1981), pp. 1011–12. For a fictional account of prophetic leadership and the divisions to which it might lead, see Walter F. Murphy, *The Vicar of Christ* (New York: Macmillan, 1979).

9. Letter to Archbishop Hunthausen to the "People of God," *Catholic Northwest Progress*, 2 July 1981.

10. One who has specified criteria for strategic action on behalf of justice is Richard P. McBrien (*Catholicism*, vol. 2, p. 720), who argues that ecclesial intervention in the political order must be governed by five criteria: (1) the issue must obviously be *justice-related;* (2) the Church should be able to deal with the issue *competently;* (3) the Church should have *sufficient resources* to deal with the issue effectively; (4) the issue should have a *prior claim* over other justice-related problems that also demand attention of the church; and (5) the *form* of the action should not be unnecessarily or unduly polarizing for the church. "A diversity of viewpoints is to be expected and tolerated, so that agreement with the specific form of social or political action selected by the church(es) should not become itself a test of authentic Christian faith and commitment."

11. Norman O. Brown, *Love's Body* (New York: Vintage, 1966), p. 245.

12. Alan R. Tom, "Teaching as a Moral Craft: A Metaphor for Teaching and Teacher Education," *Curriculum Inquiry* 10 (1980), pp. 317–24.

13. Thomas F. Green, *The Activities of Teaching* (New York: McGraw-Hill, 1971), p. 216.

14. "Instructing is transformed into indoctrinating when the concern to transmit certain beliefs because they are reasonable is changed simply into a concern to transmit beliefs. The difference between instructing and indoctrinating is a difference in the weight given to the pursuit of truth as opposed to the simple transmission of beliefs previously arrived at." (Ibid., p. 30).

15. See Paul M. van Buren, *Discerning the Way* (New York: Seabury, 1980), pp. 1–32.

16. See Robert H. Stein, *The Method and Message of Jesus' Teaching* (Philadelphia: Westminster, 1978). Stein locates forty-five times that Jesus is called "Teacher" in the Gospels, and another fourteen times in which he is called "Rabbi."

17. National Conference of Catholic Bishops, *To Teach as Jesus Did* (Washington, D.C.: United States Catholic Conference, 1972).

18. Those who establish programs for justice should obviously be mindful of these characteristics.

19. See Mark Heath, " 'To Teach as Jesus Did': A Critique," *The Living Light* 11 (1973), pp. 284–96; two issues of the *Notre Dame Journal of Education* 6 (Fall 1975 and Winter 1975) were devoted to analysis of the pastoral letter.

20. "Continuity will have to take its place alongside discontinuity as a basic category for understanding the significance of Jesus." Charles E. Carlston, "Proverbs, Maxims, and the Historical Jesus," *Journal of Biblical Literature* 99 (1980), p. 105.

21. See William Thompson, *Matthew's Advice to a Divided Community* (Rome: Biblical Institute Press, 1970).

22. Gordon J. Bahr, "The Use of the Lord's Prayer in the Primitive Church," in Jacob J. Petuchowski and Michael Brocke, eds., *The Lord's Prayer and Jewish Liturgy* (New York: Seabury, 1978), p. 149.

23. Sally McFague TeSelle, *Speaking in Parables* (Philadelphia: Fortress Press, 1975).

24. John Dominic Crossan, *In Parables: The Challenge of the Historical Jesus* (New York: Harper & Row, 1973).

25. Ibid., p. 69.

26. Samaritans were descendants of those not deported from the Northern Kingdom during Assyrian rule in 722 B.C.E. and of foreign colonists from Babylon and Media (see 2 Kings 17:24).

27. Crossan, p. 64. Cf. John D. Crossan, ed., *Semeia 2: The Good Samaritan* (Missoula, Mont.: Scholars Press, 1974).

28. See James A. Sanders, *God Has a Story Too* (Philadelphia: Fortress Press, 1980).

29. See my "Biblical Criticism in the Church Today," *PACE* (March 1980), p. 3.

30. George T. Montague, "Hermeneutics and the Teaching Scripture," *Catholic Biblical Quarterly* 41 (1979), pp. 1–2.

31. I am indebted to Jerome H. Neyrey, S.J., of the Weston School of Theology for this phrase.

QUESTIONS FOR REFLECTION AND DISCUSSION

1. What do you consider essential for teaching about the Church's tradition of education for justice?

2. How would you go about teaching these ideas, beliefs, norms, and insights?

3. How can education for justice truly be "teaching as Jesus did"?

4. What do you make of the distinction between teaching and pro-

claiming? What is your estimate of the point made in this essay that education for justice requires more attention to teaching?

5. What are some "dynamic analogies" of your own that might be used to make the biblical faith and its message of justice come alive in the experience of those with whom you work?

8. The Renewal of Education and the Nurturing of Justice and Peace

PADRAIC O'HARE

THE THESIS of this essay is that educational agencies provide environments where moral reflection, judgment, and action can grow, above all, to the extent that these agencies pursue certain traditional functions with vision and excellence.

Where ideal purposes are pursued in concrete situations, where teaching and curriculum formation are viewed as moral enterprises, and where the relationship between educators and their clients is viewed as an occasion for the establishment of genuine mutuality, there is found an educational environment in which justice may be nurtured. Though even this author has been pulled, kicking and screaming, into accepting that education is a far broader reality than those formal and informal moments of "schooling," in which emphasis is placed on exposure to illuminating knowledge and on the activation of cognitive understanding, the thesis of this essay will be elaborated with primary reference to schools. Thanks largely to the immediate influence of Gabriel Moran, I am coming to accept the definition of education as the "matrix of relations," a quality of human exchange in the context of a common life characterized by alertness and sympathy.[1] Nevertheless, schooling at all levels is a significant element or subset of education; it is important to the total education of people, and it is of great interest to me.

Two preliminary disclaimers will help to set what follows in greater relief and clarify the author's intent. The purpose of this essay is to examine the school's impact in the "nurturing of justice." It is intentional that the title of this essay does not mention "social justice," but rather "justice." I take it as axiomatic that *social* justice properly so called is the actual achievement of change along lines of greater justice in those political and economic systems that arbitrate the quality of life of aggregates of people. As such, social justice is a political enterprise occurring, or failing to occur, in those distinctly political forums where "power and conscience meet."[2] In the performance of their ordinary or internal function, schools have little direct occasion for participation in social justice. As institutions with potential "external" effects on the communities they serve, the schools must not fail to achieve an "institutional profile" that makes their commitment to social transformation unambiguous. And indeed, this exemplifying and advocacy in the larger community is part of the inevitable educational impact of such agencies. It will be better, however, to prescind from the issue of external function and consider the way schools nurture attitudes of justice in the performance of traditional educational tasks.

In limiting our scope in this way, focus can be placed on the degree to which a school nurtures the habit of accounting other people's welfare as a relevant condition on one's own behavior, or what has traditionally been referred to as "commutative" justice; to what degree it induces the habit of obeying rules that are perceived as fair, reasonable, and contributing to the common good, or what has traditionally been referred to as "legal" justice; and finally, approaching the threshold of social justice, to what degree the school environment provides at least a dawning awareness of the potential for conflict and injustice when individuals or small groups stand before powerful megastructures of a society in which rests the power to dictate who will participate in the fruits of social cooperation, or what has traditionally been identified as distributive justice. It need only be added that failure to distinguish the relatively modest goals of justice from those of social justice can result in profound disability for any effort at creating a more just world. From a theological perspective, this failure results from an inadequate appraisal of the persistence of self-seeking and the limits of human altruism. One need not accept a Reformation anthropology to assent to Reinhold Niebuhr's formulation of the relationship of such acknowledgment of limit to the actual achievement of greater justice itself:

> To understand that the Christ in us is not a possession but a hope, that perfection is not a reality but an intention; that such peace as we know in this life is never purely the peace of achievement but the serenity of being "completely known and all forgiven"; all this does not destroy moral ardour or responsibility. On the contrary, it is the only way of preventing premature completions of life, or arresting the new and more terrible pride which may find its roots in the soil of humility, and of saving the Christian life from the intolerable pretension of saints who have forgotten that they are sinners.[3]

From an educational perspective, failure to acknowledge the complexity of claims about the social good, the necessary factual basis for judgments on social justice or the need to exercise political power that the implementation of such judgment requires can only come from teacher naiveté transmitted to a new generation of disciples. In the process, a profound skepticism may be generated in a new generation whose members might have been nurtured on a more realistic idealism.

The second and final disclaimer concerns the idealistic tone of what will follow. What follows is unabashedly idealistic; it is a personal reflection on the originating ideals of a self-respecting schoolteacher.

The great English philosopher Alfred North Whitehead says that "at the heart of the nature of things there are always the dreams of youth and the harvest of tragedy."[4] He goes on to suggest that though these dreams of youth are never achieved, there is a final harmony or peace awaiting those who continue beyond the loss of innocence to act under the influence of those ideals that constitute the dreams of our youth. There is no peace for those who forget their originating ideals, and such moral and religious visions as animate the religious educator in school or any other context must be the measure of ongoing performance or else there is no reason for perseverance. Thus, what follows, though not homiletic in intent, will tie the achievement of moral formation in schools to the fidelity with which noble purposes are pursued in humane ways. On this fundamental level, rather than on the level of particular programmatic innovation, rests the schools' ability to nurture justice.

The Purposes of Education

The nobility of purpose, the quality and ethical character of motivation, the imagination and knowledge that underpin and are manifest in teaching, and the quality and tone of relationships—these generic aspects of the school are the source of its ethical efficacy.

It may be argued that a consideration of education for justice should focus earlier and more explicitly on programmatic initiatives designed to convey particular knowledge of global injustice or give the clients of a school "hands on" experience of the poor and their plight. In fact, however, it is nothing short of disastrous for justice education to be conceived *first of all* as a series of programming initiatives. The degree to which schools play a role in forming just people is first of all dependent on the foundational tone and character of the environment, its "curriculum," if you will, where "curriculum" is understood as the matrix of teaching, learning, knowledge, information, intentions, and people. Programming initiatives, like those noted above, are themselves vital, but they are secondary in importance to this hermeneutic of the school as curriculum.

There is a rich and classical literature in which the purposes of education are expressed in a manner that virtually collapses the difference between education and moral education. Three examples of this literature are noted here: Philip Phenix, theoretically retired now from Columbia University's Teachers' College, is one of the most distinguished philosophers of education this country has produced. For him, the purpose of education is to give "a sense of the whole," the perpetuation of culture against rampant "partiality of outlook." It is "to widen one's view of life, to deepen insight into relationships and to counteract the provincialism of customary existence."[5] Phenix identifies the person exposed to such educational purposes in this manner:

A complete person should be skilled in the use of speech, symbol and gesture, factually well informed, capable of creativity and appreciating objects of esthetic significance, endowed with a rich and disciplined life in relation to self and others, able to make wise decisions and to judge between right and wrong, and possessed of an integral outlook.[6]

Alfred North Whitehead expressed the noble purposes and the ennobling educational experience in terms of a liberal education, in which the goals of "culture" and "expert knowledge" are joined rather than separated.[7] "Culture is activity of thought and receptivity to beauty and humane feeling."[8] It follows from an integrated and moral view of education that "what we should aim at producing is men who possess both cultural and expert knowledge in some special direction. Their expert knowledge will give them the ground to start from, and their culture will lead them as deep as philosophy and as high as art."[9]

Finally, also under the title liberal education, the contemporary English philosopher R. S. Peters has identified the three basic lines of a mode of education that is intrinsically oriented to moral formation:

A liberal education, to start with, is one that stresses the pursuit of what is worthwhile for what is intrinsic to it. It is hostile to a purely instrumental view of activities. . . . A liberal education is secondly one that is not narrowly confined to particular perspectives. . . . I have argued for the necessity of breadth of understanding. . . . Thirdly, a liberal education is one that is incompatible with authoritarianism and dogmatism. This is because a liberal education is based ultimately on respect for truth which depends on reasons and not on the word or will of any man, body or book. This means, of course, not that there is not an important place for authority in social life, but that it has to be rationally justified.[10]

How Such Noble Purposes Are Achieved

The sentiments expressed thus far will be inert generalizations unless they point to a form of practice that recommends itself to the actual experience of those who participate in educational exchange. Further, they will have to be found adequate in expressing that experience, or else they are simply "theory" in the pejorative sense that critical thought assigns to the word. In other words, does any of what has been said so far supply direction or give an answer to the plaintive, "but how?" of the teacher and school administrator? If we take Peter's three elements of a liberal education and use them as the basis for a systematic analysis of the practice of education, especially teaching in a school context, we will find that these noble expressions of education's general purpose are indeed authentic theoretical statements, expressions of direction and ideals actually encountered in and affected by practice.

Peter's criteria are threefold: The fruits of liberal education are the appreciation of what is worthwhile for its own sake and the achievement of breadth of understanding; the context of such education is one of relative freedom. These principles may also be expressed respectively as questions of motivation, instruction, and relationships in an educational agency such as a school. So our analysis moves to these more familiar terms of all educational exchange.

The most clear, even dramatic, instance of an educational environment in which a morally destructive instrument is used unconsciously and regularly is the school in which virtually all motivation for learning and behaving in a desired manner is pinned to rewards extrinsic to either the actual achievement of some understanding or of a habit of action based on consent. Rejecting such an approach for what he calls "intrinsic motives for learning," Jerome Bruner says:

> External reinforcement may indeed get a particular act going and may even lead to its repetition, but it does not nourish, reliably, the long course of learning by which man slowly builds in his own way a serviceable model of what the world is and what it can be.[11]

On the issue of appeal to intrinsic motives for action (including certain desired learnings) rests the whole of the thesis of this essay that the normal, everyday instrumentalities of a school are the locus of its moral authority and effect. For consider a whole generation, or many generations in succession, nurtured and conditioned to respond in desired ways in reaction to external reward alone! It is the very antithesis of the intending and courageous moral agent as described by both the rational and many religious traditions of moral inquiry. (And this is not to slip unconsciously into the destructive notion of the autonomous rational *man* as the norm of moral behavior:[12] the person rooted in a common life, drawing visions and sanctions alike from the values of those around him or her, must also be a person, in John Dunne's phrase, who "has a relationship with the things of one's life."[13])

Against this manipulation, Bruner identifies certain intrinsic motives: "An intrinsic motive is one that does not depend upon reward that lies outside the activity it impels. Reward adheres in the successful termination of that activity or even in the activity itself."[14] He believes his research has established the presence of four such motives: curiosity, competence, identification, and reciprocity. Of curiosity, Bruner says: "Our attention is attracted to something that is unclear, unfinished or uncertain. We sustain our attention until the matter in hand becomes clear, finished or certain."[15] Competence is similar, he believes, to what Veblen designated "an instinct for workmanship: We get interested in what we are good at. In general it is difficult to sustain interest in an activity unless one achieves some degree of competence."[16] Identification,

refers to the strong human tendency to model one's "self" and one's aspirations upon some other person. . . . In so far as the identification figure is also a "certain kind of person" belonging to some group or category, we extend our loyalties from an individual to a reference group.

What the teacher must be, to be an effective competence model, is a day-to-day working model with whom to interact. It is not so much that the teacher provides a model to imitate. Rather, it is that the teacher can become a part of the student's internal dialogue and somebody whose respect he wants, someone whose standards he wishes to make his own.[17]

And, finally, there is reciprocity, "a deep human need to respond to others and to operate jointly with them toward an objective":

Where joint action is needed, where reciprocity is required for the group to attain an objective, then there seem to be processes that carry the individual along into learning and sweep him into a competence that is required in the setting of the group.[18]

If these are indeed the inner motives for learning, it follows that at a most basic level, education that attends to stimulating these motives and appealing to these human dynamics in the inducement to learn certain ideas or actions is ethical at the basic level of cooperating with, rather than frustrating, human nature. Further, the educator for justice will wish to appeal to these motives to frame teaching strategies and learning environment just as teachers with different goals will appeal to such inner sources of motivation. But there is a greater significance to these motives: Human beings have a right to the stimulation of their curiosity, a right to achieve rather than to bear an endless downward spiral of the most disheartening failures. Human beings have a right to find in their teachers some depth and richness of humanity, to find people to whose world view assent, however tentative, may be given (rather than, in Whitehead's droll appraisal, encountering a steady stream of pedants or fools: pedants who have knowledge but no imagination, fools who have imagination but no knowledge). Above all, human beings have a right to be, indeed social life requires that we be, appealed to in our inner desire to enter into and to grow through cooperation. The bored, frustrated, disedified individualist is the fruit of a long-term experience of schooling in which curiosity, competence, identification, and reciprocity are either ignored or systematically undermined. These are precisely the elements of a moral malaise. In a very real sense, humane and enlightened educational motivation and moral formation are identical, though the former is not sufficient to the purposes of the latter.

The second element flowing from Peters's perspective is "breadth of understanding." Here it is essential to explore the relationship between imaginative, zestful, energetic, and knowledgeable teaching and the school as an environment for the nurturing of justice. This analysis will take the form of a reflection on the ethical significance of a superior education in the general subjects that traditionally occupy the curriculum of schools.

What university people call the disciplines, and elementary and secondary school educators more typically refer to as the subjects, are:

> Those public historically developed modes of experience whose immanent principles enable individuals to build up and revise an established content and make something of themselves within it.[19]

The significance of the relationship between imaginative initiation into the mentality, methods, and ideational and factual content of these accrued and growing bodies of experience and the moral purposes of a school cannot be overemphasized. I am convinced that the imagination, insight, and knowledge of both the personal subject and the "subject matter" that teachers bring to teaching the bodies of knowledge, skill, and insight embodied in the subjects bears a fundamental relationship to the moral effects of the school. And this is true for two reasons: psychological and theological. Psychologically, the achievement of intellectual and technical competency in those areas of human endeavor enshrined in the subjects is a necessary condition for both a sense of accomplishment and a sense of appreciation of one's life. The accomplishment is the foundation of self-image. The appreciation is the foundation for zest, whose opposite is boredom and lack of interest. People who grow old with deficient levels of accomplishment and appreciation are given over to the most hauntingly compulsive modes of inner life and behavior. It is rare that such people are able to muster the heroism to make a contribution to enhancing the humanity of their surroundings or those with whom they come in contact. It is for this reason that C. S. Lewis's senior devil, Screwtape, tells his apprentice to try to keep these humans from appreciating anything, bewailing the fact that he once lost a soul simply because the fellow had a passion for liver and onions. It is for this reason that Peters says, "A minimum task of moral education is surely to equip people so that they will not be perpetually bored."[20]

Theologically, Catholics especially, though not exclusively, have formulated their theological self-understanding and made a great many pastoral decisions under the influence of the conviction that there is an intimate relationship between the quest for human understanding and God's revelation of self and of the divine will. Many religious people believe that a growing knowledge of the world around and within us, in all its scientific, historical, and aesthetic facets, can feed a religious vision of life's meaning. This vision is a powerful foundation for moral behavior. (As Peters, again, says: "Religion . . . has the function of endorsing and of emphasizing one or another of the fundamental principles of morality by placing its operation in a setting which awakens awe.")[21] This vision is only encountered in our world, the knowledge of which is the province of the subjects. This world is the locus of encounter with God, whose message is written in history and nature.

This conviction is the heart of the rationale for sponsorship by religious communities of whole schools, which advance general as well as religious education.[22] The conviction cannot, however, be allowed to devolve into an "arid intellectualism"[23] that draws a direct line between knowledge and virtue. Nor can we allow the course of studies to be denatured through narrow confessional manipulation as if we really did not believe in the relationship between human investigatory power and the achievement of religious meaning and purpose. The "love of learning," to adapt Dom Le Clerc's famous phrase, is not sufficient to the goal of "desire for God," but for participants in traditions that link nature and grace, such learning is an important element in approaching the divine.

If what has been said here is true, it follows that slippage in attention to the subjects of learning in religious or public schools is a detriment to the moral effect of these schools. As Phenix says, speaking of the disciplines, "every person is indebted for what he has and for what he is to a great network of skilled inventors, experimentors, artists, seers, scholars, prophets, and saints."[24] Robbed of the inspiration and creativity that these subjects supply (for the achievement of both culture and expert knowledge, as Whitehead says), we are individually and collectively less rich.

There is, however, no warrant here for a simple-minded "back-to-basics" movement at any level of education. The so-called basics (the concern for factual knowledge and measurable skills in schooling) got displaced in United States education in the 1960s by the eruption of a well-meaning and essentially correct personalism that sought to reorient all forms of education in the direction of respect for the authority and uniqueness of individual experience. If in some corners "experience-oriented" education became an excuse for dismissing the importance of inherited knowledge and expert skill and became the occasion for an easily caricatured naiveté about the revelatory character of each individual's experience, still, the movement properly identified the destructive character of education that simply programmed people with inert facts and skills that were disassociated from moral purposes. (As Whitehead pictured the situation, we experience, "Algebra, from which nothing follows; Geometry from which nothing follows; a couple of languages never mastered; and lastly, most dreary of all, literature represented by plays of Shakespeare, with philological notes and short analyses of plot and character to be in substance committed to memory.")[25] These personalist educators knew, as Goethe put on the lips of Faust, that the merely well informed person is the most useless bore on God's earth. Their antagonists in the back-to-basics movement are in large measure people who are motivated by educational instrumentalism, in Eliot Eisner's words, people who should be called instructors rather than teachers, "whose orientation to curriculum is technological and who want to maximize effective control over the content and form of what children learn in school."[26]

Neither an incautious personalism nor a heavy-handed back-to-basics approach will retrieve the moral focus and effect of general education in schools. The commitment to the subjects slipped because the teaching in many quarters was inert, unimaginative, uncreative, and unintegrated. Simple minded experientialism will not help, for it robs the coming generations of the foundation for their own creativity that is provided by an appreciative understanding of that which our mothers and fathers in the human quest have already set before us. The solution can be found only in a synthesis that honors inherited human knowledge and the discipline required of each new generation if that deposit is to grow, and that also attends to the demands of human imagination. In this way, there is no loss of the moral and intellectual power that has been inherited, but neither is there domination of new insight by old formulas. It is in this vein that Whitehead says:

> So far as the mere imparting of information no [school] has had any justification for existence since the popularization of printing in the fifteenth century. . . . The justification for a [school] is that it preserves the connection between knowledge and the zest for life, by uniting the young and the old in the imaginative consideration of learning. The school imparts information, but it imparts it imaginatively.[27]

And there can be no doubt about the moral significance of such a synthesis of knowledge and imagination. For imagination, bolstered by knowledge, is the source of the most profound changes in human life. And it is an axiom of the prophetic consciousness that justice always requires change, because the present level of achievement of justice is always less than that which human dignity requires.[28]

Let it stand as a postscript to this summary discussion of the relationship between learning and morality that none of it makes sense where the general subjects are taught without reference to moral or religious issues and ideas, where such questions are seen as the exclusive province of values courses or theology departments. It is disastrous to impute to some element of the instructional curriculum those moral purposes that can only be achieved when (in the form of questions) they suffuse the entire field of study in which a school is engaged. Concretely, instruction in subjects serves moral purposes to the extent that students are confronted and engaged in a long-term, multidisciplinary plot to present them with interesting scientific, historical, literary, and other ideas and information that raise moral and even religious issues.

The final element to be considered is the incompatibility of a humane and morally significant educational experience with authoritarianism. This is the question of freedom in an educational environment that I have equated with the question of relationships. A school provides an environment that nurtures justice to the extent that it provides a relatively free environment. But how is a relatively nonauthoritarian, nondogmatic, and noncompulsive environment achieved; in what qualities, primarily, does it consist? At one level, the question can be answered by reference to the earlier discussion of educational motivation: The relatively free environment is one in which desired learnings are induced and encouraged by appeal to inner sources of motivation. In this way, the subjects of such experience are schooled in responses rooted in inner conviction as well as participation in a common life and not in response to external rewards. But at a more basic level, the will to engage in educational activity in a manner that is relatively noncompulsive is, simply, a function of trust in humanity. It is related to whether one believes, as Teilhard put it, that God has truly undertaken the work of "uniting Himself intimately to created beings."[29] This talk of trust is finally reducible to the question of love.

Now, speaking of education, in any of its forms, as an act of love is easily subverted and turned into a flabby romanticism. It can become the occasion for ignoring the dimensions of challenge in education, the need for discipline, the call that education at its best always issues for people to go beyond the limitations of personal prejudice to form judgments on the basis of new knowledge and insight. And yet, if educational exchange is not finally an act motivated by love, the full power of that grace that can be shared by teacher and student is compromised. In education, as in many modes of human exchange, the act of love takes the form of resisting the typification of other human beings and seeing possibility where present actuality does not fully justify the hope one brings to the relationship. It is a process, as Paul Tillich has said, of resisting "the profanity of the everyday."

In his essay on education, Martin Buber has given evocative expression to the stance of the teacher as lover. Commenting on how easily the " 'world-historical' origin" of those with whom we work, their commonality, can hide the element of uniqueness in each human being, he says:

> This fact must not obscure the other no less important fact that in spite of everything, in this as in every hour, what has not been invades the structure of what is, with ten thousand countenances, of which not one has been seen before, with ten thousand souls still undeveloped but ready to develop—a creative event if ever there was one, newness rising up, primal potential might. This potentiality, streaming unconquered, however much of it is squandered, is the reality *child*: this phenomenon of uniqueness, which is

more than just begetting and birth, this grace of beginning again and ever again.[30]

So education and education for justice are analogous. Where learning occurs as a result of appeal to intrinsic motives, where it encompasses a broad cross section of imaginatively communicated knowledge in a relatively noncompulsive environment in relationship with people of rich and deep humanity: There moral education is occurring. Without ignoring those processes of learning about which so broad a body of research literature exists, it is true to say that the ethical effect of education is deeply intermeshed with the spirit of the teacher. For "whole" education assumes engagement with "whole" people; education that appeals to inner motivation presupposes teachers who have the zest to pursue such motivation with energy and imagination; education for breadth of understanding assumes teachers who have not given up their own quest for knowledge and understanding. And education in freedom requires teachers who are relatively free of the debilitating compulsion to manipulate others, who are free of despair about the possibilities of virtue in those with whom they work. Education in freedom demands teachers who are free to love.

NOTES

1. Gabriel Moran, *Religious Body* (New York: Seabury Press, 1974), pp. 145–86.
2. Quoted in D. B. Robertson, ed., *Love and Justice* (New York: Meridian Press, 1967), p. 86.
3. Reinhold Niebuhr, *The Nature and Destiny of Man*, vol. 2 (New York: Scribner's, 1943), p. 246.
4. Alfred North Whitehead, *Process and Reality* (New York: The Free Press, 1969), p. 410.
5. Philip Phenix, *Realms of Meaning* (New York: McGraw-Hill, 1964), p. 46.
6. Ibid., p. 9. Although Phenix's notion of education is embraced here, one can see in his stricture of "customary existence" the incipient individualist strain in Liberal notions of education. See note 7.
7. In the history of Western thought, the notion of liberal education is inextricable from the individualism that has characterized Western notions of freedom. Thus, to embrace the ideal of "liberalism" in education may be to accept the negative elements of elitism and aristocracy that characterize the origins of this mode of thought but that are not themselves simply collapsible with the notion of education for excellence. Writing of the tradition, William Reid rightly notes the historical reference to liberal education as oriented toward wholeness and autonomy, "autonomy because liberal education is education toward freedom." (William Reid, "Democracy, Perfectability and the Battle of the Books: Thoughts on the Conception of Liberal Education in Schwab," *Curriculum Inquiry* 10:3 [1980], p. 250). Thus in a simple sentence is the antithesis be-

tween most notions of liberalism and any notion of freedom as constituted by social relations revealed. Yet Reid himself notes later in the same essay, "Liberal education is an ideal and precisely because it is an ideal it can never assume any permanent embodiment . . . each age demands a reinterpretation of the idea of liberal education in terms of its own social and political order." (Ibid., p. 251). My own conviction is that reinterpretation can take the form of rejecting the destructive individualism that is the logic of early forms of liberalism in education without, however, abandoning the ideal of breadth of knowledge and education toward intentionality that are also embodied in the tradition.

8. Alfred North Whitehead, *Aims of Education* (New York: MacMillan, 1967), p. 1.

9. Ibid.

10. R. S. Peters, "Concrete Principles and Rational Passions," in Theodore and Nancy Sizer, eds., *Moral Education* (Cambridge: Harvard University Press, 1973), p. 55.

11. Jerome Bruner, *Toward a Theory of Instruction* (Cambridge: Harvard University Press, 1966), p. 114.

12. For a critique of these tendencies in the work of Lawrence Kohlberg, see Gabriel Moran, "Beyond Two-Stage Moral Reasoning," *The Living Light* (Fall 1979); Craig Dykstra, "Sin, Repentance and Moral Transformation: Some Critical Reflections on Kohlberg," *The Living Light* (Winter 1979), and his recently published *Vision and Character;* and Carol Gilligan, "Women's Place in Man's Life Cycle," *Harvard Education Review* 41:4 (November 1979).

13. John Dunne, *Time and Myth* (Garden City, N.Y.: Doubleday, 1973), p. 28.

14. Brunner. p. 114.

15. Ibid. p. 118.

16. Ibid. p. 122.

17. Ibid. p. 124.

18. Ibid. p. 125.

19. Peters, "Concrete Principles and Rational Passions," in Sizer, p. 32.

20. Ibid., p. 49.

21. R. S. Peters, *Reason and Compassion* (London: Routledge & Kegan Paul, 1973), p. 74.

22. In contrast to this most fundamental and, I think, persuasive line of justification, most Catholic school enthusiasts follow the line of justifying the alternate school system on sociological or constitutional grounds. Sociologically, the schools are pictured as a mainstay of the tribal identity of the Catholic in a pluralistic society; constitutionally, the schools are pictured as a healthy example of pluralism in a state that runs on the equilibrium of competing pressure groups. Although both these rationales have some validity, neither goes to the heart of the matter, and both tend to be expressed in a way that shows little care for notions of unity or the obligation of the U.S. Catholic to the larger social enterprise of the public education system.

23. The phrase is Joseph A. Jungmann's in *The Good News, Yesterday and Today* (New York: William H. Sadlier, 1961), p. 28.

24. Phenix, p. 24.

25. Whitehead, pp. 10 f.

26. Eliot Eisner, *The Educational Imagination* (New York: MacMillan, 1979), p. 154b.

27. Whitehead, p. 14.

28. See, for example, Pope Paul VI embrace the notion of the Church and the Christian faith as catalysts for utopian imagination in his encyclical, *Octogesima adveniens*, 1971.

29. Pierre Teilhard de Chardin, *The Divine Milieu* (New York: Harper & Row, 1957), p. 49.

30. Martin Buber, *Between Man and Man* (New York: MacMillan, 1968), p. 83.

QUESTIONS FOR REFLECTION AND DISCUSSION

1. What is the difference between education and schooling?

2. What are some concrete examples of forms of educational motivation that are ethically disabling?

3. What are the limitations of the idea that learning, appreciative knowledge of the world around us, and moral behavior are related?

4. What are the positive and negative characteristics and implications of any back-to-basics movement in any area of education?

5. How much importance do you ascribe to teacher-student relations in appraising the moral effects of a school?

9. Cold Animation Is Not Animation

MARGARET WOODWARD

Toward an Art of Justice: "Art" and "Aesthetic"

> Cold animation is not animation.
> It is a still-born child . . .

> To animate: to give life and soul to a design,
> Not through the copying
> But through the transformation of reality.[1]

That is how a group of artists from Zagreb describe the work of their art and its power as transformative communication. Perhaps educators will recognize within their own communicative efforts similar disciplined and disciplining processes—a creativity that is not abstractive from but is responsive to reality, and a seeking of ways to avoid "cold animation." If so then it seems both feasible and helpful to consider art and aesthetic more closely, to see how education can be a just art and to discover whether insights into art, aesthetic and education can issue in a more effective and significant education for justice.

Giving impetus to such considerations is the conviction that art and the arts, though they have much to teach, have no monopoly in matters of creativity, imagination, concern for integrity in forming and symbolizing, skill in crafting and development of sensitivity to people and world.[2] Indeed, to affirm a monopoly is to make art irrelevant by denying its physical existence and historical contingency. Such denial isolates art from life and divorces it from those who, as audience and consumers, recipients and participants and co-creators, are integral to the communication process. Ironically, implicit in acceptance of this "separatist" model of art is potential for socially and culturally imposed monopoly: The way is paved for aesthetic imperialism in which the world and world making of art and the arts are determined by dominant power elites.

To speak of art and education, then, is to imply a mutuality. If art and aesthetic inform the educative process, so, too, education must be attentive to and critique art and aesthetic. Some investigation of the latter seems apposite here and may serve to highlight such mutuality.

Advocacy of a place for art and for an animating aesthetic may seem antithetical to the toughmindedness, complexity, and practicality of doing justice. For some, "art" and "aesthetic" suggest an esoteric mystique alien to justice concerns. The words evoke images of the decoratively accretive and recall the axiomatic self-sufficiency of "art for art's sake." Even the artistic valuing of nonrational and imaginative elements of life may emerge, distorted, as espousal of the irrational and unreal. "Aesthetic," in this static definition, is related to activities of the nonpractitioner/critic, arbiter in matters of "good taste" and public acceptability. The idealist's preoccupation with theoretical properties may be influential here. But "aesthetic" is not "anaesthetizing." It involves action and transaction. Its concern is not just "taste" but also, and perhaps primarily, "tasting." Different, indeed, unique,[3] the artwork often moves away from the center of respectability toward a prophetic periphery. Margolis, tracing recent currents in aesthetics, delineates a developing understanding.[4] From idealism there is movement to empiricism's focus on sensory discrimination and, later, attention to the place of cultural environment in art appreciation. Phenomenology, eschewing extreme idealism and materialism, is more aware of the complexity of the artwork; it points to plural interpretative possibilities and the influence of historical flux on aesthetic responses. Most recently, and consistent with this development, there has been emphasis upon the communicative functions of art. The notion of an artwork as "fixed" and "intrinsically interesting" seems to have been expanded, relativized, and changed by the recognition that "interesting means shared."[5]

Certainly the Zagreb artists, without putting excessively pragmatic demands upon their art form, speak of the act of creating in a way that is an antidote to stereotypical concepts of art and aesthetic. Art for them is not magic; it is both hard work and gift:

> Practically, animation is a long rubbing
> of tree against tree in order to get sparkle
> or perhaps just a little smoke.[6]

Their work of art is inclusive of much more than an end product: it has to do with an active subject, with process and form, with vision, and with life itself. Its finality, therefore, is not simply an entity—this particular piece of animation or poem or musical composition—

though it is that too. It is also what has been made of reality. It is how freshly perceptive images and symbols offer to participate in a world making; how boundaries of space, time, and human possibility are extended or shattered; how a whole range of experience and of ways of experiencing are made accessible; how the past can find new expression in the present and speak with vitality into the future.

All of these dimensions of artistic communication are of importance for people involved in justice education and in education as a just art. What humans create, how and why they choose to make particular works in particular ways, their response to different media, the artwork's capacity to transcend the artist's intention, and the contexts in which the work is located, received, and experienced—these not only model processes of communication from which the educator can learn and speak, but also constitute significant fact and event. Such data demand to be read.

Contemporary social analysis, for example, stands in need of aesthetic literacy if it is to undertake such a reading. Without this, how can it identify fully the images and symbols of control? How prevent an ineffectual, inconsequent identification of these? One must also acquire specific skills, gain proficiency in left-brain activities, and have many experiences of art- and life-forming in order to combat such control creatively and effectively. "Literacy" implies language, not vocabulary. It is participative. The Brazilian peasant says he wants to learn "to read and write so that I can stop being the shadow of other people."[7] Aesthetic literacy offers an analogous empowerment.

Life, justice, art—these, like stained-glass windows, need therefore to be viewed from within, existentially. The artistic process requires an immersion, a contact with the raw materials of world, complete with all the risks attendant upon such contact. Sometimes the artist as subject[8] struggles for freedom amid the constraints of surrounding history, society, and culture. These latter can entrap, turning subject into object. Artistic freedom is negated. The milieu alone is allowed to dictate what is, what must be, what should be, and what can be. Its dictatorship extends both to a view of reality and to the artistic process itself, and so secures acquiescence of the artwork in the replicative or simplistically descriptive, the deterministic, the prescriptive, or the terminally definitive. This is parallel to what Freire sees as being "naive" rather than "critical"—an unreflective "accommodation to the normalized 'today'."[9] Such is, as one primitive poet says, "carrion" artistry, which

works at random, sneers at the people,
makes things opaque, brushes across the surface of the face of things,
works without care, defrauds people, is a thief.[10]

"Accommodation" repudiates the discipline integral to art. Significantly, Matisse speaks of the artist's great "effort" to see, and Ben Shahn relates intuition to prolonged tuition. One aspect of this discipline is its "critical" character: its way of responding to reality, how it sees.

The Russian writer, artist, and calligrapher Aleksey Remizov describes his tussle, as a youth, to meet a teacher's demands that he be faithful to nature in his drawing. For, what is "nature"? The young man studies the object he is supposed to draw. From all angles. Conscientiously. Still he cannot see it as his teacher does. He redraws. And the teacher, erasing this next effort, accuses Remizov of drawing "monsters." Aleksey has drawn what he sees. Later, he reflects:

And what is there so black about my monsters when here before my eyes I see the blackest vulgarity, and why did it never occur to anyone till now to begin by getting this kind of monstrosity out of their system? Or have we all grown so used to it, all the world has been living with it for so long that nobody notices, and they go on looking for monstrosity in quite the wrong places?[11]

For the artist, description is both a focusing and a response. Perhaps what Remizov's teacher rejects is the risk of attending: the demanding discipline of participating in the vision of the artist and of making his own response. Such vision does not ignore the literal. Rather, it recognizes and proclaims the fundamentally metaphorical nature of all reality.[12] There is an honesty in this discipline. It will not readily admit of tunnel vision nor allow the ideological treatise to represent itself as art. The act of creating is, itself, transformative. To see, in this sense, is also to discover new ways of seeing, to break down dulling complacency. The effort involved is succinctly depicted by Cortázar: "How it hurts to refuse a spoon, to say no to a door, to deny everything that habit has licked to a suitable smoothness"[13] The pain and work are in exercising the human authority of one's subjecthood: in seeing what it is that one sees.

Discipline, of its nature, implies limit. Each art—whether it be sculpture or dance or music or story or any other of the arts—knows a discipline of limit. Lu Chi describes some of the limits known by the poet:

> We knock upon silence for answering music.
> We enclose boundless space in a square foot of paper;
> We pour out deluge from the inch space of the heart.[14]

There are human limits, limitations imposed by the material with which one works, and limits of the form within which one works. Yet, as Lu Chi asserts, such limit is liberative. To work craft-ily with words, musical notations, the limits of particular possibilities, is to transcend those limits. It is to experience the giftedness of discipline, to understand why Haydn wept with wonder on hearing his *Creation.* "I cannot have written this," he said. Freeing limit thus avoids what Dewey sees as the two polarities of the nonaesthetic: rigidity and aimlessness.[15] To accept the disciplining limits of art is to experience the universe as nonmanipulable, surprising, and impervious to a mechanistic view. In one sense, the artist never does what he or she sets out to do, and so does more. The Zagreb artists, having named skills, tasks, and world-stuff particular to the animator's art, conclude:

> . . . and if you are lucky you will not get the right answer to the question.[16]

And that, paradoxically, is how solutions come to be found.

Perhaps the polarities cited above are really in relationship: efficiency and constriction give rise to aimlessness and triviality. There is a trap for educational and justice enterprises in excessive literalness and rigid pursuit of predetermined goals. Neglect of integrity of forms and materials warps communication—perhaps into overcommunicative rationality or dissipative emotionalism. This is not to claim that, for example, conceptual art or world-projections of the creator of fantasy participate in such neglect. Challenging and redefining limit, moving differently to avoid banal repetition, countering false balance with alternative works that disequilibrate, and making humanizing room for escape and entertainment and joy is not "carrion" artistry. Form is freeing, not freezing. Educators may well question their own respect for limit—and for tradition—if their enterprise is locked into a single form or process, a uni-formity. Forming is a more complex, intense, and relational activity. Thus, justice education, as a communicative art, ought not to reduce the presentational to the discursive[17] by presuming that theme and animating principle are the same. As will be shown, a revelation of injustice promotive of action demands formative defamiliarization rather than prosaic literalness.

To conclude this description it may be helpful to consider how the disciplines of "critical" vision and creative limit are applicable to cultural and structural definition of art and aesthetic. Wolterstorff[18] examines the contemporary intellectually elitist "Institution of High

Art," which isolates art objects in context-denying juxtaposition in museums and "museums without walls," and which specifies a response of "disinterested contemplation."[19] In seeing what it is that he sees, Wolterstorff sees more. Identifying criteria of "aesthetic excellence,"[20] he shows how these, applied to cities and churches, enrich aesthetically and humanly squalid environments. Art is to be lived in, as well as looked at. A critiquing art of justice will study implications of the shift to *Gesellschaft* from the solidarity of predeliberate communities where the arts, embedded in life, did not need to be named. The Eskimo ended a story with *"Chuysh wantec"* ("to chop off half the winter"); the Navajo sand painting belonged in a communal healing ritual and was not kept, but blown away. Education restricts itself to museum art if it reinforces privatizing responses; generates no communal forms; isolates itself in structure, process, and purposes; or sees world and tasks of world-forming as addenda to the educative enterprise, subject only of the sporadic project.

Education as a Just Art

> How does the pot pray:
> wash me so I gleam?
>
> prays, crack my enamel:
> let the rust in.[21]

Definitions of education are many, and are often both nonecological and glossy. They do not "let the rust in." Noncommunicative, their very completeness and specificity function as impermeable membrane, denying imagination as the capacity and quality of meeting with, hearing, creating, and responding to the actual world. Education is—or ought to be—rather more vulnerable, hand dirtying, and immersed in life than these suggest. Falsifying definition, however, may be accurate description.

Corroborating such definitions are those practices, forms, goals, and institutions that evidence the polarities of the nonaesthetic: on the one hand, a movement toward closure, finished product, dogmatic answer, blinding clarities, chaotic order, and a placing of priority on logico-rational thinking to the point of capitulation of rationality; on the other, a parallel disordering, entropy, irrationality, aimlessness, self-indulgence masquerading as attention to affectivity, and absence of critical reflection. Such extremes are, even in their own terms, self-defeating. Exclusive emphasis on the cognitive, for example, is an irrational denudation of its meaning.[22] Belief that education is contained and resides in a single, noninteractive institutional form such as the school, prevents that institution from being educative. Both polarities function irresponsibly in relation to community, society, culture, and the communicative art that such relationships require. "Separatist" is also "miseducative."

The will to care, which is an expression of subjecthood and of a growing ability to own and exercise individual and communal power toward freeing of self, others, and world, requires a different and more integrative educational art. As Ricoeur asserts: "An ethic that addresses the will in order to demand a decision must be subject to a poetry that opens up new dimensions for the imagination."[23]

Ironically, it is often possible to detect in people enculturated for Western societies a passage toward the constrictively nonaesthetic: from *infancy*, and childhood *fancy* with its unrestricted imaginings and capacity for synaesthesia, toward the abstractive *non-fancy* of productive "maturity," and eventually, to the unrecognized restorative of *fancy* ("second childhood") in unproductive old age, where memory is poetry that re-members humanness. This passage is characterized by disjunction rather than wholeness.

There is, indeed, a need for precision, for processing of images, for abstract thought. But these adult tasks require a mode that is not ultimately destructive of both imaging and subjecthood. In their valuing of productivity and devaluing of the nonproductive, cultural and institutional forms not only self-perpetuate, they impede creative and conflictual challenge. At a time, therefore, when people are most engaged in or needed for world-shaping decision making, societal and educational forms seem to leave them least equipped to make choices. "Maturity" is not only an imbalancing definition reinforcing a particular meaning of "productivity", it also functions to exclude the childlike and the wisdom of the elderly; and it describes a cyclic pattern of human development in linear terms by offering for old age images of decline and decay that it has formed people to receive rather than to critique. Fixed to one aspect of human finitude that is allowed to define worth, the fragmenting image becomes idol.

Critical vision, applied to educational paradigms that are not "subject to a poetry that opens up new dimensions for the imagination," not only shows how these paradigms may have been co-opted by the culture but also indicates some significant areas of neglect. One of these has been the failure to take into account the lateral organization of the brain and, in particular, the process specificity of the right hemisphere, which has to do with "metaphorical and poetic thought . . . [and] structure-seeking forms of intellectual activity."[24] Writing of the crucial educational responsibility to attend to left-handedness,

Bruner grimly recalls Anouilh's Creon as being "not only a tyrant but a reasonable man."[25] Contrasting with and complementing the left hemisphere's analytical, logical, sequential, and temporal operations,[26] the right hemisphere works toward holism, handling of "simultaneous patterning," processing of emotional responses, and ability to deal with the unfamiliar and with "time-independent stimulus configurations."[27]

Inattention to these processes and denial of creative interplay between right and left hemisphere functions is both impoverishing and atrophying. It impairs adult ability to *be* adult:[28] to accept multiple meanings, cope with paradox and ambiguity, and recognize and respond to those structural patterns of dependence and influence and ideologies that are witness to corporate evil. Literalness issues in facile classification, simplistic remedy, and inability to conceive of alternatives. In a museumlike rejection of life contexts, privatized efforts for individual humanization repudiate contingent corporate responsibility. Compromise—such as Reinhold Niebuhr's ethical realism[29]—is suspect because, when there is inability to handle complexity, compromise is unrelated to freedom, the partial is mistaken for the whole, and means is seen as end. Without right hemisphere education, confrontation with life issues may promote guilt rather than evoke creative and conversional action. There has been, perhaps, corresponding denudation of ability to see what is to be seen: a failure to identify the link between lack of imagination and consequent powerlessness, repudiation of personal and communal power in acquiescence and defeatism, absence of hope, and denial of subjecthood.

Art and aesthetic, per se, neither monopolize left-handedness nor exclude left hemisphere operations. But the integrative acts and disciplines of art and art forming suggest a need for, and possible modes of, educational forming that are both disciplined and imaginative. Khatibi, speaking of his own poetry, says: "We must live in the essential song to shape history within it."[30] Educational forming is concerned with the quality of the song, with that to which it gives voice, with who sings it, how education shares in the song, and how that song can reach out to shatter false limits.

Inhering in an educational quest for wholeness or unity—the "theme" of the enterprise—is an animating principle of conflict. Imagination and artistry are needed to sustain this essential paradox. Absence of conflict is as destructive as is its excess. Education that is a valuing process confronts its own limit and finds ways to disturb and critique its own in-forming bases: the symbols that may collude in seductively serene institutionalized violence and the images and beliefs that are active in its constructs, processes, and effects. Otherwise, education is mere "accommodation."

One basis-become-bias may be that of interpretations, applications, and significance ascribed to *stages* in educational development. When the patterns these delineate or that their institutional usages define are linear, sequential, progressivist, and increasingly abstractive, exploration of their links with cultural emphases on productivity, manageability, and the "reign of quantity"[31] is needed. Origins of stage theory also need to be related to how such theory is subsequently employed, and whether its historical contingency is acknowledged. The descriptive can be analyzed, as can its cultural bases. The normative is open to question and change. But stage as invariant law becomes unquestionable "given."

To avoid museumlike confinement, education will also find and value potentially educative forms in society and culture. It will be concerned with *who* sings the song. Moran suggests a creative interplay of forms of schooling, work, community, and retreat.[32] Such interplay is transformative: It subversively extends limits and generates new possibilities for education and life. Callahan and Christiansen[33] see a possible link between development of concern for diminishing energy resources and promotion of ecological consciousness, and respect for the wisdom of the elderly. It is the latter who, educated in life, may show how to live with limitation and recognize finitude. It is they who may teach play, leisure, alternative meaning. Out of such shifted recognition can come new educative forms and new symbols for the whole of life—symbols that Western society lacks.

Much else might be mentioned here. There is the value of education in the arts, ways in which these develop sensitivities, shift horizons, make traditions accessible, promote international understanding, develop right-brain activities and capacities. But there is no automatic translation of art and aesthetic into every sphere of life. Education must engage in its own art forming.

An Art of Justice Education

The function of art is never to illustrate a truth—or even an interrogation—known in advance, but to bring into the world certain interrogations . . . not as yet known to themselves."[34]

Choice of an appropriate aesthetic of justice education requires, firstly, study of present paradigms for and approaches to such education. The "bring[ing] into the world [of] certain interrogations . . . not as yet known to themselves," raises deceptively simple questions once again about the art of educative communication—about who speaks and who listens, what is spoken, and how and when and why it is spoken. The work of justice education may be to effect change in all these areas and, in so doing, to find ways to cause beauty. Perhaps the latter is one of justice education's most neglected goals.

Present foci of materials, approaches, and processes in education for justice include the informational, the action-centered and the analytical—sometimes separately, sometimes in relationship. In all of these, the problematic seems paradigmatic. Clearly, each element in this paradigm can be powerfully disclosive art. Examples abound. Fact can be gifting of life. Statistical research into Christian education in South Africa, for example,[35] brought new "interrogation" with the evidence that such education, by default, shared in the injustice of apartheld. This information issued in radically responsive change and restructuring. Fact functioned as poetry—not simply as explanatory equation, but as a new relationship between people and world.

However, as paradigm, the problematic stands in need of corrective. Otherwise it may deflect from attention to larger meanings and implications, privatize by focus on a single dimension, make solution into ultimate goal, not engage in more total and radical reconstructive efforts, and have no means of self-critique.

Illustrative of such a problematic emphasis would be an education program for potential lawyers that concerned itself only with breaches of law and with aberrations. Exclusive emphasis on these would, predictably, maim and limit meaning, educative process, and the personalities of those involved in that process. Law has a purpose beyond itself that the problem-centered ignores. Countries and peoples, too, have a beauty and a shared humanity that the problem-centered ignores. Related corrective is implied in Bruegel the Elder's depiction of "Justice."[36] She wears the headdress of a procuress precisely because, though carrying symbols of judgment, she lacks those of peace and pity, and so epitomizes justice without compassion. Protest art risks a like fragmentation if it is not somehow informed by beauty. This paradigm of the problematic may be unintentionally created by the cumulative effect of printed materials, news items, resources, and pleas for assistance sent out by justice agencies that, themselves, acknowledge larger contexts. Critical vision is needed to detect the implicit agenda—for these organizations to see what it is that they say.

How, then, may the informational, the action-centered, and the analytical escape the confines of this paradigm? Respect for the limits of form is an important discipline here. Form resists paradigmatic constraint, and the formative event enlarges possibility through sensitivity to limit. Edicio de la Torre, S.V.D., poet, priest, and political prisoner in the Philippines, records the resistance of life-forms and experience to his attempts to theologize. He speaks of

> ... the contradiction between the need to deal with life in direct, descriptive and analytic terms (scientifically, a Marxist would say) and the indirect, evocative language of what we usually call theology. Another poet-activist friend's insight into poetry proved helpful. 'There are times,' she said 'that are so pregnant with meaning that bare reportage results in a poem. There are also times that need to be related to other symbols and images to reveal their poetry.'[37]

"Bare reportage" may be fact and analysis and a theology that is theopoetic. If people in justice education do not experience this disruptive resistance of life-forms, and if they are able to follow neat or invariant procedures of justice education, it may be that they are distanced from the life-forms of their art and from the conversional richness that these offer.

If it is to be communicated, this "disruption" is sustained in the forming work undertaken by the educator. If this is not achieved, automatization can jade the capacity for active caring, or familiarization with images of local and global violence can diminish the power of these to disturb "accommodative" living. Without the creative listener, there is neither communicative act nor art.

One example of such liberating forming, from the theater, has to do with the fool, bearer of deeply human wisdom. Václav Havel, the Czech playwright, declares that it is *because* the clown's humor has pathos as one of its most basic themes that a corresponding principle of "depathetication"[38] is required. Justice educators have often presumed that pathos has as its principle "pathetication." Cumulatively, theme and principle in such literalizing correspondence have deprived fact of its poetry, making it bland or voiceless. Anaesthetic has replaced aesthetic.

Perhaps people in less affluent circumstances and those within Western society not usually accorded a voice in justice education better understand this disequilibrating movement toward wholeness. Filipino slum-dwellers, for instance, through humorous role-play that is preparatory enactment of confrontation with oppressive officials, discover in the comic theater not merely that they are oppressed—they knew that already—but that oppression is absurd. Foolishness turns meaning upside down. Though their pretentiousness suggests it, it is not the oppressors who are holders of dignity. In this inversion, this shift of context, the poor recognize and affirm their own dignity. Thus, the absurd offers a "criterion of meaningfulness"[39] that subverts assigned ideological roles of rich and poor, master and servant, intelligent and ignorant, lord and beast of burden. The imaginative shift of context produces decommitment to old contexts and a capacity to question and unmask these. A new "interrogation" is abroad. The words of an old fisherman on the Tondo foreshore take on the quality of rich insight: "We laugh because we know how unhappy we are," he says.[40]

A humorous way of viewing serious reality thus offers to be a means of achieving the objectification necessary for responsible vulnerability to meaning. Though circumstances and purposes will call for other modes—the tragic as well as the comic—justice education needs to be conscious of the interactive power of theme and principle in a communicative art productive of necessary contextual shifts. It might also question exclusive reliance upon a *single* mode. (Images for such modes need not come only from the theater—from story, for example, there is narrative, sustaining myth, challenging parable, sharp satire, etc.) Similarly, liberative limit calls for other shifts in form and context, for different community-making properties and possibilities, and for redirection that reverses roles of speaker and listener. To consider this aspect of forming might be to learn that justice education, at times, has been more preoccupied with flat "telling" than with dynamic "making."

This concern for appropriateness, which is respect for and response to world-stuff and persons, is also a concern for beauty. Schiller declares in his *Letters on the Aesthetic Education of Man* that it is only through beauty that humans "make their way to freedom"; whereas Augustine sees creation as first sacrament, disclosing its Creator, revealing a beauty "at once so ancient and so new."[41] A primary task of justice education is to communicate a sense of this beauty and an appreciation of the gifting of people and world. Only then does recognition of injustice as ugly rending of creation become apparent and the restoration of wholeness become urgent and passionately sought need.

Taeko Tomiyama's "Prayer in Memory," recalling the bloodshed in Korea's Kwangju in May 1980, captures this healing awareness of discrepancy. The beauty of the struggle for freedom contains both judgment and promise of resurrection. Seiji Utsumi's accompanying photographs, nonliterally, and in language of people and a country, speak both grief and hope.[42] The third artist, united with these two in responding to an event, was a composer, Yuji Takahashi. It is perhaps worth noting here that the Kwangju event was presented to

光州・五月の血

1980年5月の光州で流された血──街上に流されたたくさんの若い血。鳥も泣き、麦も涙した。光州の死者たちの魂は雨粒になったようだ。その雨は、熱い心の種子となって乾いた心に降りそそぎ、やがて新しい種子をはぐくむであろう──いつの日か芽ぶくために。そしてまた雨粒は岩を砕くだろう。

Bloodshed in Kwangju in May 1980

A great deal of young blood was shed on the streets. Birds cried and barley wept. However, the spirit of the dead in Kwangju seemed to become raindrops. This raindrops will wet dry minds, and eventually bring up new seeds, to put forth buds someday in the future.
Furthermore, those raindrops will also eventually crush solid stone.

From *Kwangju: Three Messages* (Tokyo: Hindane Production). Art by Tomiyama Taeko.

Western society largely through the eyes of Western photographers and news reporters. Thus, it remained possible to stay at some distance, safe, untouched by the claims of such an event. Why is Asia not imaged to us through Asian eyes? How else can its beauty be discovered? What happens to the people who respond as did Tomiyama, Takahashi, and Utsumi is also significant. In entering into the experience, they also became *more* themselves: the musician made more music, the photographer new images, the artist wrought his visual prayer.

It is only education toward appreciation of this wholeness, this essential integrity of the beautiful, that can sharpen perception of evil. And perhaps it is only possible to be truly oppressive when a rich sense of giftedness is lost. Sin is corruption of beauty. For those who have come to know the beautiful, the military in El Salvador *"lie [their] most terrible truth"*[43] by using Beethoven's *Ode to Joy* to summon Salvadoreans from the Cathedral after the carnage at Archbishop Romero's funeral. Hymn singing, murder, and Beethoven—it is a "terrible" liturgy indeed.[44]

Beauty gives impetus to action. Dorothee Sölle's poem, "Ernesto Cardenal," has the poet explain how he came to be priest, poet, and revolutionary. His answer is "love of beauty":

> This led him he said
> to poetry
> (and beyond)
> it led him
> to god
> (and beyond)
> it led him
> to the gospel
> (and beyond)
> it led him
> to socialism
> (and beyond)[45]

To apply considerations of art and aesthetic to education as a just art and to education for justice is, perhaps, to discover the deeply religious dimensions of all three. It is also to come to recognize the pain and tough work of participating in creating selves, worlds, persons, and the Kingdom already begun among us; it is to know some of the disciplines involved and to experience a restlessness, disquietude, and hopefulness as aspects of the art of redemptive humanness.

NOTES

1. Group of unnamed artists, Zagreb, Yugoslavia, quoted in *RISK* 12:3–4 (1976), p. 38.
2. Cf. N. Wolterstorff, *Art in Action* (Michigan: William B. Eerdmans, 1980), pp. 5–7. Wolterstorff discusses contemporary grouping of phenomena as major arts and cites other, earlier groupings—for example, music and mathematics.
3. Cf. A. Isenberg, "Critical Communication," in J. Hospers, ed., *Introductory Readings in Aesthetics* (New York: Free Press, 1979), p. 213, for discussion of this characteristic uniqueness.
4. Joseph Margolis, "Recent Currents in Aesthetics of Relevance to Contemporary Visual Artists," *Leonardo* 12 (1979), pp. 111–19.
5. S. Moore, *The Fire and the Rose Are One* (New York: Seabury, 1980), p. 52.
6. *RISK*, p. 38.
7. *The New Internationalist* 8 (October 1979), p. 15.
8. Cf. P. Freire, *Pedagogy of the Oppressed* (New York: Seabury, 1968), pp. 100–101.
9. Ibid., p. 81.
10. Aztec poem, English version by Denise Levertov, in J. Rothenberg, ed., *Technicians of the Sacred* (New York: Doubleday, 1968), p. 361.
11. A. Pyman, "Aleksey Remizov on Drawings by Writers with Particular Reference to the Interrelationship between Drawings and Calligraphy in His Own Work," *Leonardo* 13 (1980), pp. 234–40.
12. Cf. J. D. Crossan, *Cliffs of Fall* (New York: Seabury Press, 1980).
13. Julio Cortazar, *Cronopios and Famas* (New York: Random House, 1969), pp. 3–4.
14. Lu Chi, translated by Achilles Fang, in C. I. Lee and F. Galati, *Oral Interpretation* (Boston: Houghton Mifflin, 1977), p. 2.
15. J. Dewey, *Art as Experience* (New York: Paragon, 1979), p. 138 f.
16. Op. cit.
17. For elaboration and application of S. Langer's distinction between the presentational and the discursive (S. Langer, *Philosophy in a New Key*, [Cambridge: Harvard University Press, 1942]), see Maria Harris, "A Model for Aesthetic Education," in G. Durka and J. Smith, eds., *Aesthetic Dimensions of Religious Education* (New York: Paulist Press, 1979) p. 147.
18. *RISK*, p. 38.
19. Wolterstorff, pp. 34–39.
20. Ibid., pp. 163–68. Criteria identified include: unity (modes of which are coherence and/or completeness); internal richness, variety, and complexity; and "fittingness" to outside qualities.
21. A. R. Ammons, "Utensil," *Contemporary Literature* 21:2 (Spring 1980).
22. Cf. E. W. Eisner, *The Educational Imagination* (New York: Macmillan, 1979), p. 84 f.
23. Paul Ricoeur in P. Ricoeur and E. Jungel, *Metephor: Zur Hermeneutik Religioser Sprache*, Munich, 1974, p. 70; quoted in translation in F. Herzog, *Justice Church* (New York: Orbis, 1980) p. 87.
24. E. W. Eisner, p. 85.
25. J. Bruner, *On Knowing: Essays for the Left Hand* (London: Belknap Press of Harvard University Press, 1979).
26. E. W. Eisner.
27. G. Rico, "Metaphors and Knowing: Analysis, Synthesis, Rationale," doctoral dissertation, Stanford University, 1976, pp. 41–44. Quoted in E. W. Eisner, p. 85.

28. Cf. G. Moran, *Education Toward Adulthood* (New York: Paulist Press, 1979), especially the discussion of the four operative meanings of adulthood in chapter 2.

29. Cf. Reinhold Niebuhr, *Moral Man and Immoral Society* (New York: Charles Scribner's Sons, 1962).

30. Abdelkebir Khatibi, *Modern Poetry in Translation* no. 37/38 (Winter 1979), p. 62.

31. Rene Guenon.

32. Moran.

33. S. Callahan and D. Christiansen, "Ideal Old Age," *Soundings* no. 57 (1974), pp. 1–16.

34. A. Robbe-Grillet, in K. Baynes, *Art in Society* (London: Lund Humphries, 1975), p. 24.

35. Research undertaken at the request of the South African bishops by Sr. Marie Augusta Neal.

36. Bruegel the Elder, "Justice," 1559, engraving, Bibliotheque Royale, Brussels.

37. In his Introduction to *Pintig: Sa Malamig Na Bakal* [Lifepulse in Cold Steel] (Hong Kong: Resource Centre for Philippine Concerns, 1979), p. 9.

38. Václav Havel, "The Anatomy of the Gag," translated by Michal Schonberg, *Modern Drama* 23:1 (March 1980), pp. 13–24.

39. Ibid., p. 21.

40. This example is drawn from personal experience of meeting with the poor in Metro-Manila.

41. Cf. Aiden Nichols, *The Art of God Incarnate* (New York: Paulist Press, 1980), chapter 9, where this is related to what the author describes as "the essentially aesthetic structure of revelation."

42. T. Tomiyama, Y. Takahashi, and Y. Utsumi, *Kwangju: Three Messages* (Tokyo: Hidane Productions, 1980). On May 27, 1980, martial law troops besieged Kwangju, with an all-out assault on the city. The death toll was said to amount to as many as two thousand. Thus ended a bid for freedom in which on May 19, 1980, two hundred thousand of Kwangju's citizens actively resisted martial law troops, and on May 22, 1980, Free Kwangju was born.

43. J. Cortazar, p. 11.

44. This incident was documented in *The Guardian* at the time.

45. Dorothee Sölle, *Revolutionary Patience* (New York: Orbis, 1977).

QUESTIONS FOR REFLECTION AND DISCUSSION

1. What do you consider to be the place of art and the aesthetic in your own society and culture?

2. What is the significance of the "community-making properties" of art and art forming?

3. How would you apply the disciplines of art to education for justice?

4. What is meant by describing artistic action as the "pain and work" of exercising the "human authority of one's subjecthood."?

5. What are the justice implications of the notion that art and engagement in the aesthetic are more about tasting than mere taste?

10. Christian Education for Peace and Social Justice: Perspectives from the Thought of John Dewey and Paulo Freire

RUSSELL A. BUTKUS

Part I: Introduction

Christian education for social justice is still a new phenomenon. Although good and provocative programs abound, there is still work to be done in the area of curriculum development and pedagogical guidelines. Many Christian educators who have attempted to "teach" a course or program in social justice know of the difficulty and resistance that is often encountered. Yet, the task is a critical one. It may be the most important challenge of our educational ministry.

My reading of John Dewey and Paulo Freire suggests that these educational giants can inform our quest for better and more effective ways of educating for social justice. Thus, the major purpose of this essay is to discuss and analyze the major pedagogical principles of Dewey and Freire, critique their usefulness for social justice education, and propose a tentative pedagogical foundation for Christian education for social justice. However, before I undertake this important task, I would like to share several assumptions I bring to my analysis of Dewey and Freire.

These assumptions emerged and became crystallized in my consciousness largely as a result of critical reflection upon my work and the work of others in Christian religious education. My assumptions have, in a significant way, influenced my reading of Dewey and Freire; however, the readings have also shaped or altered my assumptions. I acknowledge the fact that we are limited by our assumptions, so I will depend upon dialogue with others to enlarge my horizons and to prevent my perceptions from becoming overmyopic. Furthermore, I make no claims for originality or complete truth. My assumptions are simply reflections of my truth, and they may or may not contribute to the overarching truth we seek as Christian religious educators. My six assumptions for Christian religious education for social justice are as follows: First, Christianity is primarily a way of being and doing in the world. Christianity can never be embodied in a set of propositional statements or truths about Christianity, nor can it be reduced to an ideal or theory of how to live. Contrarily, Christianity is a practice, a unique and profound way of living in the actual context of the world. Christian faith must be lived faith in response to our encounter with Jesus Christ and the Kingdom of God. Therefore, Christian religious education cannot be solely interested in orthodoxy —right belief. It must be equally concerned with orthopraxy—right action, if we are to promote the complete version of the Christian story and vision.

The second assumption follows from the first. Christian education for social justice must employ an epistemological paradigm that unifies theory and practice, idea and action. A "theoria" approach to justice education is inadequate. Justice is not justice until it is done. Christian education for justice must be grounded in a reflective/active model of knowing.

However, a reflective/active way of knowing is insufficient by itself. This leads to the third assumption: Christian education for justice must utilize a critical principle that fosters critical analysis and the unmasking of ideological assumptions and vested interests that underlie present action or inaction in behalf of justice. The importance of a critical principle lies in the fact that our present action is often controlled and shaped by a hardened, reified past. Critical reflection is a process involving critical remembering, in which we attempt to uncover the genesis of present assumptions and action. This can lead to liberation from a reified past and promote a reshaping or a reconstructing of present action. Critical reflection must have a personal as well as a social dimension.

The fourth assumption is that all of Christian religious education should be education for social justice. I do not mean that all of the content of our educating can simply be reduced to issues of social justice. I do, however, believe significant connections and parallels can be made with justice themes. I am specifically referring to method or approach rather than to content. Regardless of content, the approach we take in our educating will implicitly promote or inhibit justice. This leads to the fifth assumption: Christian education for social justice must be done justly. How we teach is as important as what we teach. We can not presume to do justice education by means that are inherently unjust. Our practical approach, technique, or strategy must be consistent with the Christian community's understanding of justice. This assumption demands departure from traditional models and structures of educating.

Our concern for social justice, which must permeate the entire Christian "curriculum" of thought, life, and practice, is the final assumption. We must become aware of and critique the "hidden agenda" that promotes injustice in our common life and practice as Christians. This is a primary task and responsibility of Christian religious educators and is one aspect of the prophetic dimension of Christian education.

It is with these assumptions that I begin my analysis of John Dewey and Paulo Freire. In discussing these two giants of twentieth-century education, I will not try to present a complete picture of their thought and work. In the case of Dewey that would be impossible, since the man's works are voluminous and volumes have been written about him. My major interest is to focus on and analyze their major pedagogical insights that can inform us in doing education for justice. I will do this in a dialectical fashion. Both Dewey and Freire have much to offer us if we are willing to listen. On the other hand, both men have limitations that we must recognize and move beyond.

Part II: Major Pedagogical Insights from John Dewey and Paulo Freire

Regardless of the controversy and confusion that often surround the educational thought of John Dewey, no one can possibly deny the enormous impact he has had on twentieth-century North American education. No single person has done more to shape and influence educational theory and practice than John Dewey. Given the depth of his thought and the richness of his insights we, as Christian educators, would be irresponsible if we did not give him a fair hearing. His thought can inform and enlarge our own educational practice.

Dewey's Epistemology

The foundation of Dewey's educational thought is his epistemology, which is usually termed instrumentalism, experimentalism, or pragmatism. His epistemological interest was in emphasizing the unity and continuity rather than the duality in human knowing. Dewey's primary reason for rejecting epistemological dualism and accepting a coherent unified process of knowing was the development of the scientific experimental method. For Dewey it is "the method of getting and of making sure it is knowledge and not mere opinion—the method of both discovery and proof."¹ According to Dewey, the scientific method has done more to warrant a transformation in the theory of knowledge from dualism to experimentalism than any other single phenomenon.

Besides the scientific method, Dewey's epistemology is also grounded in a biological anthropology. For Dewey, a human person is a dynamic, biosocial creature, a future-oriented experimenter, who does not live his or her life as an unconcerned spectator but as an actual participant in the world of events. "If," as Dewey says, "the living experiencing being is an intimate participant in the activities of the world to which it belongs, then knowledge is a mode of participation."² Human knowing, for Dewey, is grounded in an experimental interaction between the self and the social environment.

The process of coming to knowledge, in Dewey's perspective, is future-oriented. Human knowing is less retrospective and less concerned with antecedent reality than it is with the anticipation of future consequences. This is not to say that Dewey ignored or negated the past. On the contrary, antecedent experiences are an important aspect of the process of knowing. However, knowledge is pre-eminently valuable because of its applicability to the world. This does not mean applicability to what is past and gone but to what is still going on and is as yet unfinished. Applicability to the world is the true test of genuine knowledge. Dewey placed great emphasis on knowing as a practical activity that purposely modifies the environment. The process of knowing involves the transformation of the knowing subject and the transformation of the world through practical, meaningful activity.

Dewey rejected any theory of knowledge that separated knowing and doing and did not promote practical action upon the world. In response to epistemological dualism, he emphasized the continuity between theory and practice. Human knowing, for Dewey, is a reflective/active process grounded in the person's interaction with his or her social and natural environment. The medium of exchange between the knowing subject and the world is what Dewey called experience. All genuine knowledge in Dewey's epistemology is ultimately experiential.

It is obvious that Dewey's epistemology is heavily grounded in the scientific method. What he proposed was a paradigmatic shift away from dualistic models of knowing to a model of knowing that unified reflection and action. It was this reflective/active epistemology combined with his understanding of experience that provided the basis for his idea of education as the reconstruction of experience.

Education as the Reconstruction of Experience

John Dewey was an outspoken critic of traditional education. His educational thought is largely a response to the deficiencies and inadequacies that he perceived in the normative practice of education. Specifically, he rejected the practice of separating subject matter from actual lived experience. He saw the primary concern of traditional education as the transmission of past information to the new generation. In this context, teaching became the imposition of adult standards, subject matter, and methods upon the young. Learning required an obedient, docile receptivity; there was no room for active student participation in the learning process.

In contrast to traditional education, Dewey argued, education must be primarily based on experience, not on subject matter derived from the past. The challenge of progressive education was to effectively and creatively combine present and future experiences with subject matter. However, Dewey did not claim that all experience was educational. In fact, experiences can be miseducational: if they are disconnected; if they arrest or distort growth; if they produce a lack of sensitivity to future experiences; or if they cause an individual to fall into a rut.[3]

As a corrective to miseducational experiences, Dewey believed education's task was to provide organization, direction, and continuity to experiences. Dewey's primary criterion for creating and analyzing educational experiences was what he called the continuum of experiences or the principle of continuity. By this, Dewey meant that present experience is derived from or linked to previous experiences and in turn modifies to some degree subsequent experiences. This continuous process is what Dewey called the reconstruction of experience. Education as the reconstruction of experience is Dewey's understanding, in capsulized form, of what education should be. In *Democracy and Education*, Dewey offers us a technical definition of education: "It [education] is that reconstruction or reorganization of experience which adds to the meaning of experience and which increases ability to direct the course of subsequent experience."[4]

There are three important variables in the reconstruction of experience. The first is the past experience, which refers to past knowledge or disciplines. The second, and the point of departure, is the learner's present experience. The third, and future-oriented, variable is continued growth and social progress. Experience is reconstructed when the student re-invents or relearns in a new way the inherited disciplines and past knowledge for the purpose of growth and social progress. Past knowledge, if it is to be useful, must be made applicable to ever new demands and situations. However, the "funded capital" must be modified or recreated to meet the new conditions that have arisen.

Dewey attempted to combine the three main variables of the classic curriculum debate into a creative tension. He rejected any theory that overlooked or denied the significance of one over the other. Of course, for Dewey, the starting point in the curriculum was not the past disciplines or the future social needs but the present experience of the learner.

Child/Learner-Centered Education

Dewey rejected the notion in traditional education that the curriculum must begin with the past disciplines of knowledge. Instead, he firmly believed that the child's needs and interests should be the foundation for curriculum development. He had a great deal of respect for the child's individual personality, intelligence, and capacity to be an active participant in the educational process. According to Dewey, it is the educator's responsibility to carefully observe the child's needs, interests, and capacities in order to determine the child's readiness for the learning process. Furthermore, it is also the educator's responsibility to organize and direct the medium of experience out of which reconstruction can occur. In Dewey's thought, the child/learner was the hope for social reconstruction and progress. He believed that the child's social activities should be the true center for the subject matter of the school curriculum. He also believed that the reconstruction of experience was not only a personal process but a social one as well.

Social-Centered Education

Education as a social process resided, for Dewey, primarily in the school. Dewey saw the school as the most effective way of bringing the child to share in what he called, the "funded capital of civilization." Dewey also recognized that education as it occurs within the school will be a reflection of the quality of social life. Dewey was aware of the socializing nature of the school environment. He believed that the school should be intentionally organized around a particular social ideal, to promote the most positive and beneficial qualities of that ideal. In Dewey's mind the social paradigm that best fit his ideal was democracy, and he understood democracy to mean more than a particular form of government. He believed the school should be structured upon four democratic principles: moral equality, mutual respect, participation, and cooperation.

Dewey's understanding of education as a social process also demanded a social dimension for subject matter and curriculum. As stated earlier, the starting point was the child's needs and interests. Therefore, the curriculum should be grounded in the child's experience of existing social life. The educator's task was to select, organize, and direct the social experiences to be encountered and reconstructed. Moreover, the curriculum should be developed "with the intention of improving the life we live in common so that the future shall be better than the past."[5] Dewey's intention was to promote social as well as personal reconstruction. He strongly believed that education was the main impetus for social progress, reform, and reconstruction. In Dewey's view education would reconstruct North American society in two ways. First, schooling would create a new generation of individuals who would acquire, through democratic experiential education, the capacity for scientifically organized intelligence. Second, these individuals would intervene in the social structure and promote reconstruction on the social, political, and economic levels of society. Dewey was convinced that freed, organized intelligence was the primary method for social action and change.

There is no question that Dewey had a high regard for the potential power of this educational process to effect constructive change in society. He also had a high regard for the teacher in this process. In closing this brief sketch of Dewey's educational thought, I quote him from the essay "My Pedagogic Creed,"

> Every teacher should recognize the dignity of his calling; that he is a social servant set apart for the maintenance of proper social order and the securing of the right social growth. In this way the teacher always is the prophet of the true God and the usherer in of the true Kingdom of God.[6]

*   *   *   *

Unlike John Dewey, Paulo Freire is not a North American; his cultural experiences, interests, and assumptions therefore differ significantly. Freire's educational thought is rooted in his experience with adult literacy programs for Brazilian peasants during the early 1960s. Out of this experience, he concluded that Brazil needed a new type of education that would "lead men to take a new stance toward their problems, one oriented toward research, instead of repeating irrelevant principles. An education of 'I wonder,' instead of merely, 'I do.' "[7] He discovered the political dimension of education and concluded that no type of education was politically neutral. According to Freire, all forms of education are based on a particular political stance or ideological position. Freire saw two possible options for education as a political act: Education was either for domestication (this predominated in Brazil) or education was for liberation and humanization. For Freire, authentic pedagogy must emerge from and with oppressed peoples in their struggle to regain their humanity. Authentic pedagogy makes injustice and its causes into objects of reflection by the oppressed. Underlying Freire's understanding of education are several pedagogical principles. The first and most foundational is his epistemological perspective.

Freire's Praxis Epistemology

The bedrock of Freire's epistemology is a particular anthropological vision. Freire understands humans as relational, dynamic beings who can intervene in reality in order to change it. According to Freire, "to be human is to engage in relationships with others and with the world."[8] For Freire, a person's relationship with the world is active and creative. Human beings have the capacity to recreate and transform the world and thereby build a humanizing future. Human beings come to be and know themselves through their interaction with the world.

Like Dewey, Freire rejects the objective and subjective extremes of the epistemological question. Objectivity and subjectivity, he believes, cannot be dichotomized. Only when their unity is preserved can authentic knowing occur. If the unity is broken, false and inaccurate modes of knowing are created. Authentic knowing results only when a dialectical unity is maintained between objectivity and subjectivity grounded in action upon the world. There are two assumptions behind Freire's claim for objective/subjective unity. First, there is an objective reality that can be known, and second, human consciousness plays a significant role in transforming it.

Knowing, for Freire, is the process of interaction between a subject and his or her objective world. In other words, knowing involves a twofold movement of reflection and action that means that Freire's epistemology is a method of praxis. A praxis way of knowing involves a dialectical process from action to reflection and from reflection upon action to a new action. Freire maintains that objectivism and subjecti-

vism cannot result in a true praxis. Praxis is central to Freire's liberating pedagogy because it is through praxis that human beings
become conscienticized. Through praxis human beings become empowered to critically evaluate reality and thereby recreate it through
liberating action. However, praxis by itself is not automatically emancipatory. As a corrective to this problem, Freire combines praxis with
a critical principle.

Conscientization

Freire holds that, besides the ability to know reality, human beings
also have the capacity to critically apprehend it. In applying a critical
principle to reflection, Freire is taking reflection a step deeper. In
praxis, the reflective moment is the capacity to objectify an action or
situation and analyze its antecedents, its inner connectedness, and its
future consequences. It is the ability to analyze the various components of an experience and come to a new clarity of understanding
about it. On the other hand, critical reflection is the capacity to analyze the underlying structure of an action or experience. It is the
ability to unveil and apprehend the causal relationships, the hidden
motives and interests of present action. However, critical reflection is
not only an individual process but a social one as well. It is the capacity to unmask assumptions and ideologies that are socially and culturally mediated. Freire is convinced that when oppressed people arrive
at a critical awareness of reality they will commit themselves to liberating action.

The Freirean conception of praxis begins with critical reflection
upon present action, which leads to liberating action and thus to further critical reflection, and so on in a dialectical process. The process
of critical reflection and liberating action is what Freire calls conscientization. According to Freire,

> Conscientization refers to the process in which men, not as recipients, but
> as knowing subjects, achieve a deepening awareness both of the socio-cul-
> tural reality which shapes their lives and their capacity to transform that
> reality.[9]

Conscientization is the emergence from silence and domination to political engagement for freedom. It is, as Freire says, "a critical self-
insertion into reality."[10]

Like Dewey's, Freire's epistemology provides the foundation and
the method for his educational thought. Conscientization is the sub-
structure for his idea of dialogical/problem-posing education.

Dialogical/Problem-Posing Education

Freire abhorred traditional forms of education because they employed what he called a banking approach to education. Banking education is best characterized by a strict dichotomy between teacher and students. The teacher is the sole possessor of knowledge, and it is his or her task to "deposit" this information into the student's minds, which are perceived as empty, passive receptacles. According to Freire, the interest of banking education is to adapt students to the world. Its purpose is to make students "fit" into existing social structures. For Freire, banking education is ultimately domesticating and oppressive. It is utilized by those who serve to maintain social structures.

Freire proposes a method of problem-posing education in contrast to banking education. Problem-posing education dissolves the teacher/student dichotomy. The educational process is seen as a partnership of mutual cooperation between teacher and students. Problem-posing education is based on Freire's anthropological vision: Human beings are knowing subjects committed to naming and transforming the world through dialogue with one another.

According to Freire, "dialogue is the encounter between men, mediated by the world, in order to name the world."[11] As Freire sees it, dialogue is the antithesis of the banking method of education. Banking education employs hierarchical, vertical, antidialogical means to "educate." There is no cointentionality or mutuality in this approach. It negates the dignity of the human person as a knowing subject. In contrast, problem-posing education utilizes dialogue as the primary methodological tool.

Freire's understanding of dialogue is based on Buber's I-Thou relationship. Dialogue is rooted in a horizontal relationship between two subjects. It is a process based on mutual equality with the intention of discovering the truth cooperatively.

In Freire's pedagogical process, there are several essential criteria or prerequisites for dialogical education: love, humility, faith, trust, hope, and critical reflection. Although all are essential, love seems to be pre-eminent. Unless there is a profound love for people and the world, dialogue will be impossible. It is the foundation for dialogue, and it entails commitment to the cause of liberation. Freire says, "If I do not love the world—if I do not love life—if I do not love men—I can not enter into dialogue."[12]

Dialogue, then, is Freire's central methodological principle for his liberating pedagogy. A genuine act of knowing, that is, an authentic praxis and, therefore, conscientization, can not occur unless there is a dialogical pedagogy. Educator and educatees must encounter one another as equals in a genuine relationship of dialogue. This brings me to the last major pedagogical principle of Freire's educational thought: his utopian vision.

Utopian Education

Freire claims that his liberating pedagogy is utopian in nature. By this he means the educational process must be imbued with and empowered by a vision of a humanizing future. Without such a utopian vision there would be no recourse, no alternative but to submit to hopelessness and despair. Freire's utopian vision is not a naive millennialism. As Denis Goulet points out, Freire's utopianism emerged "out of his practical involvement with oppressed groups in a process of struggle."[13] Freire's utopian pedagogy means to engage in prophetic denunciation and annunciation. Authentic education requires historical commitment in which a dehumanizing reality is denounced and its transformation announced in the name of human liberation. Freire's utopian vision is also infused with hope and risk. However, hoping does not mean a passive waiting. Rather, it means actively working toward the announced future. Utopian education occurs when educators and educatees, engaged in actual praxis, risk the denunciation of a dehumanizing present and the annunciation of a humanized future.

Part III: Critique

At first glance, one can detect several significant parallels and similarities between John Dewey and Paulo Freire's educational thought. Although the interest of this essay is not a comparative analysis of Dewey and Freire, it is pertinent to this discussion to briefly delineate the similarities. First, both educators see human knowing as an experiential process grounded in the interaction between people and their environment. A reflective/active epistemology is the foundation for both Dewey's and Freire's pedagogy. Second, both claim that education must begin with the present needs, interests, and experiences of the learner. That is the only legitimate point of departure for education. Third, Dewey and Freire claim that education must be genuinely democratic in structure. This, they believe, must be based on a profound faith in the capacity of human beings to be creators and remakers of culture. Last, both believe in the power of education to effect positive social transformation.

There is little doubt that several key aspects from Dewey's and

Freire's pedagogical thought can inform and enrich our educational work, especially our task of Christian education for social justice. Both present several challenging and provocative insights that we as Christian educators can not ignore. I will focus on three insights from each that we must affirm and upon which we can build.

The first pedagogical principle that we must seriously consider is Dewey and Freire's epistemological position. Dewey proposed an experimental epistemology as the basis for education. For the purpose of justice education, we must affirm, along with Dewey, that true knowledge only emerges in reflection/action upon the world in order to transform it. Likewise, Freire promotes a reflective/active epistemology. However, Freire takes Dewey's position a step further by combining a reflective/active epistemology, that is, praxis, with a critical principle. For our purpose of social justice education, a process of critical reflection is necessary to unmask socially mediated assumptions and idealogies that promote and legitimate oppressive and unjust social structures. Therefore, we must affirm and investigate ways of utilizing and expanding Freire's notion of conscientization.

A second principle for our affirmation is Dewey and Freire's prescription that education begin with and build upon the learner's present experience, needs, and interests. Philosophically and theologically this assertion tends to affirm the dignity of the learner, and it also promotes the belief that people are knowing subjects capable of recreating society. Pragmatically, the learner's present experience and interests are the best point of entry for doing social justice education. It is at this point that people will be most open and responsive to issues of social justice. Furthermore, Freire combines learner-centered education with dialogue. If our desire is to educate justly, then we must seriously attempt to do our educating as a dialogical process.

The third area of pedagogical insight that we must affirm is Dewey's understanding of education's social dimension and Freire's notion of utopian education. Dewey placed great significance on education as a social process, especially in two ways. First, we must consider his democratic principle as the basis for intentionally structuring the educational process. Second, we can be empowered by Dewey's belief that education can lead to social reconstruction. After all, that is our main goal in educating for justice: to motivate people to act in behalf of justice.

We can be powerfully informed by Freire's utopian vision and its prophetic dimension. Freire's utopianism complements the Christian hope of the Kingdom of God. The medium for promoting justice as "good news" lies in our hope for a humanizing future. The power to motivate requires a positive apprehension of the future. This aspect is clearly evident in Freire's pedagogy, as it must be in our own. Furthermore, justice education must be a dual process of challenge (denunciation) and consolation (annunciation).

My analysis of Dewey and Freire would be incomplete if I stopped here. There are also several elements of their educational thought that must be critically evaluated and perhaps denied. Again I will focus on three aspects from each author's position, in this case, aspects that we must question and move beyond. In Dewey's case the first criticism, and perhaps the most important, is the fact that his epistemology lacks a critical principle. Dewey himself was critical of the educational, social situation of his day. However, his epistemology does not provide a way of standing outside the educational process by critiquing underlying assumptions, interests, or ideologies. For our purpose we must recognize this as a serious defect in his pedagogical thought.

A second criticism of Dewey is the fact that he is overcentered on child and school. I am not certain to what extent justice education can be done with children and I am even less certain that authentic justice education can occur through institutionalized schooling. These are questions that must receive greater attention. A final criticism of Dewey is that his use of democracy is ambiguous and perhaps naive. In *Democracy and Education* he claims that the social paradigm we use to structure education must be rooted in actual societies. Yet he also claims that school must be an ideal version of society. He misunderstands the powerful negative influence that society exerts upon the school. It is correct to assume that his conception of democracy is rooted in U.S. democracy. But, he is unwilling or unable to recognize the deep and serious political/economic interests that underlie North American democracy and education.

Freire must also be critiqued. We must remember that his social milieu is quite different from our own. It would be dangerous to uncritically appropriate or translate his pedagogy to our cultural situation. The first problem is with Freire's assumption that critical reflection will lead to liberating action. He is silent on the emancipatory dynamics of the critical process. I am convinced that his assertion is based not on theory but on his own praxis with oppressed peoples. In Freire's experience, conscienticized victims of oppression were motivated to political action in behalf of their own liberation. But our culture is much different. The psychic boundaries between oppressed and oppressor are much less distinct. The truth is that we are working with people who are predominantly motivated by Freire's conception of the oppressor consciousness. How will critical reflection motivate people to liberating action when they have so much to lose? I am hopeful that critical reflection can lead to action in behalf of justice but I am less optimistic than Freire is.

A second criticism of Freire is his overemphasis on the present situation and his lack of attention to the past story in the pedagogical process. Again, this is largely conditioned by the cultural situation of his praxis. Both present and past are perceived by him as oppressive realities. However, he too readily dismisses the past for its controlling influences, and in the process he overlooks the possible liberating characteristics. We too must begin with present action, but I am unwilling to ignore the liberating potential of our past story as Christians.

Finally, Freire must be critiqued for his overoptimism about the revolutionary capacity of education. I believe education for justice can make a significant impact on the way people live and act. However, we must reject the underlying Pelagian illusion of Freire's pedagogy. We, in a very real way, cooperate in building God's Kingdom when we promote and work for liberation from injustice. When all is said and done, though, we have neither the tools, the character, nor the wisdom to initiate the final inbreaking of God's Kingdom.

Part IV: Tentative Pedagogical Foundations for Christian Education for Social Justice

Both John Dewey and Paulo Freire provide us with rich possibilities that can inform and empower us in our educating task for social justice. There are five pedagogical principles, grounded in the thought of both educators, that should be incorporated and enlarged upon where necessary in our Christian education for social justice. I see these five principles on a skeletal framework, that is, a foundation upon which actual, specific programs can be built.

The first principle is concerned with the context or setting of the educational experience. Both Dewey and Freire imply that the context for authentic education must be a democratically structured community. Programmatically, this means that we will have to relinquish educational models that are hierarchical and vertical in nature. This type of structure does not promote equality, mutual respect, participation, or cooperation. In other words, hierarchical structures can not provide a sense of community or promote justice.

The second foundation is concerned with methodological procedure, and it is based on and flows from the principle of community. This is the principle of dialogue for which we are primarily indebted to Freire. Christian education for justice must utilize a dialogical method and process. There are several consequences for this claim. First, program leaders will have to learn how to be good dialoguers. Second, it will require the dissolution of the traditional teacher/student dichotomy. Finally, the physical environment must be comfortable, nonthreatening, and capable of promoting dialogue.

The third pedagogical principle concerns our underlying epistemology. If our intention is to provoke critical awareness of injustice and to motivate to action in behalf of justice, then we must utilize a critical praxis epistemology. Freire's principle of conscientization can be the epistemological foundation for any sound program for social justice. There are two significant ramifications for this claim. First, there will have to be some point in the program when participants are encouraged to critically evaluate their present action or inaction in relation to justice. Second, a praxis approach will require mandatory action for justice as an actual part of the program. It must be sufficiently "praxeological." This will demand that the educator be prepared to offer concrete proposals for action. Specific action must be a final outcome of the program.

The fourth principle is the point of departure for the pedagogical process. Both Dewey and Freire claim that education must begin with the learner's present needs, interests, and experiences. Programs for justice must also begin with present action. It is the only legitimate point of entry in the pedagogical process. To begin elsewhere is to negate the significance of the concrete, existential reality in which people find themselves. Any hope of sponsoring people to critical consciousness and social action is directly related to their capacity to reflect on experiences and situations that deeply touch their lives.

The final pedagogical principle is concerned with our future vision, the Kingdom of God. Like Freire's pedagogy, education for justice must be utopian in nature. That is, we must be empowered by our vision of the Kingdom of God. If doing justice is going to be perceived as "good news," then it must be proclaimed in relation to the "good news" of God's Reign. Hope can be great motivation. As Christians it is the hope of God's Kingdom that infuses our lives with meaning and purpose. It is that hope that is truly realizable when we hunger for, work for, and educate for justice.

NOTES

1. John Dewey, *Democracy and Education*, in *John Dewey, The Middle Works*, vol. 9: 1916, edited by Jo Ann Boydston (Southern Illinois Press, 1980), p. 347.

2. Ibid., p. 347.
3. Elmer L. Towns, ed., *A History of Religious Educators* (Grand Rapids: Baker Book House, 1975), p. 324.
4. John Dewey, *Democracy and Education,* (New York: Free Press, 1957), p. 82.
5. Ibid., p. 199.
6. John Dewey, *My Pedagogic Creed,* in *Three Thousand Years of Educational Wisdom,* edited by Robert Ulich (Cambridge: Harvard University Press, 1947), p. 638.
7. Paulo Freire, *Education for Critical Consciousness* (New York: Seabury Press, 1973), p. 36.
8. Ibid., p. 36.
9. Paulo Freire, "Cultural Action for Freedom," in *The Harvard Educational Review,* Cambridge, 1970, p. 27.
10. Ibid., p. 76.
11. Paulo Freire, *Pedagogy of the Oppressed* (New York: Seabury Press, 1970), p. 76.
12. Ibid., p. 78.
13. Paulo Freire, *Education for Critical Consciousness,* p. xiii.

QUESTIONS FOR REFLECTION AND DISCUSSION

1. What is the meaning of Freire's notion of conscientization?

2. Why is a reflective/active or critical praxis epistemology essential for social justice education?

3. Why is it necessary for justice to be promoted as "good news," and how is our hope and vision of the Kingdom of God central to this assertion?

4. What differences and similarities are readily noticeable between Dewey's and Freire's pedagogical perspectives?

5. What are the practical implications of the basic ideas of Freire and Dewey for those involved in education for justice?

11. Moral Education, Peace, and Social Justice

MARGARET GORMAN

CONSIDERABLE INTEREST in moral education has been generated in the past decade among educators, parents, and ministers of all persuasions. This has been due not only to the growing concern about the decline in traditional moral values but also to the work of developmental psychologists. By proposing developmental schemas of cognitive, moral, and even faith development, they have shifted the focus of moral education from an imparting of content (moral commandments, moral theories, etc.) to the developing of the capacity to make moral judgments and moral decisions. Moreover, since the theories are not linked with institutional religions, but make the claim that the development is a natural psychological process, public school systems have made use of their theories and proposed and introduced educational practices without fearing that they have violated the separation of church and state.

The moral development has been formulated largely by Lawrence Kohlberg. Former students of his (Scharf, in the context of prisons, and Paolitto, in education) have gone on to develop specific educational practices for teachers derived from his theory.

Therefore, when we speak of education and social justice, it is inevitable that we look at what the insights of Kohlberg can contribute. But we must keep in mind the limitations of this model:

1. Kohlberg's theory has three components: philosophical, psychological, and educational. It is possible to take advantage of the psychological and educational insights while at the same time recognizing the limitations of his philosophical approach. We will discuss this further.
2. Kohlberg's theory is limited to the development of moral *judg-*

ment. Moral judgment is but one necessary component in the development of *conscience*, which, I would assume, is the real goal of moral education. Other components are:

a. the need level of the child.

b. a hierarchy of values that enables one to *want* what one judges is morally right. Unless one values human life more than money, one can reason about social issues but may never decide upon acting to improve the quality of life of others. (Here role models with social justice values are very necessary. For the Christian, the gospel values as lived by Jesus and his followers should be presented.)

c. self-esteem or a healthy sense of self-worth. Its importance in moral education lies in the fact that maturity of moral judgment, and even a Christian hierarchy of values, will avail little unless one feels that the action judged and valued is consistent with one's sense of self as one is now and as one could be. We will discuss this later more fully.

These limitations have already been recognized by some of Kohlberg's critics. Simpson[1] has criticized Kohlberg for omitting a consideration of the need level in his theory, whereas Meacham[2] has pointed out the significance of self-esteem in making mature moral decisions.

Thus, when we consider the relation of moral education research to social justice education, we must clarify and distinguish terms. If the goal of moral education is the development of conscience, and moral judgment is but one component in conscience, then moral education should also consider the other components. The definition of conscience is taken from the *Sacramentum Mundi:*

> Conscience is distinguished from moral knowledge (consciousness of value), on which it constantly draws and for which it provides the most vital content, by its immediate reference to one's own concrete action. . . . A careful analysis shows that in conscience man has a direct experience in the depths of his personality of the moral quality of a concrete personal decision or act as a call of duty on him, through his awareness of its significance for the ultimate fulfillment of his personal being.[3]

It is clear that conscience, in this understanding, implies judgment and a knowledge of who one is and can be. Hoffman also indicates a developmental process that he describes as moving along the lines described by Kohlberg:

> Beginning with the adoption of external patterns and norms of conduct and the acceptance of moral attitudes and values from others (authoritarian,

legal conscience), it progresses to the point where an independent position is adopted as a response to one's appreciation of the claim of moral values (personal conscience).[4]

Hoffman also speaks to the training of conscience:

> The training of conscience, the aim of which is the fully developed conscience functioning in terms of autonomy (independence), intensity (depth, immediacy, vitality of experience) and extent of moral knowledge at one's command, is only partly the result of moral instruction and incomparably more the result of the encouragement of genuine activity of conscience implemented throughout the entire field of conscience.[5]

The three broad levels of Kohlberg's model of moral development are very similar to the phases described by Hoffman—an egocentric level, followed by a group authority conforming phase, leading finally to principles recognized as universal and not arbitrarily imposed.

This paper, then, will consider the insights of Kohlberg and his critics, including the criticisms of Carol Gilligan, and will consider briefly the need and self-esteem components of conscience development. Following the exposition of the theory and research, some educational techniques will be discussed, since they are derived from Kohlberg's theory. Finally, there will be an attempt to indicate the applicability of the theory and research to social justice education, drawn especially from my own attempt to do just this in a college course. It is necessary to emphasize that I believe that one can derive much that is educationally sound in Kohlberg without having to agree with his philosophical views of morality.

The Kohlberg Theory of Moral Development

Kohlberg's theory is a cognitive structural developmental model based on Piaget's theory of cognitive development. Piaget's theory of cognitive development states that in development

1. there is an invariant sequence of stages that cannot be altered or skipped;
2. that this sequence is moving from simple structures to more complex and integrated structures; and
3. that disequilibrium occurs whenever an existing cognitive structure is confronted with an event that it cannot assimilate—the structure then breaks up, and a new structure emerges that is more complex, integrating all past structures.

The function of the educator, then, is to present those events or challenges just one step above the present cognitive or moral structure of the students, in order to create disequilibrium. Then the teacher should guide and help the students as they strive to develop the next cognitive structure. In other words, the aim of education is *development* not *imparting of content*.

These are the central ideas behind the educational theory of Kohlberg regarding the *process* of development. He posits that the goal or content of the higher stages is justice, based on social contract theory and respect for the rights of each human being. We are far more concerned with his description of the process of moral development and feel that an understanding of the process will be very helpful to those who wish to educate to social justice, even though they may disagree with Kohlberg's analysis of the content of the notion of justice. From his doctoral research, presenting ten moral dilemmas to young men of various ages, Kohlberg posited three levels of moral judgment, within each of which there are two stages. They are listed below.

PRECONVENTIONAL LEVEL

At this level, the child is responsive to cultural rules and labels of good and bad, right or wrong, but interprets these labels in terms of either the physical or the hedonistic consequences of action (punishment, reward, exchange of favors) or in terms of the physical power of those who enunciate the rules and labels. The level is divided into the following two stages:

Stage 1. The Punishment and Obedience Orientation

The physical consequences of action determine its goodness or badness regardless of the human meaning or value of these consequences. Avoidance of punishment and unquestioning deference to power are valued in their own right.

Stage 2. The Instrumental Relativist Orientation

Right action consists of that which instrumentally satisfies one's needs and occasionally the needs of others. Human relations are viewed in terms like those of the marketplace. Elements of fairness, reciprocity, and equal sharing are present, but they are always interpreted in a physical, pragmatic way. Reciprocity is a matter of "You scratch my back and I'll scratch yours."

CONVENTIONAL LEVEL

At this level, maintaining the expectations of the individual's family, group, or nation is perceived as valuable in its own right, regardless of immediate and obvious consequences. The attitude is not only one of conformity to personal expectations and social order, but of loyalty to it, of actively maintaining, supporting, and justifying the order and of identifying with the people or group involved in it. At this level, there are the following two stages:

Stage 3. The Interpersonal Concordance or "Good Boy—Nice Girl" Orientation

Good behavior is that which pleases or helps others and is approved by them. There is much conformity to stereotypical images of what is majority or "natural" behavior. Behavior is frequently judged by intention—the judgment "he means well" becomes important for the first time. One earns approval by being "nice."

Stage 4. Society Maintaining Orientation

There is an orientation toward authority, fixed rules, and the maintenance of the social order. Right behavior consists of doing one's duty, showing respect for authority, and maintaining the given social order for its own sake.

Postconventional, Autonomous, or Principled Level

At this level, there is a clear effort to define moral values and principles that have validity and application apart from the authority of the groups or people holding these principles and apart from the individual's own identification with these groups. This level again has two stages:

Stage 5. The Social Contract Orientation

Right action tends to be defined in terms of general individual rights and in terms of standards that have been critically examined and agreed on by the whole society. There is a clear awareness of the relativism of personal values and opinions and a corresponding emphasis on procedural rules for reaching consensus. Aside from what is constitutionally and democratically agreed on, the right is a matter of personal "values" and "opinion." The result is an emphasis on the "legal point of view," but with an emphasis on the possibility of changing law in terms of rational considerations of social utility (rather than freezing it in terms of Stage 4 "law and order"). Outside the legal realm, free agreement and contract are the binding elements of obligation. This is the "official" morality of the American government and Constitution.

Stage 6. The Universal Ethical Principle Orientation

Right is defined by the decision of conscience in accord with self-chosen ethical principles appealing to logical comprehensiveness, universality, and consistency. These principles are abstract and ethical (the Golden Rule, the categorical imperative); they are not concrete moral rules such as the Ten Commandments. At heart, these are universal principles of justice, of the reciprocity and equality of human rights, and of respect for the dignity of human beings as individuals.[6]

It is evident from the above descriptions that Kohlberg's schema does in fact resemble the broader description of Hoffman (see above). In fact, most of Kohlberg's critics will agree that the first four stages really do not describe morality itself but rather the reason why people act "morally"—out of fear of punishment; for personal gain, group pressure, and role demands; or because authority decreed it. It is on the third, the postconventional level, that his critics are most vocal, for here Kohlberg moves from describing what *is* (why people act) to stating what *ought to be* moral.

For the educator of elementary and secondary school children and even for those who teach college students, insights into these first four stages are most helpful, especially since research has shown that one can only understand the thinking one stage above where one is. It would be inappropriate and educationally unwise for a first grade teacher to expose pupils to stage four thinking. They will not understand it.

Several techniques have been developed to help the child become aware of ideas on a stage higher than his or her own. Research has been done in public schools and religious schools where moral discussions were held. The children definitely moved to a higher stage of moral thinking than those children who were not engaged in discussion. Some of the techniques suggested are:

1. introduction of moral dilemmas from literature, history, and social sciences;
2. role-playing;
3. getting the students to tell about acts or situations of injustice in their own experience or in the newspapers and to reflect on them in light of justice issues;
4. service programs.

I will discuss these techniques further and relate some of them directly to social justice education. One of the key components in the movement from one stage of moral judgment to the next, particularly in the movement from stage two to stage three, is the growth in the capacity to take the perspective of another person, or the role-taking perspective. Those on stages one and two see moral actions only in terms of the effect on themselves and on no one else. In order to make judgments at stage three, a student has to see the effect of actions on others and be aware of the feelings of others as well as their rights. As a child develops this capacity she or he will be able to sense the effect of actions, not only on individuals, but on different classes of people, until the perspective encompasses the whole human race. It is fairly evident that this perspective-taking is also an important component of social justice education. One needs to gain experience with people with different viewpoints from one's own in order to mature in this ability.

In fact, in my own research on the moral development of seventeen-year-olds,[7] those children in a segregated wealthy suburb were on significantly lower moral stages than children in a less homogeneous area on the same socio-economic level. Ironically, the efforts of the parents in the suburb to keep their children away from inner-city experiences or any other experiences of diversity only kept their children on lower stages, because no disequilibrium occurred. Cognitive dissonance or the challenge to one's existing cognitive structures regarding right and wrong are essential to growth in moral maturity.

The teacher can help the child grow in this capacity to take the perspective of others through the use of moral dilemmas together with skillful questioning aimed at getting the child to become aware of the feelings and viewpoints of others. In *Promoting Moral Growth* the authors recommend "in-depth questioning strategies."

> Questions should probe many sides of the same issue. A "should" or "why?" question is not sufficient to stimulate stage change. Students need to hear extended arguments from one another so they can understand the reasoning and challenge each other's logic. Five kinds of in-depth probing questions have been identified by moral educators interested in effective questioning strategies: clarifying probe, issue-specific probe, inter-issue probe; role-switch probe, and universal-consequences probe.
>
> A *clarifying probe* asks students to explain the terms they use, especially when the meaning of a statement is ambiguous or does not convey the reasoning behind the content. A clarifying probe is important if teachers are not to impart their meaning to students' words because of the differing stages of development between teacher and student.

STUDENT: *No, he shouldn't tell on his friend who cheated on the test. He might get in trouble.*

TEACHER: *What kind of trouble?*

STUDENT: *Well, his friend won't like him anymore. He might get back at him in some way.* (Elements of stage 2)

> An *issue-specific probe* is a question or statement that asks students to explore one moral issue related to the problem in question. "Issues" are different areas of focus in our moral judgment. We have seen how Kohlberg uses these issues in scoring a Moral Judgment Interview. A few such issues are authority, roles of affiliation and affection, contract obligations, and the value of life. By focusing on a particular issue in depth, students have the opportunity to explore fully the reasoning behind their beliefs. They apply their thinking beyond the immediate moral problem that confronts them.

> *Do you have any obligation to a stranger? What is the difference between one's responsibility to family or friends, and to a stranger?*
>
> *Why do people have a responsibility to obey legal authority?*

> An *inter-issue probe* is one that seeks to stimulate the resolution of conflict

between two moral issues. Often the priority of one issue over the other reflects a difference between two contiguous stages of moral reasoning (e.g., the value of friendship at stage 3 is more important than protecting one's own interest at stage 2). This kind of probe thereby causes cognitive conflict, because students have to test the adequacy of their reasons in choosing one issue over the other.

What is more important, loyalty to a friend, or obeying the law?

If it becomes necessary to steal in order to save someone's life, could you justify that decision? How?[8]

Role-playing is another technique whereby the student can be helped to understand the feelings and thinking of those less fortunate than she or he. It can also enable them to understand the thinking of those in authority when they play the role of parent or teacher or school administrator.

Research has shown that the discussion of moral dilemmas drawn out of the personal experience of the students themselves is more effective than discussions of made-up dilemmas or dilemmas proposed by the teacher. This would then point up the value of service experiences in which the students would encounter directly people who have been or are being treated unjustly—either by other people or by social systems.

Research has also shown that experiences of serving others (the elderly, the mentally retarded, the sick) are of little value in moving students to a higher level of moral judgment unless the experiences are reflected upon, in order that the students see the issues involved and integrate these insights into their perspective.

I have been teaching a course in social justice on the college level for the past four years. The course requires (in addition to the reading of Aristotle and Plato on justice and McGinnis and Hollenbach on social justice, among others) ten hours of service in a supervised setting (with the elderly, with prisoners, with retarded children, etc.). Reflection on the experience is an essential element in the course and is carried out by weekly discussion groups and weekly journals. The journal format is carefully structured to develop both the awareness of injustice and role-taking or perspective-taking. The students are asked to report on an event in their service setting or in their own dormitory or personal life according to the following format:

1. Describe the event briefly.
2. List the persons involved.
3. List the rights and feelings of each person in the situation.
4. What conflict of rights is involved? Is it violation of rights by other individuals or by the social or political system?

5. What might Plato or Aristotle or any other theorist we are studying say?
6. What options are possible? What are the consequences of each of the options?
6. What is your choice and why?

In this very structured way, I am endeavoring to develop the moral judgment of the students and stimulate them to think of constructive alternatives as well as give some hope to them that the system can sometimes be changed. Some students are working with consumer advocacy groups or legal services and share these experiences with the other students. This enables them to see social justice in action as "a standard which seeks to guarantee human dignity by specifying forms of governmental intervention which are appropriate for the protection of minimum standards of well-being, access and participation for all individuals."[9] The course aims, then, at developing moral judgment and perspective-taking through the interaction of service, reading, and reflection.

Service experiences, then, can be a means of helping the student be aware of injustice. Several students who had been very sheltered experienced real cognitive dissonance as they worked with alcoholics and saw people in conditions very different from their own. Through discussion, reflection, class lectures, and experience, the students are helped to make increasingly mature judgments on the justice and injustice of systems.

Service experiences can also help in the other two components of conscience—need level and self-esteem. According to Maslow, when a lower need is satisfied relatively, the next higher need becomes stronger. When the physiological needs are relatively satisfied, the security needs emerge. When these are relatively satisfied, the belonging need emerges. The need for belonging is strongest in high school students and in many college students. As Simpson[10] points out, a student could be on stage four in moral judgment but, because his or her need for belonging is so strong, the student will go against what his or her own moral judgment says and follow the crowd in order to satisfy the need for belonging. When the students are engaged in some form of service, they usually are working in groups and become aware of their membership in the larger human family. Teenagers usually set up their own peer groups and are very sure about who is in, and who is not in, the group. Service to people beyond their own particular group can break up their elitism and help them have experience of people with values other than their own. All of this widening of their perspective would help them want to join groups with a purpose beyond the mere enjoyment of the members. It would lead them to expand their group membership and transcend their local groups and to work toward autonomy, the goal of conscience development.

Self-esteem, as Meacham points out, is necessary for a mature stage of morality.

> Mature moral behavior thus depends upon a synthesis of principles abstracted from the course of social interactions with a self-concept which reflects the construction of evaluative relationships with other persons . . . moral behavior is dependent upon two dialectical processes, one involving subject and object, the individual and that which is judged, and the other involving a synthesis of moral principles and self-concept. Thus for the morally mature person, there is no longer a contradiction between, but rather a unity of, moral concerns and the concerns of the self. For the individual who has not achieved this synthesis, an inconsistent morality may be displayed as the person conforms to various pressures which reinforce his self-esteem. Further, attempts to boost self-esteem may include the definition of moral principles in terms of self, rather than the self-concept being a reflection of moral principles.[11]

Self-esteem is derived from significant others and from some kind of achievement. Although the significant others are primarily parents, teachers, and respected elders, students who have been engaged in service programs consistently report how much the experience has helped their self-esteem. Moreover, a certain sense of achievement naturally ensues that can be recognized especially when these students are contrasted with classmates who are not doing some form of service. By serving others, the students strengthen their own sense of themselves, open their horizons to groups larger than those of their own age and background, and begin to be concerned about justice to groups other than their own.

This in no way implies that service programs are ways of using the less fortunate in order to aid the moral development of the more fortunate. I merely wish to point out that, in addition to helping the less fortunate, the student also inevitably develops morally if he or she is helped to reflect seriously on the experience. Service programs are valuable in that they help others; they can also be very valuable educationally.

Carol Gilligan and the Two Types of Adult Morality

One last contribution of moral development research and theory is that of Carol Gilligan, who has criticized Kohlberg for his narrow view of the higher stages (five and six), as well as for his view of women's moral stages. She has indicated that Kohlberg states that stage five and stage six are a morality of rights and noninterference: "I respect your rights and I will not violate them." This seems to be a morality more characteristic of most men. Women seem to have their higher stages of morality based on a sense of care and responsibility quite aware of the contextual ambiguities of all moral judgments. Gilligan does indicate that these are two types of adult morality, that of rights and that of care and responsibility. Her description of the morality of care and responsibility would seem to be what those concerned with social justice education might like to develop in students.

After giving the answers indicating one woman's conception of morality, she comments:

> These responses also represent a reflective reconstruction of morality following a period of relativistic questioning and doubt, but the reconstruction of moral understanding is based not on the primacy and universality of individual rights, but rather on what she herself describes as a "very strong sense of being responsible to the world." Within this construction, the moral dilemma changes from how to exercise one's rights without interfering with the rights of others to how "to lead a moral life which includes obligations to myself and my family and people in general" . . . The problem then becomes one of limiting responsibilities without abandoning moral concern. . . .
>
> Thus, while Kohlberg's subject worries about people interfering with one another's rights, this woman worries about "the possibility of omission, of your not helping others when you could help them."[12]

Whereas Gilligan is concerned with expanding the description of stage five and stage six to include not only a morality of respect for human rights but a morality of care and responsibility, Kohlberg himself has raised an important question about the role of the moral environment of the school in helping or preventing the moral growth of its students.

What would happen, for example, if in all the classrooms of a certain high school the teachers endeavored to raise the moral judgment level of the students from stage three to stage four? The questions and discussions in all classes would be geared to probing the role of the system of laws and legitimate authority in protecting human rights in order that the students could better understand the value of law. But what if, in this school, the disciplinary level is that of punishment and reward, stage one and stage two of moral development? As Kohlberg pointed out, quoting Dr. Philip Jackson, 90 percent of what is learned in the classroom is not specifically taught but is communicated through the moral environment. Kohlberg goes on to say:

We believe that what matters in the hidden curriculum is the moral character and ideology of the teachers and principal as these are translated into a working social atmosphere which influences the atmosphere of the children.[13]

The need to make the hidden curriculum an atmosphere of justice, and even care and responsibility, and to make this hidden curriculum explicit in the intellectual discussions of justice and morality is one of the most important components of social justice education. For, educators for social justice may find their teaching undone if the students perceive that the moral environment of their school contradicts its teachings.

Although Kohlberg has not been explicit about fitting the moral environment to the level of moral development of the students, I believe that to be consistent with the developmental theory and research that reports that students can only understand one stage above where they are cognitively and morally, the discipline of an elementary school would have a different emphasis than the discipline of a secondary school or a college.

Since those in an elementary school would largely be on stage one or stage two and moving toward stage three, the need for extrinsic punishments and rewards would be greater than for those in junior high school, where the greater emphasis can be put on group standards and group loyalty. Certainly, even these children can be exposed to the morality of law, human rights, and care, but the emphasis should be on those stages of loyalty, group membership, and so on, that they can more easily understand. In the high schools and colleges, opportunities for student government and for participation in the establishment of a just, caring community would be an excellent means of social education. I have actually seen a model for student government for the first four grades, carefully matched to the kind of thinking these students are capable of doing.

Moreover, research has shown that one person is seldom or never purely on one moral stage, but has within himself or herself the capacity to make moral judgments on any of the stages lower than his or her dominant stage, and even on one stage above the dominant stage. The same could be true of institutions. I therefore propose for the consideration of school administrators an approximate scale for the weight or emphasis to give to each stage in the moral atmosphere of their school. (See Fig. 11.1.)

Figure 11.1. A Proposal for the Relative Emphasis on Different Stages in the Moral Environment of Schools at Different Levels.

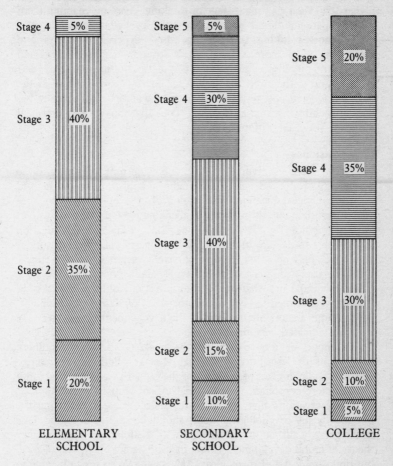

For example, an elementary school principal would give greater emphasis to stage two—extrinsic rewards—than would a high school principal. She or he might emphasize stage three—group membership and community—as well as stage four, emphasis on student government. On a college level, 50 percent of the approach should be toward principle and human rights and perhaps only 10 percent on punishment and reward. Even adults act on stage one to avoid getting a ticket for speeding, for example.

Thus, the moral atmosphere of the school could also foster growth, opening the students to experiences of moral judgments on stages higher than their dominant stage of thinking. Also, by enabling them to participate in student government at the level consistent with their level of moral thinking, they could get direct experience in helping to make institutions more socially just. Were the older high school and college students also to experience in the moral atmosphere of their school some of the adult morality described by Carol Gilligan as the morality of care and responsibility, there would be consistency between teaching and action in the school that could be a powerful means of social education.

Conclusion

Thus we have endeavored to indicate how current research into the psychology of moral development might be applicable to and helpful in social justice education. The notion of developing more mature cognitive judgments through the challenging of one's existing way of judging moral actions is a helpful one. Since social justice education would want to develop the capacity to judge moral issues maturely, Kohlberg's insights into the stages of development should help educators. The use of discussion, role-playing, and service helps.

But it is important that we do not ask of the Kohlberg model what it has never claimed to give: a total theory of *conscience* development. Several other factors are involved in the development of conscience as we have indicated very briefly here.

It is important, too, to note that the greatest criticism of Kohlberg has been of his description of the highest stages. Perhaps the description that Gilligan gives of her view of the higher stages of moral judgment is more consonant with the goals of social justice education.

The reservations that any educator should have in adopting too uncritically any psychological theory should be applied here, too. One of the greatest difficulties in wholeheartedly adopting a psychological theory of moral development is that morality is not only psychological but philosophical and theological. As yet, no one seems to be able to totally integrate these disciplines, so methodologically different and yet so concerned with the same phenomenon—the moral person. I would only hope that the reader can be selective in examining the psychological research into moral development and applying it in the work of social justice education.

NOTES

1. E. L. Simpson, "A Holistic Approach to Moral Development and Behavior," in *Moral Development and Behavior*, edited by Thomas Lechone (New York: Hall Renehart & Winslow, 1976), especially chapter 9.
2. J. D. Meacham, "A Dialectical Approach to Moral Judgment and Self-Esteem," *Human Development* 18 (1975).
3. R. Hoffman, "Conscience," in Karl Rahner, ed., *Encyclopedia of Theology, The Concise Sacramentum Mundi* (New York: Crossroads, 1975), p. 283.
4. Ibid., p. 283.
5. Ibid., p. 283.
6. L. Kohlberg, *The Philosophy of Moral Development* (San Francisco: Harper & Row, 1981), pp. 17–20.
7. M. Gorman. "Moral and Faith Development in Seventeen-Year-Old Students," *Religious Education* September/October 1977.
8. R. Hersh, D. Paoletto, and J. Reimer, *Promoting Moral Growth* (New York: Longman, 1979), pp. 149–65.
9. D. Hollenbach, S. J., *Claims in Conflict* (New York: Paulist Press, 1979), p. 154.
10. E. L. Simpson.
11. J. D. Meacham.
12. C. Gilligan, "Woman's Place in Man's Life Cycle," *Harvard Educational Review* 49 (1979), p. 443.
13. L. Kohlberg, "The Moral Atmosphere of the School," in N. Oberlg, ed., *The Unstudied Curriculum; Its Impact on Children*, monograph of the Association for Supervision and Curriculum Development (Washington, D.C.: 1970).

QUESTIONS FOR REFLECTION AND DISCUSSION

1. What are some concrete challenging experiences that can be offered to elementary school, secondary school, and college-aged persons that will help them grow in moral awareness and that are appropriate to their level of cognitive and moral development?

2. How does an elementary or secondary school or a college fit its administrative and disciplinary policies to the moral and cognitive levels of development of its clientele?

3. In what ways can participation in student government be a method of education for social justice?

4. How can we help students at various cognitive and moral levels reflect on their experiences and observations of injustice?

5. How can we convey to our students the confidence that their work for social justice can and will have an impact on social structures?

12. Parameters, Principles, and Dynamics of Peace Studies

JOSEPH J. FAHEY

> Disagreements must be settled, not by force, nor by deceit or
> trickery, but rather in the only manner which is worthy of the
> dignity of man, i.e., by a mutual assessment of the reasons on
> both sides of the dispute, by a mature and objective investiga-
> tion of the situation, and by an equitable reconciliation of differ-
> ences of opinion.
>
> Pope John XXIII, *Pacem in terris*

WHEN ANGELO RONCALLI, the son of Italian peasants, was elected
to the papacy in 1958 few expected John XXIII either to live long or
to produce any significant changes within the Catholic church. But
John's conviction was that the *mentalité Maginot* that characterized so
many in his church and in the world would, if not challenged, lead to
the destruction of both. He shocked his church by calling the Second
Vatican Council and he delighted many in the world with the publication of his encyclicals *Mater et magistra* (1961) and *Pacem in terris*
(1963). The latter encyclical, issued less than two months before his
death, stimulated great discussion and debate not only within the
Catholic church but also among leading world intellectuals and political leaders, which was practically unparalleled in the history of the
papacy. In 1965, in New York City, a group of world leaders (including Barbara Ward, U Thant, Paul Tillich, George F. Kennan, Earl
Warren, N. N. Inozemtsev [USSR], and Arnold Toynbee) gathered
to assess the significance of *Pacem in terris*. A small group of Manhattan College faculty attended this convocation, and as a result, the idea
for courses in peace studies was conceived.

The quotation that begins this essay particularly struck the faculty
members, and they immediately sought to establish courses that
would examine the causes of war, the roots of injustice, and the path
to peace. In 1966 an interdisciplinary course was established in the

history department entitled "The Anatomy of Peace." The course was taught by a historian, a biologist, an economist, and a theologian. It was team-taught out of necessity: no one faculty member knew enough to offer a complete course! But the situation quickly changed, and within two years there were seven independent courses in peace studies along with a continued interdisciplinary analysis. In 1970 a student said he would like to receive a degree in peace studies, and with the full support of the college's administration (which has always been exceptionally supportive), a B.A. in peace studies was first offered in 1971.

But there were (and still are) many questions to be answered about this strange new discipline. Is it in fact a discipline at all, or is it a "hodge-podge collection of mickey mouse courses" (in the words of one critic)? What are the parameters of the subject? How can you research something that has no subject heading in the library? Is not this subject politically motivated and subjectively biased? What are people going to do with this worthless degree? We haven't adequately answered all those (and more) questions, but I am now convinced that it really has been an adventure (for both faculty members and students) to seek their answers. Accordingly, I am grateful to Padraic O'Hare for the opportunity to share some of the adventure of peace studies with the readers of this volume and to address myself to some of the principles and dynamics of peace education.

The Parameters of Peace Studies

Above all, peace studies is a "problem-centered" discipline. It is based on the conviction that education must respond to the great social problems of our (or any) age through a multidisciplinary analysis that can go much further in contributing solutions to our problems than if the problems were studied by one traditional discipline alone. Further, as with all new courses of study, peace studies is very much an experimental discipline, and its parameters and methodologies have been established through trial and error—and sometimes by accident.

After our fifteen or so years in this experiment our faculty and those in other programs, along with the Consortium on Peace Research, Education, and Development (yes, there is even a professional association!), have identified five key areas of investigation that at present constitute the problems and opportunities associated with peace education and research. It should be stressed here that the five concerns we shall presently discuss are the results of a phenomenological investigation of the current art of peace education: they are not normative and we must still be open to new problem areas in the future. But they are, nevertheless, considerably broader in their scope than we first began and have often been accepted only after sometimes vigorous debate on the part of our faculty and students.

A brief discussion of these five areas:

1. *War, the arms race, and disarmament.* In addition to the influence of *Pacem in terris* on our program we must not forget the historical context of the origins of peace studies at Manhattan College. Just a few years before, our country had survived the Cuban missile crisis, in which reckless conduct had almost led to a nuclear war. In addition the war in Indochina was raging with its consequent turmoil and violence at home. Obviously, these events provided a strong impetus for the study of the causes of war, including arms races, which are almost invariably major causative factors of war. Research on these problems has been a hallmark of many peace studies programs and courses and continues to this day. But if arms races lead to war is there any evidence that disarmament is a causative factor in preventing war and securing peace? There is still very little research in this area, but at least what exists raises the question of whether there are not other forms of "defense" besides those that threaten to kill one's opponent. A preliminary judgment is that disarmament coupled with positive economic and social relationships is indeed a more practical program of security than is a continued arms race, which can enkindle war not just through intention but through accident, miscalculation, or terrorism as well. Finally, what about the study of peaceful societies, that is, societies and cultures that can be considered "healthy" in that they have a minimum of war and social violence? Peace studies thus has its "preventive" side, and we can learn much from those apparently strange people who somehow have managed to survive without war. The research must continue.

2. *Social and economic justice.* Both common sense and empirical evidence increasingly demonstrate that there can be no true peace without cultural values and social institutions that foster human rights and the myriad works of justice. One must first discover, of course, the causes of injustice, should they arise from a faulty estimate of human nature, from power and greed, from sexism, racism, or simply from institutions that are anachronistic (such as the nation-state). Obviously, this study is not only relevant to the First and Second worlds but to the Third and Fourth worlds as well. In fact, the study of justice is particularly relevant and urgent necessary concerning the socially and economically poor of the earth. And we must always link the vast expenditures on armies and weapons with the terrible injus-

tice suffered by so many on our globe. The Vatican, for example, has stated that the arms race is a *crime* even when the weapons are not used, for they directly "kill the poor by causing them to starve" (cf. *Statement of the Holy See to the United Nations*, 1976). Human dignity and the sacredness of human life, in short, must be the leitmotif of the quest for a positive peace.

3. *Dispute Settlement.* Although we must end war and strive for justice we cannot adequately do so unless we discover practical methods to settle the inevitable disputes that will continue even after we have (we hope) ended the institution of war. Conflict is natural to the human animal not only because there appears to be a biological basis for the necessity of conflict in order to survive but also because our free will (limited though it may be) provides us with the opportunity to use many different methods to settle disputes. Hence, the study of mediation, conciliation, arbitration, and legal sanctions (to name a few) are essential components of peace education. The creative resolution of conflict, which relies on sound reason, thorough investigation, and the use of parties neutral to the dispute, is not only theoretically possible but eminently practical, since it is practiced daily by literally billions of people. (One unscientific study I did revealed that, on the average, my students used five nonviolent methods each day to settle disputes and few ever engaged in violence. That's good news; more research is needed.)

4. *Philosophies and strategies of nonviolence.* Mohandas K. Gandhi was fond of saying that "I have nothing new to say to you. Nonviolence is as old as the hills." Anthropological evidence indicates that the human animal probably practiced nonviolence before violence and certainly before the advent of war as a social institution. The thorough study of the great (and not so well known) practitioners of nonviolence should occupy a very central place in a peace studies curriculum. For all of my years of teaching I am still amazed at how the students become truly stimulated when they study Dorothy Day, Martin Luther King, Jr., or Mohandas K. Gandhi. "Now I know there is another way!" so many of them tell me but then sadly lament: "Why didn't I hear this before? Why doesn't everyone—especially world leaders—take a course on nonviolence?"

Although dispute settlement and nonviolence have much in common, the distinction between them is not merely one of reason. Dispute settlement generally assumes that both sides *willingly* agree to a particular method of conflict resolution whereas nonviolence is a form of "direct action" to secure justice. Nonviolence becomes operative where one's opponent does not willingly act justly. It is, therefore, a form of force or coercion to establish justice and peace when voluntary methods fail. But the goal of nonviolence is to secure a victory for *both* sides in a given struggle. (Should nonviolence be used to further injustice or to "conquer" a foe, it then becomes merely another expression of violence.) Ideally, nonviolent direct action results in a physical victory for the oppressed (freeing their bodies from chains) and a spiritual victory for the oppressors (for when they cease the act of oppression they free their souls from bondage). It is no wonder that both Gandhi and King could assert that the "real victors" in their struggles for justice would be the English in the one case, and white people in the other.

5. *World Order.* The quest for a governed world is not, of course, novel in human history, but it is receiving far greater attention in this century since, for the first time, we have the capacity to annihilate that very history. Many are coming to realize that we simply cannot have authentic global peace while we continue to live in international anarchy because we are largely slaves to the nation-state form of human social institution. "Total" war as we know it—and total injustice as well—are by-products of nationalism. To establish a globally governed world in which human rights are guaranteed, economic justice is fostered, and war is outlawed is certainly no easy task given the vast divisions in economic, political, and social philosophies that at present exist. But we should take heart, for even today's nation-states are largely the product of earlier forms of evolution that have fairly consistently resulted from people binding together (often, tragically, through violence) in larger groups to serve the common weal.

The study of shared global values (and there are many), as well as concrete proposals for creating global institutions that can regulate everything from the environment to space, *is* a human possibility but one that many still lack the imagination or moral imperative to seek. It is my view that we shall evolve to larger forms of social interdependence out of necessity rather than through moral suasion; but whatever the impetus, the time to study this question is now. For, as with much in the field of peace studies, we are sowing the seeds the harvest of which we hope our children's children will reap.

Principles

It is rare that academics begin a new course of study without first reflecting on an appropriate educational philosophy and methodology to undergird and guide that study, but that is essentially what happened with the development of peace studies. We were so anxious to begin the experiment that we assumed that the question of principles that would guide our study would eventually be addressed and answered. Although this question is by no means fully resolved, it is possible, nevertheless, to state several principles that have emerged from our experience. This is what we have gleaned to date:

1. *Peace education, above all, must be solidly academic in nature.*
Both the administration and the faculty at Manhattan College knew from the very beginning that success or failure would be determined by the degree of academic excellence that characterized the peace studies program. The program still has its critics in this area, but when those same critics take the opportunity to examine exactly what we are doing they often become staunch supporters. We were, however, fortunate from the beginning in two key areas: first, since we were an institute we were free to pick and choose from among the best on our faculty; second, we have fairly consistently attracted some of the most intellectually stimulating students on campus.

The academic nature of peace studies cannot be stressed too much. Our students are told that they must study those "boring" textbooks, they must know the library like their own room, and they must be as precise and accurate as possible in their research. Since the "objective" nature of any research requires as many views as possible to be consulted before arriving at a conclusion, we require our students to be as familiar with military (and multinational, and so on) perspectives as they are with those that come from peace researchers. In short, there are no less rigorous academic requirements in peace studies than there are in any other discipline.

2. *Peace studies is multidisciplinary in method.* As we have stated above, peace studies is "problem" centered and therefore requires that the problem under examination be examined by as many traditional disciplines as possible. Take war, for example. To attempt to predict the possibility of war by merely consulting a country's history may result in an accurate prediction, but the chance of accuracy will be dramatically increased by examining a particular country's political system, its relationships with other states, its economic philosophy and condition, its educational system, the level of violence found internally in the country, the diversity of its religious and ethnic populations, its "value" system, and the relationship of its military spending to its GNP. In short, the disciplines of political science, economics, education, international relations, religion, philosophy, and sociology (and others, obviously) are *essential* components of any examination of this sort.

Methodologically, such an examination calls for a broad range of multidisciplinary courses as well as interdisciplinary seminars and supervised research. At Manhattan College the humanities, the social and physical sciences, business, and engineering all contribute to the peace studies program. There is almost no subject that cannot contribute to a peace studies curriculum!

3. *Peace studies is "reconstructionist" in nature.*   Although education certainly has a more than legitimate "socializing" function, it merely serves the status quo if it does not also challenge a student to reconstruct or reform his or her given society and world. All education should have a "futuristic" orientation and perspective and peace studies is uniquely suited to this task. To educate for the future one must be prepared for and welcome change, and to inspire students to accept risk and uncertainty as essential to human survival is the goal of all education and of peace studies in particular. A former professor of mine, who had suffered under the Nazis, once remarked that all education should be education for "courage." Much more thinking needs to be done in educational philosophy about this concept.

4. *Peace studies requires a moral commitment.*   While peace studies must be academically "objective," it cannot be morally neutral. The purpose of peace studies is to serve the cause of life at both physical and spiritual levels. The sacredness of the human person and the survival of the species demand that those who engage in peace studies commit themselves to a kind of humanism that can be found in our world's great religious traditions. There exist on our own faculty Christians, Jews, and humanists, who although they worship differently, share a concern about the survivability of our universe. At times outside observers comment on the "religious" nature of our faculty and students because of the depth of their moral commitment to life. Peace studies is *for* peace and life and *against* violence and injustice. Although this moral "bias" may sometimes affect the objectivity of research (but I wonder if it does not make one *more* academically objective), it is, nevertheless, a posture that is essential to the peace studies enterprise.

5. *Peace studies must have a "practical" orientation.*   Although there is a legitimate place in education for the philosophy that holds that knowledge is an end in itself, it is also imperative that knowledge should be directed toward some end that will benefit the human species. Consequently, students should be taught the art of dispute settlement and the science of economic and political justice. There are already careers in diplomacy, conciliation, mediation, arbitration, education, and economic development that attract many peace studies students. To prepare them academically and professionally for these

(and other) careers is a more than legitimate goal of any peace studies program.

Since the vast majority of our students are not peace studies majors (many take only one or another course in the area), students in other fields also benefit from a dispute settlement or justice perspective that is not only relevant to their chosen career but to their daily life as well. Education that enables people to be creative and practical problem-solvers contributes significantly to a more humane society. Although the peace studies program at Manhattan College is essentially an academic one, students are required to participate in "practical" internships as well.

The Dynamics of Peace Studies

We turn now to a discussion of the operational dynamics of a peace studies program. Although we will specifically refer to the Manhattan College experiment, it should be noted that other peace education programs have similar characteristics and modes of operation.

There are two major reasons for the existence of peace studies courses at Manhattan College: to offer a broad variety of courses on justice and peace concerns to *every* undergraduate at the college, and to offer specific training for the student who chooses a major in peace studies. The purpose of the Peace Studies Institute is to act as a catalyst and to stimulate departmental offerings in the areas of justice and peace. Thus, although there are specific courses, seminars, and internships that are proper only to the Institute (they are for the major or minor in the field), the bulk of the peace studies courses are offered by individual faculty members and departments in the college. Hence, it is relatively "easy" to institute such a program since hardly any new faculty members have to be hired and there are relatively few budgetary concerns to block the operation of an institute such as ours.

The peace studies program consists of four major components: individual courses, interdisciplinary seminars, independent research, and external field work internships. The student major in peace studies (thirty credits, or ten courses) must take two interdisciplinary seminars (six credits), pursue an internship (three to six credits), an independent research project (three credits), and six other courses offered by individual departments (eighteen credits). Students are encouraged (but not strictly required) to pursue another academic major in addition to peace studies. Dual majors that have proven to be popular with our students are government and politics, religious studies, history, philosophy, sociology, communications, and management.

Although the program is offered through the School of Arts and Sciences (and is supervised by the dean and the director of the Peace Studies Institute respectively), students from the schools of Engineering, Business, General Studies, and Teacher Preparation have pursued both the peace studies major and, especially, the minor (fifteen credits). We shall now discuss individually the four major components of the program. As we do so, it will be helpful to consult the flowchart on peace studies requirements (Fig. 12.1).

Interdisciplinary Seminars

The introductory seminar on "Problems of Peace and Social Justice" and "Senior Seminar in Peace Studies" are offered respectively at the beginning and the end of the major. (The introductory seminar is normally taken in the sophomore or junior year whereas the senior seminar is taken the second semester of the senior year.) The purpose of the introductory seminar is to acquaint the student with the nature, scope, and methodology of peace studies, and normally a research paper is required that focuses on a specific problem that is then examined through an interdisciplinary analysis. The seminar is principally conducted by one faculty member, and anywhere from four to six other faculty members participate through lectures on the significance of their field for peace research or on the general methodology of interdisciplinary studies.

Individual Courses

An individual course offering from any department that devotes a significant amount of its content to one or more of the five problem areas discussed earlier in the section titled, "Parameters of Peace Studies," is acceptable for credit toward the peace studies major (thus making the professor a member of the peace studies faculty). Peace studies courses have arisen in one of two ways: they have either been newly created with the purpose of the program in mind (e.g., The Anatomy of Peace, Religious Dimensions of Peace, or the Economics of Peace), or they are traditional course offerings that have been specifically adapted to the philosophy of the peace studies program (e.g., International Relations, Biology of Human Behavior, or The Sociology of Social Problems). Overall, about fifteen new courses have arisen as a result of the peace studies program's presence on campus. Aside from the peace studies major (which generally has a steady enrollment of only about ten students), we estimate that about 25 percent of the students in the college (we have about four thousand

Figure 12:1. Peace Studies Major, Manhattan College

GENERAL REQUIREMENTS FOR ALL STUDENTS
30 credits divided as follows:
1. Nine required credits:
   Three credits from Peace Studies 201 or 202: Problems of Peace and Social Justice

   Three credits from Peace Studies 401 or 402: Senior Seminar in Peace Studies

   Three credits from Peace Studies 451 or 452: Peace Studies Field Project

2. Twenty-one elective credits chosen from among the listed courses

ELECTIVES

Biology
   215: Biology of Human Behavior

Economics
   320: Economics of Peace
   331: World Economic Geography
   412: Economic Growth and Development

Fine Arts
   335: War, Peace and the Arts

Government
   441: International Relations
   442: International Organization
   445: Latin American Politics

Philosophy
   414: Philosophies of Nonviolence

History
   403: History of Diplomacy
   431: Anatomy of Peace
   473: The Art of War to 1713
   474: The Art of War Since 1713
   479: Cold War and After
   452: American Foreign Relations

Psychology
   340: The Psychology of Social Problems

Religious Studies
   353: Hindu Religious Traditions
   354: Buddhist Thought and Literature
   433: Religious Dimensions of Peace
   434: Non-Violent Revolution
   438: Business Ethics

World Literature
   307: Literature and the Great War

Sociology
   301: Sociology of Social Problems
   302: Sociology of Minorities

Managerial Sciences
   450: Behavioral Dynamics

Peace Studies
   301: Peace Studies Seminar: Pilgrimage to Humanity
   421–422: Independent Studies in Peace Studies
   303: The Thirty Years War in Fact and Fiction

undergraduates) are enrolled in a peace studies course in any one academic year—thus every student in the college is (we hope) exposed to at least one course before she or he graduates. In addition, there is evidence to suggest that other college course offerings devote more time to the issues of peace and justice than they did, let us say, ten years ago. (But it would be rash to conclude that the presence of the peace studies program is solely responsible for this—both world events and the general trend to examine social problems undoubtedly should receive major credit here.)

Though it is impossible in many colleges and universities (and even primary and secondary schools) to institute new courses on a peace and justice theme, it is *always* possible to add a justice and peace dimension to already existing courses. We are limited merely by our imagination and willingness to experiment or to be controversial. Education for the present is really (for our students) education for the past, whereas education for the future mandates that we sensitize our students to the demands of a globally interdependent society whose chief hallmarks must be the nonviolent resolution of conflict and the presence of economic and political justice.

Further, even if a given professor refuses to examine the challenge of the future, there is still much that the individual student enrolled in a given course can do to increase his or her awareness of justice and peace issues. Term papers, outside reading, and even questions in class can raise the consciousness of many while contributing to greater personal knowledge in this area. (I especially encourage graduate students—who generally have more academic autonomy than under-graduates—to turn even a traditional degree into a peace studies degree by carefully choosing the kind of research they will pursue.) It is important to recall what we have said above: Almost any course of study can be channeled toward peace and justice concerns. We do well here to recall the ancient Latin proverb: *"Aut inveniam viam, aut faciam"* ("Either I will find the way, or I will make it").

Independent Research

Although the peace studies major is not strictly required to pursue an independent research project she or he is strongly encouraged to do so. Normally, the project is done in the senior year and serves, in effect, as a senior thesis. The project is supervised by one or more faculty members, and although the topic is of the student's own choosing, it must be specific in nature and fall within one of the parameters of the peace studies program. Recent topics have included

"Nonviolence in the Thought of Mohandas K. Gandhi," "United States Diplomatic and Military Support for Multinational Corporations in Latin America," "Dorothy Day: Peacemaker," "Roman Catholic Perspectives on World Order," "The Role of the American Arbitration Association in Dispute Settlement," "Bottle-Fed Babies: The Nestle Controversy," "Feminist Perspectives on Human Rights," and "The Non-political Contributions of the United Nations." Although some of the above topics admittedly sound more like doctoral dissertations, they nevertheless do provide students with the kind of in-depth experience of research that may well have a profound effect on their future careers. One of our students even won a Gandhi Peace Prize in India for his research, and a few have published their work. These are no small accomplishments for undergraduate students!

Field Work Internships

Each student is required to spend at least a portion of a semester in a practical internship that, although educational in nature, gives the student firsthand experience with a major issue of justice and peace. Some students have traveled in the summer to such places as Northern Ireland, Peru, Jamaica, and various locations in the United States for their internship. Internships vary widely and have included work at the United Nations, with the American Arbitration Association, the American Friends Service Committee, Covenant House/Under 21, the Better Business Bureau, Fellowship of Reconciliation, the Mayor's Volunteer Task Force, and the Institute for World Order. In addition, students have tutored Hispanic children in the South Bronx and taught (or helped to teach) peace studies courses in area high schools and senior citizens' homes; one has even worked with the New York City Police Department (in family disputes).

The importance of the internship cannot be stressed too much. In almost every case it has helped students to understand the relevance of their academic preparation to "real life" issues, and has inspired them to take their courses very seriously upon their return to the college. In addition, many have actually pursued careers in the area of their chosen internship.

We might say a word here about the kinds of careers our graduates have pursued. Almost to a person they have pursued graduate studies or taken jobs in areas that are directly related to their training in peace studies. The fields of law, education, dispute settlement, communications, and social work have proven to be particularly attractive to our graduates. Some of our students are peace activists; some individuals work at the United Nations and the American Arbitration Association; still others are employed in business or by the United States government. One graduate is an assistant professor of psychology; another works with handicapped children. Despite the diversity of their careers, the most impressive thing about our graduates is the level of commitment to justice and peace concerns in their careers. A graduate who is a Legal Aid attorney was representative when he recently wrote to me:

> The challenge of implementing Christ's call for social justice and to become a peacemaker, Gandhi's teachings, [my internship in] Northern Ireland, and my Peace Studies courses have all laid the foundation of my commitment and dedication to work for social and economic justice in which peace will flourish.

It has been a singular privilege to serve our dedicated graduates during their undergraduate years; though their number is small, their impact is large, and if we are ever to achieve peace I am confident that our peace studies graduates will somehow be actively and creatively involved in the process.

Conclusion

Peace studies is above all an adventure, an adventure in education and in life. In this essay we have discussed the parameters, principles, and dynamics of peace education and of the peace studies program at Manhattan College in particular. All of what we have discussed has been directed to stimulating, enhancing, and invigorating the life process. It is hoped that some of the insights contained here—gleaned over almost two decades—will inspire others to engage in a similar educational adventure. Though the night is dark and the storm is imminent, there is nevertheless hope, and if education does not provide hope it is doubtful if future generations will have any. We may be entering a new age in human existence that is characterized by wholly different values and "weapons" than those we have found in the past. The spiritual value of compassion and the "weapon" of nonviolence, if fully pursued, can dramatically alter the lives of many in our own generation and those that lie in the future. Each individual human being is sacred and has a cosmic destiny and it is only when each person is treated justly that the elusive goal of peace can be secured. Programs and courses in peace studies are a modest attempt to empower people to alter our bloodstained history, and it remains to be seen if they shall be employed in time.

But while time is still with us we must use every bit of knowledge and every talent to labor for a world that is free of war and secure in justice. To accomplish this noble task, a special responsibility rests on the reader of this volume. Only when *you* do all in your power to further the cause of peace through education and action will there be cause for hope. Only when *you* combine your talents with those of others to labor for justice at home and abroad will the virtues of love and reconciliation become universally accepted cultural values. Join us in this adventure. The children of the future are eager for your positive response.

QUESTIONS FOR REFLECTION AND DISCUSSION

1. Discuss the degree to which economic justice and peace are related. What concrete examples of absence of peace because of deprivation of economic justice can you identify?

2. Do you agree that when those who exercise oppression and violence toward others cease such oppression, they themselves are beneficiaries? Can you think of examples of this from your own life?

3. Reflect on the relationship between academic objectivity and moral commitment. How is it possible to remain objective without becoming morally neutral?

4. Reflect on the person or persons in your life who have served as beacons of nonviolence and prophecy. Are there Gandis, Days, or Kings in your experience? What are the sources of their strength and peace?

5. How can you implement, however modestly, the goals and dynamics of peace studies in your situation?

III

RELATED

MINISTERIAL ISSUES

13. Liturgy, Justice, and Peace

KATHLEEN HUGHES, R.S.C.J.

Introduction

The renewal of the Church's liturgical life must be counted among the distinct achievements of the Second Vatican Council. It has been a renewal that, in varying degrees, has affected all of the Christian churches as each has pondered and probed the integral relationship between word and sacrament, the nature of the assembled church, the many modes of the presence of Christ in the worshiping community, and the symbolic language or ritual action. Printing presses shifted into high gear, scarcely able to keep up with the new service books of the various communions that were issued in the late 1960s and throughout the 1970s. Worship offices and liturgy committees sprang up. Liturgical studies programs trained professional theologians and practitioners who, in turn, offered study days and workshops and ground out reams of treatises dealing with the history and theology of worship and practical guides to its concrete expressions. Whatever one may think of its results, the fact is undeniable that the worship life of the Church has been radically altered.

The liturgical movement corresponded in time to the increased concern for issues of social justice. During this era of liturgical renewal the churches simultaneously became more involved in the needs of the human community. The liturgy committee found its analogue in committees for peace and justice. Study days and workshops raised the consciousness of thousands who, in turn, participated in peace marches and demonstrations, joined the Catholic Committee on Urban Ministry (CCUM) or Bread for the World, supported the Equal Rights Amendment or Ban the Bomb, wrote members of Congress or newspaper editors—in diverse ways probing and picketing and prophesying the Christian response to the injustices in our world. Whatever one's position on individual issues, the fact is equally undeniable that the Christian social conscience has been pricked.

Two movements. Two realities. Consciousness was being raised on two levels. Rare, however, has been the dialogue and interchange between such groups. One had only to be present during a summer session at the University of Notre Dame in the late 1970s to discover how antithetical was the perceived relationship between liturgy and social justice. The participants in the liturgical studies program celebrated morning and evening prayer and a full Sunday Eucharist in Sacred Heart Church with vestments and incense, dignity and formality. They understood themselves as participants in the recovery of the Church's tradition of worship who were, at the same time, contributing to its adaptation through model celebrations. Meanwhile, the participants in the CCUM summer session met in lounges, celebrating alternative, experimental worship services created around justice themes.

The latter group saw the former as "playing church with bells and smells," unconcerned with, or even oblivious to, real human issues, tinkering with trifles while cities burned and hearts eroded. The former saw the latter as "mucking around with the tradition," creating liturgies *ex nihilo* and manipulating participants by using worship as a weapon of social transformation. The lines were clearly drawn.

This vignette, though a caricature of extremes, provides some truth and insight into the complexity of the relationship between worship and justice, between liturgy and life experience. For, on the one hand, the temptation to religious ritualism remains a constant threat to genuine liturgical renewal. It *is* possible to delude oneself, to worship different gods on Sunday and during the week, to count oneself part of the Body of Christ yet remain unmoved by the needs of his members. On the other hand, to superimpose "themes" on the celebration of liturgy is to distort the experience of worship in a different way. We gather for worship to celebrate not an idea but a Person, not what we can, should, or will do but what God has done and continues to do for us in Jesus, dead and risen. Anything less is neo-Pelagian.

We will first look more closely at these two distortions of authentic liturgy that seem to hamper a true rapprochement between liturgy and justice. In a later section it will be proposed that the relationship between liturgy and justice is intrinsic to both realities and that the way to bridge the gap between them may lie in taking seriously the meaning of participation in the Paschal Mystery that liturgy makes present, a participation that would issue in conscious Christian commitment to that vision of justice inherent in the celebration.

The Gap Between Liturgy and Living Justly

The temptation to religious ritualism is not a new problem stirred up by the liturgical renewal. It was a temptation to which our ancestors in the faith succumbed, as witness the stinging rebuke that the prophet Amos places on Yahweh's lips:

> I hate, I despise your feasts,
>   and take no delight in your solemn assemblies.
> Even though you offer me your burnt offerings
>   and your cereal offerings,
>   I will not accept them,
> And the peace offerings of your fatted beasts
>   I will not look upon.
> Take away from me the noise of your songs;
>   to the melody of your harps I will not listen.
> But let justice roll down like waters,
>   and righteousness like an ever-flowing stream.
> [Amos 5:21–24][1]

In the book of Micah, the prophet considers the perennial human dilemma: What kind of worship, what sacrifice of praise should be offered to God? What liturgy does God desire of us?

> With what shall I come before the Lord,
>   and bow myself before God on high?
> Shall I come before him with burnt offerings,
>   with calves a year old?
> Will the Lord be pleased with thousands of rams,
>   with ten thousands of rivers of oil?
> Shall I give my first-born for my transgressions,
>   the fruit of my body for the sin of my soul?
> [Micah 6:6–7]

And Yahweh responds, but not with a solution. We are offered, instead, a way of life: to do justice, and to love kindness, and to walk humbly with our God (Micah 6:8).

What Micah and Amos provide is a very salutary warning. They are not condemning ritual worship out of hand. They are condemning religious formalism. They oppose a cult performed with mechanical exactness but no inner devotion. They decry external rites unrelated to interior morality. The prophets remind us that there is an intrinsic relationship between cult and conduct—that worship is an expression of, and not a substitute for, social responsibility.

Care for libation of oil and fattened cattle, for albs and incense and programs and pauses is commendable. But more is surely required, says Yahweh. Worship is rooted in justice; that is, worship is an expression of right relationships or it is worse than worthless: it is an abomination to the Lord.

Justice cares for the establishment of right relationships. Justice is about the recognition within us and among us of our growth as unique human beings with gifts and grace, with potential and desires, with anxieties and hopes and fears. Justice is about unity and solidarity, about the linking up of our destinies, about rising and falling together without domination or constraint, without exploitation or manipulation, without discrimination or violence. Justice concerns that blessed hunger and thirst when human rights are violated in various ways, when discrimination is encountered in its numerous forms, when situations are burdened with injustice in whatever guise—a hunger and thirst for the indispensable transformation of the structures of social life so that each person may find him- or herself in Christ, and may mature, through Christ, in the one body of the human community.

Whereas justice cares for the establishment of relationships, *liturgy* is their celebration. We gather to give praise and thanksgiving, to recall the mighty acts of God in human history, to make the memorial of Jesus' victorious death, to pray for the needs of our world, and to celebrate the kingdom of justice and love that is already and that is yet to be. Liturgy is our activity, our service, as human beings in all of our fragility and weakness, our hunger and thirst for justice still unsated, yet struggling as we are to give expression to the life we are shaping in Christ. Liturgy is not a stepping outside of daily life into some mystical realm but a lifting up of our dailiness, recognizing that we are God-touched yet incomplete. It is a gathering of people who need to let go, to give themselves over, to surrender to the God of Mystery, and to receive grace and strength to keep going. And in the very process of confessing the one true God and Jesus Christ whom God has sent, the confessing community's self-awareness is purified and deepened, its commitment to justice re-affirmed.

Sometimes this commitment is made explicit in the language of our prayer:

> God our Father,
> your Word, Jesus Christ, spoke peace to a sinful world
> and brought [hu]mankind the gift of reconciliation
> by the suffering and death he endured.
> Teach us, the people who bear his name,
> to follow the example he gave us:
> may our faith, hope and charity

turn hatred to love, conflict to peace, death to eternal life.
We ask this through Christ our Lord.

The Sacramentary
Fourth Sunday of Lent
Alternative Opening Prayer

Keep, O Lord, your household the Church in your steadfast faith and love,
that through your grace we may proclaim your truth with boldness, and
minister your justice with compassion; for the sake of our Savior Jesus
Christ, who lives and reigns with you and the Holy Spirit, one God, now
and for ever.

The Book of Common Prayer
The Season after Pentecost
Proper 6

Eternal Lord, your kingdom has broken into our troubled world through
the life, death, and resurrection of your Son. Help us to hear your Word
and obey it, so that we become instruments of your redeeming love;
through your Son, Jesus Christ our Lord, who lives and reigns with you
and the Holy Spirit, one God, now and forever.

Lutheran Book of Worship
Third Sunday of Lent
Prayer of the Day

"Followers," "ministers," "instruments"—keeping the memorial of
Jesus' death and rising places obligations on the people who bear his
name. Confessing faith in God has social implications.[2]

As the liturgical renewal has progressed, various criteria have been
proposed to measure the quality of the celebration, for example, careful planning, artistic integrity, theological accuracy, appeal to the
senses—a whole series of objective criteria that formed a kind of liturgical examination of conscience, a way of judging the progress of the
reform. But there are larger questions:[3] Does this progress, of which
we may be the promoters, make human life on earth more human? In
the context of this progress are we becoming truly better; more mature spiritually; more aware of the dignity of our humanity; more
responsible; more open to others, especially the neediest and the
weakest; and readier to give and to aid all? Is there a growth of social
love, of respect for the rights of others, for every person; or on the
contrary, is there an increase of various degrees of selfishness, the
propensity to dominate, the propensity to exploit? Can we speak of
progress in the liturgical "renewal" at all unless the liturgy has had a
profoundly humanizing effect in our lives as well as in our celebrations?

These larger questions having been asked, it must also be stated that the claims the liturgy might make upon our lives sometimes cannot be heard because of the way in which they are delivered to us. The words and the gestures will only mediate the presence of the transforming Christ if they are spoken in a language that can be heard and appropriated by the entire community:

> Liturgy requires the faith community to set aside all those distinctions and divisions and classifications (stemming from color, sex and class). By doing this the liturgy celebrates the reign of God, and as such maintains the tension between what is (the status quo of our daily lives) and what must be (God's will for human salvation—liberation and solidarity).[4]

The language of prayer, both the words and the ritual action, cannot transform the human heart if they are not heard; they cannot be heard if spoken in a way that excludes anyone in the community from full participation.[5]

The prophets' warning must sound again in our ears, urging us to examine not simply the quality of our celebrations (including their inclusive dimensions) but the quality of our Christian lives as well. Throughout human history ritualism has been a temptation. It is no less a temptation today.

The Manipulation of the Liturgy

Worship can be distorted in another far more subtle way, and this second problem is of recent origin: It is the superimposition of a theme on the celebration of liturgy.[6] This is a new threat to genuine liturgical renewal and, in the context of the present discussion, a threat to genuine social justice as well, for it promotes a truly superficial idea of Christian justice and of its celebration.

The process of thematizing looks something like this:[7] A group gathers to plan a worship event. A theme is proposed, say, for example, one or another of society's ills and the appropriate Christian response. The group chooses Scripture passages that "speak to the issue," songs and prayers that support it. And lest the theme is not already crystal clear, the sermon is designed to drive the point home. It is all very tidy. The choice of justice themes, it is anticipated, will fire up the community to do works of justice. The problem is, that is not how the liturgy works, nor how women and men become just.

We do not gather in the presence of the Holy One in order to discuss what we intend to do but to surrender to God's designs for us, a surrender that cannot be predetermined or controlled because it is not up to the initiative of the community. Liturgy is God's initiative. It is a response to the God who gathers a people, who counts us worthy to stand in the divine presence and to serve, not because of anything we have done or intend to do but because of the Victim whose death has reconciled us to God, in whose Spirit we become one. The celebration of ideas will not make us just; Jesus Christ will make us just, and so we pray to God: "*May he make us* an everlasting gift to you."

Liturgy is not logical explanation, nor can its end be reduced to a political or ethical "goal"—a series of "shoulds" or "oughts." Theme liturgy, whether it be "right to life" or "hope" or "disarmament" or whatever, makes of the liturgy an exposition of ideas. There are other more appropriate forums for such discussion. We do not celebrate the liturgy in order to think about ideas, however worthy, but to place ourselves in contact with the person and work of Jesus Christ and to submit to Christ's action in our lives. Liturgy is less a matter of the head than of the heart, an experience less of formation than of transformation, *if* we will let God work the divine will with us.

The liturgy has a unique potential for inviting transformation in the Christian community. The liturgy gives expression to the community's faith experience; or to borrow a phrase from Victor Turner, the liturgy transmits the community's "deep knowledge" from one generation to another.[8] In this function, it is true, liturgy is formational. At the same time, liturgical prayer deepens and enlarges the community's experience of faith, depicting what the community is summoned to become in the power of the Spirit, inviting wholehearted response. It is this second function of the liturgy that is potentially transformational:[9]

> Transformation is a total personal revolution. It begins with repentance—the rejection along with actual sins of the whole apparatus of natural virtue as irrelevant and misleading—and proceeds eventually to the desired dissolution of all that ordinary people ordinarily value in themselves or others. The result of this dissolution, this death of the natural man, is the birth of the whole human being, the perfection of man, meaning both man as an individual and man as a race, because this process is at once personal and communal. And it takes place in Christ and nowhere else. It is what Christians call the resurrection, or eternal life.[10]

The insights of Victor Turner and Rosemary Haughton will help to clarify how the community may be transformed through its ritual prayer. For Victor Turner, nearly all rituals of any length and complexity have the function of placing men and women temporarily outside of everyday structural positions and demands—what Turner calls "status incumbencies"—and into a liminal betwixt-and-between state.

In specifically religious rituals, the liminal interval may be an experience of stripping and leveling before the transcendent:

> In liminal sacredness many of the relationships, values, norms, etc., which prevail in the domain of pragmatic structure are reversed, expunged, suspended, reinterpreted, or replaced by a wholly other set. . . . Men who are heavily involved in jural-political overt and conscious structure are *not* free to meditate and speculate on the combinations and oppositions of thought; they are themselves too crucially involved in the combinations and oppositions of social and political structure and stratification. They are in the heat of the battle, in the "arena," competing for office, participating in feuds, factions and coalitions. This involvement entails such affects as anxiety, aggression, envy, fear, exultation, etc., an emotional flooding which does not encourage either rational or wise reflection. But in ritual liminality they are placed, so to speak, outside the total system and its conflicts; transiently, they become men apart—and it is surprising how often the term "sacred" may be translated as "set apart" or "on one side" in various societies. If getting a living and struggling to get it, in spite of social structure, be called "bread," then man does not live "by bread alone."[11]

Liminality for Turner describes the state of freedom and creativity realized by people set apart for a while from inhibiting "status incumbencies" in order to contemplate "the mysteries that confront all men, the difficulties that peculiarly beset their own society, their personal problems and the ways in which their own wisest predecessors have sought to order, explain, explain away, cloak, or mask these mysteries and difficulties."[12]

Haughton might agree that ritual liminality provides an opportunity for contemplation, but she would emphasize that the point of such contemplation would be decision for action. In her schema, ritual provides the medium for the experience of withdrawal from and indifference to inhibiting social structure in order to afford a frame for encounter with the sacred—encountered only in the breakdown of structures. Such liminality she describes as "wilderness," "ambiguity," "in-betweenness." For Haughton, the point of ritual withdrawal and the point of encounter with the sacred in the breakdown of ritual structures is the possibility of transformation: "[Ritual] is directly and solely concerned with the occurrence of transformation,"[13] its limits only the willingness of human response to the invitations to a real, personal surrender. Participation in liturgy demands decision. God's covenant with humankind requires the response of the obedience of faith. The event of liturgical prayer invites conversion and transformation, and the words and the gestures of the liturgy contribute to the invitational process.

Haughton proposes that it is in embracing *ambiguity* that transformation happens. The basic ambiguity upon which Christianity is based is Christ Himself who belongs securely to no category whatsoever:

> He cannot be thought of as a divine being, in human form, nor as a man seized by divine inspiration, but is a disconcerting complex that nobody has even managed to define satisfactorily, because the whole point is that you can't. He wasn't a priest yet offered sacrifice, he was ruler yet ended up on a gallows. Master and servant, carpenter and king, a dead man who was known and recognized as living. A total failure and a total success. These are ideas to which we are well accustomed, so they don't easily feel contradictory. But if one reflects on any one of these points it can be seen that while each member of each pair is clearly a true description, the truth of each one is a totally different mental and emotional "area" from the other. If both are put into one sphere of thought they are really contradictory, really nonsense. For each has to be kept in its own proper sphere in order to be true, and the mental shift from one to another, if one really makes this move and doesn't merely slide over the top of both, involves a kind of psychological distortion.[14]

The ambiguity of Christ shatters all categories. It makes of *all* Christian language an experience of ambiguity, a challenge to its hearers, a summons to transformation in Christ.

The liturgy provides numerous invitations for transformation. The language of ritual prayer, reflecting as it does God's saving encounter with humankind in and through Christ, deliberately shatters our ordinary categories, using ordinary words and gestures in extraordinary ways, often presenting logic-defying irreconcilables in juxtaposition. The community is sinner and saved, powerless and graced by God, active subject of the praise of God and needy receiver of empowering grace.

The liturgy invites the praying community, bound to God by covenant love, to let go of all other ties that bind; to become powerless that God might fill it with power; to be utterly confident not because of its own worth but because God is faithful; to be leveled and to be lifted up by the God whom it encounters in its prayer. The liturgy of the Christian community is at one and the same time an expression of its experience of faith and a summons to conversion and transformation in Christ.

The summons will not come because of carefully crafted but, in the last analysis, extrinsic "themes" that are imposed on the celebration. The summons to transformation is intrinsic to genuine worship. Only as we open ourselves to the event of Jesus' death and rising and as we allow ourselves to be purified in His abundant and life-giving presence shall we grow in holiness and justice. We shall, in fact, overcome. But let there be no illusion. We shall overcome by God's transforming grace.

Make of Your Lives a Living Worship

In the celebration of the liturgy, Jesus' death for the life of the world becomes available to us. Jesus, the Just One, the perfect response to his Father's will, the source of God's continued gift to us, becomes present in the celebration and in the people celebrating—in the words and gestures, the sacrifice and the meal. The liturgy summons us to *become* the sign of his presence to and with one another. Such is our *participation* in the worship of the Church.

There is perhaps no statement from the Second Vatican Council's *Constitution on the Sacred Liturgy* more often quoted and more frequently misunderstood than that which refers to "participation":

> Mother Church earnestly desires that all the faithful should be led to the full, conscious, and active participation in liturgical celebrations which is demanded by the very nature of the liturgy, and to which the Christian people, "a chosen race, a royal priesthood, a holy nation, a redeemed people" (1 Pet. 2:9,4–5) have a right and obligation by reason of their baptism.[15]

Full, conscious, and active participation—our right and duty by reason of baptism. How easy it is to water down that statement! How easy it is to be full-throated in our singing, to follow along in our "participation aid," to make all the appropriate responses, to give a warm and friendly greeting of peace, to receive the Eucharist—and to walk away, untouched at the core of our being. How easy it is to participate with a certain mechanical exactness, like Pavlov's dogs, scarcely aware of what we are doing, glad that the sermon is brief on hot summer days, wondering what we should serve next Wednesday when company comes, making mental notes to catch so-and-so in the parking lot . . . all the while muttering our "Amen's" and "And also with you's." How easy it is to come away unscathed by the reality of what we are doing when we gather to make his memorial.

On the other hand, what would it be like if we took the liturgy seriously, or rather, let the liturgy take us seriously—take us, for example, into that world of justice and love as expressed in the words of one of the Roman eucharistic prayers:

> To the poor [Jesus] proclaimed the good news of salvation,
> to prisoners, freedom,

and to those in sorrow, joy.
In fulfillment of your will
he gave himself up to death;
but by rising from the dead,
he destroyed death and restored life.
And that we might live no longer for ourselves but for him,
he sent the Holy Spirit from you, Father,
as his first gift to those who believe,
to complete his work on earth
and to bring us to the fullness of grace.[16]

Participation in the liturgy means participation in the life, death, and rising of Jesus, truly dying and rising with him, truly laying down our lives. Participation means working mightily for the establishment of the kingdom by letting the Spirit of God work in us to complete Christ's work on earth. Participation means living Christ's life: pouring ourselves out for the poor and the imprisoned and the suffering. Participation means living "no longer for ourselves but for him." Otherwise, how can we say "Amen" to such a prayer?

Participation in the liturgy means hearing the Word of God as it is proclaimed in our midst week after week and letting that Word take root in our lives. Participation means saying "Our Father" and recognizing ourselves as sons and daughters, brothers and sisters, consciously embracing the relationships implied. Participation means taking up the cup of salvation, remembering it is the cup of suffering as well, and not drinking unworthily. Participation means *meaning it* when we say of the Body of Christ: "Amen." So be it. Yes, it is. Yes, I will be, with God's grace.

With every "Amen" we join ourselves to the Paschal Mystery and pledge ourselves to that vision of justice and love that is inherent in the celebration. "Amen" is an act of faith and an act of commitment. Full, conscious, and active participation in the liturgy means that we will, *in deed*, live what we proclaim.

Liturgy and justice have an intrinsic relationship to one another precisely because liturgy places us before the Just One to whom we say "Amen." We need not change the liturgy in order to highlight themes of justice. We need simply to celebrate the liturgy with genuine participation and allow the Just One gradually, almost imperceptibly, to change us.

NOTES

1. Scripture citations are taken from The Holy Bible, Revised Standard Version, Ecumenical Edition.

2. In the prayers here cited the community expresses its understanding of its mandate to just action, asking God for those graces necessary to strengthen it in its resolve. It is interesting to note in some recent compositions how the focus of prayer has shifted from asking God to take care of those in need, thus perhaps relieving the community of its obligation, to asking God to make us agents of change. See, for example, the prayer "In Time of Famine" in *The Sacramentary* Approved for Use in the Dioceses of the United States of America by the National Conference of Catholic Bishops and Confirmed by the Apostolic See, English translation prepared by the International Committee on English in the Liturgy (Collegeville Pa.: The Liturgical Press, 1974); the prayer for "The Oppressed" in *The Lutheran Book of Worship*, prepared by the churches participating in the Inter-Lutheran Commission on Worship (Minneapolis: Augsburg, 1979); the prayer for "Social Justice" in *The Book of Common Prayer* and Administration of the Sacraments and Other Rites and Ceremonies of the Church, According to the use of the Episcopal Church (New York: The Church Hymnal Corporation and The Seabury Press, 1977).

3. The questions that follow have been inspired by the First Encyclical of John Paul II, *Redemptor hominis*, March 4, 1979, in which he examines modern developments as progress and threat, if not examined in the light of the gospel.

4. Bishops' Committee on the Liturgy, *Environment and Art in Catholic Worship* (Washington: National Conference of Catholic Bishops, 1978), no. 32.

5. It is impossible in the present article to treat either the question of the inclusion of women in the ministries of the liturgy or the question of language that discriminates because it is racist, sexist, clericalist, or anti-Semitic. These issues are, however, pressing justice questions in light of the paper's thesis, namely, that the liturgy is a summons to *everyone* in the assembly to transformation into Christ, a summons that must not be muted by any word or action that tends to exclude. See Kathleen Hughes, "Women and Eucharistic Liturgy," *New Catholic World* (July/August 1981), pp. 161–64.

6. "Theme" celebrations are not limited to any one sector of the church. The United States Catholic hierarchy broadly promotes the use of themes by specifying National Catechetical Sunday, National Mission Sunday, National Vocation Sunday, and so on. Furthermore, a Jewish colleague confided to me that his Reform congregation was also busy at the copy machine with celebrations such as "Manger, Mistletoe, and Menorah."

7. There is an appropriate way to understand "theme" celebrations. One might think of the Mystery of God or the person and work of the God come among us in Jesus as compared to a prism with many facets, only a few of which are visible to the eye at any one time. If every eucharistic liturgy celebrates the event of Jesus, dead and risen, it is the Scripture passages of the day that highlight one or other facet of this many-faceted mystery. It is the Word of God that gives the "theme" or lends the nuance to a celebration and differentiates celebrations one from another.

8. Victor Turner, "Passages, Margins and Poverty: Religious Symbols of Communitas," *Worship* 46 (1972), p. 399.

9. The words and the actions of liturgy participate in the functions classically ascribed to all sacramental life: *exprimit, causat.*

10. Rosemary Haughton, *The Transformation of Man* (Paramus N.J.: Deus Books, 1967), pp. 7–8.

11. Turner, pp. 393, 402.

12. Ibid., p. 402.

13. Haughton, p. 248.
14. Ibid., pp. 277–78.
15. Vatican II, *Sacrosanctum Concilium*, no. 14, translated by Austin Flannery in *Vatican Council II: The Conciliar and Post-Conciliar Documents* (Collegeville Pa.: Liturgical Press, 1975).
16. Excerpt, Eucharistic Prayer IV, *The Sacramentary*.

QUESTIONS FOR REFLECTION AND DISCUSSION

1. How would you specify the relationship between liturgy and living justly?

2. In relation to the goal of a just life, what does the term *ritualism* imply?

3. Also in relation to this goal, what does the term *activism* imply? And, can there be an "activist" orientation to the liturgy?

4. Why is the celebration of theme liturgy and extrinsic and superficial solution to bridging the gap between liturgy and social justice?

5. What kind of catechesis would you design to help communities participate in the liturgy internally as well as externally?

14. The Pastoral Care and Counseling Relationship

CLAIRE E. LOWERY

Introduction

Though the pastoral counseling movement has been proclaimed as coming of age in the 1980s,[1] debate and misunderstanding still surround its newly established identity. The controversy can be divided into two schools of thought: those that advocate an "ecclesial" model and those who practice a "psychotherapeutic" model for pastoral care and counseling. If one follows an ecclesial model, the social dimension of pastoral care and counseling is very important. If, however, one follows a psychotherapeutic model the social dimension remains outside the scope of this profession. The central reason for this is that pastoral counselors (of the latter school) choose to separate their counseling from their ministry. They speak of a conflict of interest. A director of a pastoral counseling center was recently quoted as saying: "I refuse to wear both hats and be both therapist and pastor for the people. Here in my parish my job is pastor," he explains, "I think that the type of relationship that a pastor has with his parishioners needs to be different than the kind of relationship that a counselor has with a client."[2] This separation between church and practice limits the effectiveness of the pastoral counselor.

An ecclesial model of pastoral counseling would claim that the faith identity of the pastoral counselors and their ministry are key to an effective counseling relationship. Here, pastoral counselors not only work with their clients toward personal growth and wholeness but confront the needs of the community—the social ills that frequently cause personal pain and struggle—through the ministry of pastoral care and counseling.

The debate that surrounds these conflicting opinions has not been fully settled yet. Its resolution bears a direct influence on whether or not the societal context for the pastoral counseling relationship is recognized or dismissed. This essay will look at these questions in relation to the ministries of pastoral care and counseling. If pastoral counseling has "come of age" in the eighties, then a new agenda must be set. This agenda must find a more explicit way to address the societal ills that bear a direct influence on the pastoral care and counseling relationship.

Conflicting Opinions

In today's society, we recognize a growing interest in pastoral counseling. Though the goals and methods of pastoral counseling are being affirmed as a major new development in the health care field, they are being challenged by both psychologists and psychiatrists who ask whether or not clergy have the right and expertise to practice counseling. Skeptics claim that counseling and church don't always mix and that this combination can often create confusion for both the counselor and the counselee. Observers ask the question: "Can the pastoral counselor separate moral and religious precepts from the issue at hand?" They presume that moral and religious values obstruct good counseling.[3] In response, others proclaim that pastoral counseling, though primarily focusing on the dynamic issues in a person's problem, *must* be surrounded by a clear and discernible moral context. These writers assert that it is insufficient for pastoral counselors to adopt a "guiding process" that provides, "information," "knowledge," or other resources. They emphasize that a moral framework or a procedure for resolving moral issues together with a re-incorporation of theological understanding are integral to the pastoral care process.[4]

The latter group fear that pastoral counseling has become secularized by claiming a psychotherapeutic model and leaving ministry behind. They question why the words *pastoral counseling* have been substituted for *pastoral care*.

These questions are not new; they have been central to the conflict surrounding the struggle, growth, and development of pastoral counseling. In response to these conflicting opinions, it is necessary to explore two aspects of the pastoral care and counseling relationship: pastoral care in an ecclesial model and pastoral counseling as a healing ministry within pastoral care.[5]

Pastoral Care: An Ecclesial Model

Since the early 1950s, Seward Hiltner, pastoral theologian, has been at the forefront of those who assert the ecclesial model. He has

constantly challenged pastoral counselors to construct a pastoral counseling relationship out of their theological and spiritual concerns and
not solely from a psychological and medical framework.[6] Hiltner's
concern for the theological emphasis rests on his conviction that all
ministers are called by vocation to the ministry of pastoral care, and
that the "professionalization" of the specialized ministry of pastoral
counseling should not remove the minister from his or her major
responsibility of pastoral care. Edward Schillebeeckx, an internationally respected theologian, would agree with Hiltner when he cautions
against the possible dangers of overspecialization within the context of
ministry that both isolates and removes one from participation in the
total mission of the church.[7] Counseling is only one of the ministries
of pastoral care, which includes preaching, teaching, administering,
and leading the community in worship. Professionalization should not
place the pastoral counselor apart from the total ministry of pastoral
care.

Pastoral care is performed to some degree by all baptized Christians
who participate in the church's mission of healing, sustaining, guiding, and reconciling troubled individuals whose difficulties occur in
the context of ultimate meaning and concern.[8] The pastoral care relationship is based on mutual trust that seeks to care for others because
of God's care. The ministry of pastoral care is to give guidance, encouragement, and leadership to a congregation of people who seek as
a community to live as committed Christians. It is faith that calls all
Christians to caring activities. The two essentials for the pastoral care
relationship are the faith identity of the care giver and the informed
manner in which one practices care.

Walter Brueggemann describes the pastoral care relationship well.
He identifies the significance of faith identity in this relationship by
using the biblical metaphor of covenant as the "grounding in another
vis-à-vis self-groundedness."[9] His intent is not to specify any technical sense or particular biblical interpretation. Rather, he uses this
metaphor for the most fundamental affirmation of biblical faith. He
primarily claims covenant as a way of understanding pastoral care in
that "human persons are grounded in Another who initiates personhood and who stays bound to persons in loyal ways for their well-
being."[10] This affirmation of persons contradicts the current temptation to self-groundedness that he would equate with narcissism. The
primary elements of the mature convenanted personhood are found in
a "hope" that God's promise and purpose will not fail, a "listening"
that moves one in a decision to concede to the voice of Another who

calls us by name, and the action of "answering" that may be summarized as the doing of justice and righteousness.

Brueggemann sees in each element of covenanting a protest against self-groundedness. For the self-grounded person is "hopeless," "must always do the speaking," and "hears nothing to which to make answer." Pastoral care is concerned with the issues of how people who are hopeless, persistent speakers, and faithless listeners can be brought to faithful convenanting.[11]

A recent survey makes these issues of "covenanting" more explicit when it identifies the typical problems brought first to ministers as, in 42 percent of the cases: (1) depression, (2) marital problems, (3) premarital problems, (4) guilt, and (5) feelings of inadequacy.[12]

The ministry of pastoral care will assist people seeking help in the faithful actions of covenanting. It leads people in the way of Christian vocation by helping them come to terms in free ways with the givenness of God's purpose in their lives.

According to Brueggemannn, the ministry of pastoral care is to assist each person in both "listening" and "answering." This action of covenanting must be evident in the teaching, preaching, administering, counseling, and calling to worship ministries of pastoral care.[13] The ministry of pastoral care is to give guidance, encouragement, and leadership to a congregation of people who seek as a community to live as committed Christians. Christian community is central to the ministry of pastoral care, and the spirit of the community is as much a concern of pastoral care as are the special problems of the individual. Pastoral care enables each person to find a sense of direction amid his or her own personal struggle. Through membership in a community, one's attention does not remain solely with self but is directed toward the tasks of Christian community.[14] Though pastoral care is not the same as social change, when it sees the need for social action in specific situations, pastoral care will assist the community in both listening and answering.

Seward Hiltner furthers this understanding of pastoral care by emphasizing the tender and individualized care by the "shepherd" for the sheep. He identifies the basic principles of shepherding as "concern" and "acceptance."[15] Here Hiltner extends his concept of pastoral care to include the minister's ability to see and experience the class structure in which people who need care must live. General knowledge is no substitute. Ministers must recognize the specific impact of these structures upon the person's identity. This emphasis in pastoral care helps to establish a more systematic and social orientation to one's caring for both the individual and the community. The problems that address us in pastoral care are "collective" as well as "individual." Depression, feelings of inadequacy, quilt, marital struggle, and so on are often related to social ills in our society. Here one must also recognize that the social problems can also arise from individual maladjustments, mental stress, and psychological illness. An example of this is the twentieth century's inability to live in covenant relationship as noted in the societal problems surrounding family life today. Thus, whereas the minister must focus on the acute need of individuals who come for care, the metaphors of "covenant" and "shepherd" must be active and operative in preaching, teaching, administration, and worship.

The principle that must guide the tasks of pastoral care is that the maturity of Christian life, personal growth, and social responsibility belong together in the integrity of the person. Social responsibility includes here the sharing in movements toward social alleviation or reconstruction and the wider sense of any deliberate effort to bring Christian faith to bear on the way we live together our lives of covenant. The church's mission of healing, sustaining, guiding, and reconciling is the mission of strengthening the Christian community. It must always remain the foundation stone for the ecclesial model of pastoral counseling.

Pastoral Counseling: The Healing Ministry of Pastoral Care

Those who have contributed to the growth and development of pastoral counseling throughout the last two decades look with pride on their accomplishments.[16] Pastoral counseling is a well-respected profession for which ministers are skillfully trained and educated. Churches are slowly recognizing the importance of this specialized ministry within the context of the church's overall mission. But with this growing recognition and endorsement, there still remains a tension. Pastoral counselors give evidence of tending toward isolated professionalization rather than strengthening the specialization of pastoral counseling within the total context of pastoral care. Both the churches and the pastoral counselors are to blame for this lack of relationship. Indeed, some well-respected pastoral counselors argue that pastoral counseling is an extension of the Christian community, and that pastoral counselors may not operate a private practice.[17]

The starting point for the desired relationship between pastoral counselors and the church must be mutual recognition and acceptance. If this were the case, we would see a growing number of churches seeking to have professionally trained pastoral counselors as members of their staffs. At present this is not the reality. Instead of this close working relationship, we have a growing number of pastoral counseling centers that function independently of the churches. These counseling centers establish themselves as communities apart, rather than incorporating themselves into the primary church community. Instead of mutual enrichment, we have rivalry. Furthermore, pastoral counseling, when it overprofessionalizes, loses two things: first, a faith basis that people who come to pastors or ministers expect, and second, a community basis, a believing and sustaining community that would nourish both client and counselor.

Paul N. Pruyser, clinical psychologist at the Menninger Foundation in Kansas, rightly expresses concern that ministers and theological students doing pastoral training in his institution show little inclination to talk with clients or parishioners about faith, God, or religion, or even to think about their ministries in religious or theological terms.

> They do not quite trust their parishioners' occasional use of theological language and their presentation of theological conflict. Issues of faith were quickly "pulled" into issues of marital role behavior, adolescent protest against parents or dynamics of transference in the counseling situation. There seemed to be an implicit suspicion of the relevance of theology, both to any client's life and to the method and content of the pastoral counseling process.[18]

Pruyser concludes that it is a "jarring note" when any professional person no longer knows what his or her basic science is, or finds no use for it.[19]

Statements like this focus the need for pastoral counselors to reinsert themselves into the ministry of their calling, the mission of pastoral care. This does not mean that ministers should not specialize or become proficient through professional and academic training in counseling. On the contrary, it demands not only that they be well trained in counseling theory but also that their theological vision be kept alive. Professionalization can lead to separation, and pastoral counseling becomes a process of the natural order with little or no witness to its unique identity. But if pastoral counseling has "come of age" then its true identity must be evident in a ministry of faith. This need for a renewed faith basis for pastoral counseling leads us to a second point: Pastoral counseling needs a community basis.

Just as pastoral counseling once needed to separate itself from other ministries in order to establish its own identity, now pastoral counseling faces the challenge of integrating its identity with other ministries within the church like teaching, preaching, administering, and calling to worship. Only as it does this, can it overcome the obvious limits and dangers of a psychotherapeutic model.

Here too the social context of pastoral counseling would be clarified, and pastoral counselors would be more able to deal constructively with questions of social justice. As women and men of faith they would not ignore the social context. They would offer an alternative to the danger that Christopher Lasch describes so well in *The Culture of Narcissism: American Life in an Age of Diminishing Expectations.*

> Americans have retreated to purely personal preoccupations. Having no hope of improving their lives in any of the ways that matter, people have convinced themselves that what matters is psychic self-improvement, getting in touch with their feelings, eating health food, taking lessons in dancing, immersing themselves in the wisdom of the East, jogging, learning how to "relate," overcoming the "fear of pleasure." Harmless in themselves, these pursuits, elevated to a program and wrapped in the rhetoric of authenticity and awareness, signify a retreat from politics. While this ideology of personal growth is superficially optimistic, it radiates a profound despair and resignation. *It is the faith of those without faith* [emphasis added].[20]

The unique and primary responsibility of the pastoral counselor is to bring the strength of her or his faith to the individual. This does not mean a presence that leads to moral exhortation. Rather it is a presence that establishes "covenant" and brings about the empowerment for "hoping," "listening," and "answering" in the life of the person. The individual person's experience of brokenness must be listened to in relation to the total deviant social process that surrounds the person. This social dimension must be addressed in order for people to re-assert the inner strength and ability that will allow them to cope with the difficulties that press upon them. The ability to do this depends not only upon the faith identity and counseling skills of the pastoral counselor but also on the effective relationships that he or she has established with other ministries in the church. In the context of the church's mission, pastoral counselors would not separate love and justice, personal and social relationships. In recognizing that the health or sickness of the individuals is inescapably bound up with the justice or injustice of society, they would begin work with other ministers of the church to deal effectively with the unjust structures whose victims counselors treat.

In conclusion, this essay has tried to show the value of an ecclesial model for pastoral counseling. Pastoral counseling needs to re-establish its roots within pastoral care and explore its interconnections with other aspects of ministry that will allow pastoral counseling to overcome the dangers of a narrow professionalism and to address itself to concerns of social justice. In reclaiming their faith identity, pastoral counselors have a unique opportunity to draw on the communal resources of the church.

The church, for its part, needs to recognize and reward the profession of pastoral counseling in its potential for *revitalizing the healing ministry of the church.*

An agenda for the eighties calls for a new vision that will make visible the working relationship between the church's ministry of pastoral care and the specialized ministry of pastoral counseling. It is the first step toward an effective response to the social dimensions of the pastoral care and counseling relationship.

NOTES

1. John Patton, "Pastoral Counseling Comes of Age," *The Christian Century*, March 4, 1981.
2. Editorial, "How well does the clergy treat its flock?" *The Boston Phoenix*, October 27, 1981.
3. Ibid.
4. Don Browning, "Images of Man In Contemporary Models of Pastoral Care," *Interpretations* 33:2 (April 1979).
5. Prior to the 1950s "pastoral counseling" was not recognized as a professional practice by either schools of counseling theory or the churches. It was the pioneer work of Seward Hiltner (pastoral theologian at the University of Chicago Divinity School) that brought together the significance of counseling theories and pastoral theology to strengthen the healing ministry of pastoral care within the churches. The goal of his study was to strengthen the foundation of pastoral care through an interdisciplinary approach to counseling psychology and pastoral theology. In the thought of Seward Hiltner, "pastoral care" is the pastoral ministry of the church. Pastoral counseling is the healing ministry of pastoral care.
6. For a fuller understanding of the development of pastoral care and counseling and the significance of theology, I refer the reader to: Seward Hiltner, *Pastoral Counseling* (Nashville: Abingdon, 1952).
7. Edward Schillebeeckx, "A Creative Retrospect As Inspiration for the Ministry in the Future," in *Minister? Pastor? Prophet?* edited by Lucas Grollenberg, (New York: Crossroads, 1981).
8. William Clebsch and Charles Jaekle, *Pastoral Care in Historical Perspective* (New York: Aronson, 1975), pp. 56 ff.
9. Walter Brueggemann, "Convenanting As Human Vocation" (a discussion of the relation of the Bible and pastoral care), *Interpretations* 33:2 (April 1979).
10. Ibid. pp. 124 ff.
11. Ibid.
12. Survey Report published by *Ministers Life* (Minneapolis, Minnesota: November 1980).

13. Brueggemann, Ibid., pp. 121 f.

14. Daniel Day Williams, *The Minister and the Care of Souls* (New York: Harper's Ministers Paperback Library, 1961). In this book, Williams makes a significant contribution to pastoral counselors by addressing the essential relationship between the individual and the community for effective human wholeness.

15. Seward Hiltner, *The Christian Shepherd: Some Aspects of Pastoral Care* (Nashville: Abingdon Reprint Library, 1980).

16. For a complete understanding of the advancements made in the field of pastoral counseling, I refer the reader to Howard Clinebell, *Basic Types of Pastoral Counseling: New Resources For Ministering to the Troubled* (New York, Nashville: Abingdon, 1966).

17. Patton, Ibid.

18. Paul Pruyser, *Minister as Diagnostician* (New York: Westminster Press, 1976), pp. 27 ff.

19. Ibid.

20. Christopher Lasch, *The Culture of Narcissism* (New York: Warner Books, 1979), pp. 26 f.

QUESTIONS FOR REFLECTION AND DISCUSSION

1. How is pastoral counseling, as practiced in the Church, saved from individualism?

2. Discuss the ways in which a closer relationship between pastoral counseling and pastoral care furthers the Church's mission of social justice.

3. How do the life and work of your Church either succeed or fail to reflect the covenant actions of "listening" and "answering" within the Christian community?

4. Choose one problem or need proper to the pastoral counseling relationship, and show how the Christian community can support both the counselor and the individual in working toward wholeness.

5. Discuss the elements that help or hinder the realization of wholeness in our society today. In what ways can the ministries of teaching, preaching, administering, counseling, and calling to worship work together more effectively in the cause of justice?

15. Sing a New Song unto the Lord: The Relationship Between Spirituality and Social Responsibility

MARGARET BRENNAN, I.H.M.

ONE MONDAY morning in October, I viewed an extraordinary and touching story on *The Today Show*. For about five minutes the attention of the viewers was diverted from the bad news of rising interest rates, violence in the Middle East, and famine in northern Kenya desert areas. The TV cameras took us to Chicago where a black girl, severely retarded and unable to speak, was giving a piano concert. A social worker, who made frequent visits to the home where this young "artist" lived with her grandmother, had begun to sense that the more or less constant banging the girl made with her hands had a kind of rhythm to it and arranged to have music lessons given to her. The piano instructor discovered that she had perfect pitch. The disruptive and discordant banging on whatever surfaces were available had become harmonious tones when transferred to piano keys. An excited, and what appeared to be a thoroughly intelligent, smile played across the face of this young girl as she struck the keys. She was at last able to communicate outside of herself what had seemed to others only frustrating and discordant attempts, and what was in reality a harmonious whole.

This story spoke to me in a kind of parabolic way about the difficulty of articulating the relationship between Christian spirituality and social justice responsibility. The need to find a harmony embracing classical and time-honored understandings of spirituality, on the one hand, and the clear call to be consciously committed to creating a new world, on the other, has produced a variety of "sounds" that have yet to result in a fully integrated whole.

To continue in the framework of the story, it would seem that we are still struggling to hear a rhythm between the differing tones that will enable us, not only to put the sounds together, but then to play them in such a way as to engage others as well as ourselves in the expression of such an experience.

This is not surprising, as it is only within the last two decades that serious attempts have been made to establish an intimate relationship between spirituality and commitment to justice. At the same time, it would be naive and even untrue to suggest that Christian men and women of previous generations have not struggled with the question, as the love of God has always expressed itself in the love of one's neighbor. The words of Jesus in Matthew (25:31-46) have not only inspired heroic commitments of selfless service on behalf of the poor, the maimed, and the marginal but have also given testimony that God has been experienced as well as served in such encounters.

However, what adds a new note, a new "sound" to the traditional expressions of Christian faith, spirituality, and service today, is the insight that lies behind the statement articulated by the bishops in the 1971 Synod on "Justice in the World":

> Actions on behalf of justice and participation in the transformation of the world appear to us a constitutive dimension of the preaching of the gospel, or, in other words, of the Church's mission for the redemption of the human race and its liberation from every oppressive situation.[1]

Christians are called not only to alleviate the needs of those who are the victims of oppression, but to turn their efforts as well toward the elimination and correction of structures that make such injustice an accepted way of life. For Gustavo Gutierrez, this means the "efforts to abolish the present injustice and to construct a different society, freer and more human . . . where the oppressed will be agents of their own destiny."[2] This is what he understands by commitment to a praxis of liberation.

Entering into such a commitment has brought about a crisis for many Christians. Faith and piety, as they have been known and practiced, have not for the most part led Christians to a commitment that has challenged political and economic structures that keep whole peoples oppressed and living in conditions that denigrate their human dignity and their ability to work out a God-given destiny.

In Latin America the crisis has taken on sharper contours because, as Segundo Galilea has pointed out:

> the faith of the average Latin American has until now been very clearly defined by his culture. His family, his education, his social environment and the sociological primacy of Catholicism, which gave him a certain image

of Christ, ethics and faithful practice all formed part of this traditional faith. But as soon as the traditional Catholic commits himself to the liberation of the workers or the peasants in tasks of an educational or political nature, he finds himself in a way exiled. The categories of his faith—sin, salvation, charity, prayer, etc., do not inspire or illuminate sufficiently his commitments.[3]

In North America the context is more subtle and, as a result, perhaps less easy to delineate. The parameters of faith and spirituality on the one hand and commitment to the cause of justice on the other are not so easily defined by a culture that is at once individualistic, pluralistic, and capitalistic and that, in the United States, clearly separates the relationship of church and state. As a result, Catholic teaching for the most part, until recent decades, did not stress commitment to social action and the challenging of unjust structures as an integral part of faith education.

The challenge to search out and examine the meaning of spirituality from within the North American cultural context in which we live out our faith and the challenge to confront the commitment to make spirituality operative in the framework of social responsibility is the challenge to make of differing "sounds" a harmonious integrated whole.

The purpose of this essay is surely not to attempt to do what has only just begun. I wish only to separate and clarify ever so little the variety of notes that can make the "sounds" more harmonious and to suggest ever so tentatively how we can learn to play the music.

There are many ways of defining spirituality. Very simply put, a person's spirituality can be considered the way that he or she more or less consciously relates to God in all the human dimensions of life. If the person is a Christian, then that relationship with God is mediated through Jesus Christ and the presence of his Risen Spirit received as gift. The author of the Johannine Gospel articulates this relationship in a reflection that takes the form of a discourse placed on the lips of Jesus. God, Who is Creator, Redeemer, and life-giving, comes in us, abides in us, dwells in us. The sign that God lives in us is the love we have for one another, even to the laying down of our lives (John 14:23; 15:12-13).

In the Matthean Gospel, the lived expression of this relationship is described in very concrete terms. Chapter 25 measures our ultimate beatitude in direct proportion to the service of one another because of Jesus. "Truly, I say to you, as you did it to one of the least of these, you did it to me" (Matt. 25:40).[4] How consciously we realize the meaning of these encounters with God measures the depth and vigor of our Christian spirituality.

In a way, there are as many expressions of Christian spirituality as there are people, for each of us relates to God within our own human experiences and within the human encounters with others that touch our lives each day. It is to experience what Gerard Manley Hopkins has described in a poetic fashion: "Christ plays in ten thousand places, lovely in limbs, and lovely in eyes not his to the Father through the features of men's faces."[5] Christian spirituality, then, is a concrete way of living out the gospel inspired by the Spirit who dwells within us. It is not grasped in abstract terms nor can it in itself be held out to be studied. It is not created by taking theological concepts and applying them to life. It is embodied in people, and it is found only in the concrete context in which people live out their faith.

The object of spirituality is religious experience—that is, a heightened knowledge of awareness of God. As Christians we believe that we can experience God in Jesus Christ in whom God also experiences us, coming very near to us; taking on our humanity; sharing in our joy, our pain, our hopes and fears. Moreover, in Jesus we can approach God who created us in the divine image and likeness, endowing us with that capacity for perfect freedom to consent to the divine life in God and in others and gifting us with the ability to love God and others for their own sake and not our own. For Thomas Merton, it is this understanding of Christian anthropology that is the foundation and basis of commitment to social action.

> "Whatever I may have written, I think it all can be reduced in the end to this one root truth: that God calls human persons to union with Himself and with one another in Christ. But if I have written about interracial justice, or thermonuclear weapons, it is because these issues are terribly relevant to one great truth: that human persons are called to live as sons and daughters of God."[6]

No person today can be unaware of unjust situations and structures that have reduced countless thousands of human beings to living lives less than human. Racist and sexist attitudes reduce whole classes of men and women to a status of subjugation and second-class citizenship. National security state values emphasize escalating military expenditures and nuclear proliferation that endanger the very existence of our planet and pollute our life systems through ecological destruction and waste. At the same time, a philosophy of consumerism confronts us in the mass media with captivating catch words and slogans, while a higher cost of living makes us restless and resentful that we cannot have what we are lulled into thinking we cannot live without. A world context of such catastrophic and discouraging dimensions coupled with the seeming inability to do anything about it have prompted one segment of the Christian community to search for an experience of the Transcendent in prayer forms and communities concerned with individual and interpersonal needs while ignoring the infrastructural idealogies and institutions from which these very needs proceed.[7] Such people view the spiritual life as something lived apart from political and economic realities rather than in the midst of them.

At the other end of the spectrum are those whose commitment to justice has denigrated and dismissed the necessity of a contemplative stance, placing emphasis instead on an experience of God that can only be realized in the historical dimensions of daily life. The attempt to mediate the extremes in a somewhat simplistic statement—yet provocative for all that—is related in an incident told by Ernesto Cardenal:

> A young supporter of the revolution told me they can't get Catholic books in Cuba. He asked me to send him some. He wanted modern Catholic books that were up to date. "Social books?" "No, I don't need those. In that field we're more modern here than elsewhere. Nothing from the outside could make me more revolutionary. I want books on mysticism. To learn how one can be a mystic and also a revolutionary."[8]

This young man's search for an integration of faith and life will not become a reality achieved once and for all through a new knowledge acquired by reading the mystics. It will demand further a kind of dialectical interplay correlating and calling forth an experience of God on the one hand with a commitment to social responsibility on the other.

Spiritual formation today is challenged by this process. Active involvement in the struggle for justice and liberation is no longer an option. It is a condition to knowing and realizing Christian love. A holistic and contemporary spirituality is contingent upon it. What procedures does such a situation suggest for those entrusted with spiritual formation, those whose ministry is to educate the faith and/or spiritually assist in focusing the direction of another's life?

Among the various perspectives of such a task I would like to single out two that not only intersect with each other but also interact in the life of a Christian today. The first is what I consider the need to reformulate the meaning of spirituality in the framework of the public, communal, historically rooted nature of biblical faith. The second is to deepen the realization that personal human experience in the struggle to be free and to love is the privileged locus of God's revelation and the framework of spirituality.

The Public, Communal, Historically Rooted Nature of Biblical Faith

The most basic biblical truth, fundamental to all spirituality, is that we are created to God's image and likeness—called to union with God not just as individuals but as members of the human family. "It is not good for man to be alone" (Gen. 2:17). Xavier Lèon-Dufour, in reflecting on the biblical notion of solitude, surprises us when he concludes that being forced to live alone and isolated is a sin—an evil that comes from the fragmentation, isolation, and alienation caused by sin.[9] To be created in God's likeness is to share in the superabundant fruitfulness of life and of love that is the nature of the Creator. Later, Jesus, in whom God incarnates this Word, will say, "I have come that they may have life, and have it more abundantly" (John 10:10). Whole peoples and classes, as well as individuals, can be forced to live in a state of alienation and isolation deprived of ever becoming fully themselves, of ever realizing their own dignity and meaning—estranged from themselves and others, and as a result, estranged from God. For such persons a truly religious experience is impossible.

The People whom Yahweh formed, to whom God made a commitment in covenantal love, were a people caught in bondage and oppression. Slave labor had reduced them to a state of indigence and indignity. The cries of the Israelites for release began the historical rootedness of God with those whose lives are deprived of that self-awareness through which true destiny and ultimate meaning are expressed, that is, the opportunity to live as they have been created, in the image and likeness of God. In the theophany of the burning bush Moses heard the words that initiated the Exodus. "I have heard the cries of my people and I have a mind to set them free" (Exod. 3:7). In the desert a crowd of refugees met God and were formed into a People convenanted not only to Yahweh but to one another. Here we behold a God passionately involved with the world, a God reacting intimately to the events of history, not standing outside the range of human suffering and sorrow, but entering into it. The words of Yahweh, "I will be your God, and you will be my People" (Jer. 7:23; 11:4; 24:7), also contain a command to witness to that same solidarity with and commitment to one another. Protectors of the orphaned and the widowed are regarded as sons and cherished more than a mother. "To the fatherless be as a father and help their mother as a husband would. Thus you will be like a Son to the Most High and He will be more tender to you than a mother" (Sib. Or. 4:10). Special care is to be rendered to the stranger, the outsider. "You shall not oppress or molest an alien for you were once aliens yourselves in the land of Egypt" (Exod. 22:20).

The laws of Yahweh were not prescriptions laid down in order to insure obedience and the acknowledgment of sovereignty. Rather, God's Law was a precious gift by which the People could create and sustain a harmony among themselves in the life they shared together. Biblical justice calls us to render to each one his or her due as persons precious to Yahweh, as part of the People chosen by God. It can also be described as fidelity to the demands of a relationship to God and to one another.[10]

The spirituality of the Judaic tradition, then, is one in which the conscious relationship with God is evidenced, expressed, and realized in the human experience of life together in community, a community called into being and formed by God, marked by steadfast love, mercy, and fidelity to the covenant sealed with the sprinkling of blood, the symbol of life given over and surrendered. The spirituality of Jesus continues in this tradition and brings it to fulfillment in the covenant made in his own blood, the laying down of his life that we may have life in him as a new People in whom he lives and with whom he identifies. God in Jesus becomes one with us that we may experience and become one with the divine. Our righteousness, our justification, is rooted in this relationship. The tender, merciful, and compassionate love of God, God's reigning and in-breaking into our world in the words and actions of Jesus, is announced first to those who most need this good news of salvation. In Luke's Gospel, Jesus announces this proclamation by applying to himself the consoling words of Isaiah. "The Spirit of the Lord has been given to me, for He has anointed me. He has sent me to bring the good news to the poor, to proclaim liberty to captives and to the blind new sight, to set the downtrodden free, to proclaim the Lord's year of favor" (Isa. 61:1–2).

What stands out in the passage and in Jesus' application of these prophetic words to himself are the verbs that suggest the meaning of ministry to the poor: being *sent*, to *bring* good news, to *proclaim* the meaning of this good news. Michael Crosby suggests that the content of such a message of good news to the poor might well have implied "a reversal of ideas and institutions which will restore the poor to wholeness."[11]

In another set of passages Jesus addresses those who are not poor in the sense of being marginated, dispossessed, or deprived and gives motivation as well as counsel for a right attitude toward wealth and possessions. In the Sermon on the Mount the multitudes are instructed not to hoard the treasures of the earth, since they have no lasting value and are only destined for destruction or the envy of those who will attempt to acquire the treasures for themselves (Matt. 6:19–21). In a later pericope Jesus tells the rich young man seeking perfection and discipleship to sell what he owns and give the money to the poor. His reward will be treasure in heaven (Matt. 19:20–22). In the kingdom parables Jesus uses the metaphor of a treasure to image the possession of the heavenly kingdom (Matt. 13:44–46). In one case it is found quite gratuitously. In the other it is sought after—a pearl of great price. But in both cases the seeing and experiencing of the treasure's shimmering beauty is enough to prompt the selling of all one's goods to possess it. Following the logic of these passages, Crosby suggests that solidarity with the poor is the way to have treasure in heaven, to experience God. But, he warns,

> We will never have the courage to render our personal, communal and collective lives on behalf of the poor unless we have first sought the treasure. We will not be able to part with those things that give us security, those things that the unbelievers of the world are running after until we have discovered the reign of God's presence (Mt. 6:32–33), which is found in religious experience. We are poor in spirit when we seek God in ever deepening moments of contemplation and mystical experience. Experiencing God as Father, Son and Spirit in prayer, we are disposed to reorder our lives, sell what we do not need, and give to those who do not have what we formerly thought to be so important.[12]

Perhaps it is here that we can see the intersection and interaction of those elements through which spirituality and social responsibility will become a harmonious sound. We can only be motivated to sustain a commitment to justice, that is, to live out and pursue the relationships due to God and one another because of the demands of covenantal love, if we have known and experienced the God of the covenant.

And herein lies the second challenge: the deeper realization that human experience is the locus of God's revelation.

Human Experience as the Privileged Locus of God's Revelation

Where and how do we experience God in our lives and in our prayer? Foundational to any transcendental experience is, as has been said many times, the realization that we are created in the image and likeness of God, and that God dwells within us as ground of our being and ground of our beseeching. Teresa of Avila, a woman fully human and fully alive, whose common sense, understanding of human nature, and union with God touch the reality of our world, has written most simply and yet profoundly about the basis of prayer:

> Do you suppose that it is of little importance that a soul should come to understand this truth and find that, in order to speak to its Eternal Father and take delight in Him it has no need to go to Heaven? We need no wings to go in search of Him but have only to find a place where we can be alone and look upon Him present within us.[13]

The truth is simply enough said and the reality an object of belief, yet the realization of what it means existentially more often than not eludes us. If God dwells and abides with us and within us, then God's Presence is not removed or apart from the human experiences that make up the daily fabric of our lives. Even more intimate is the realization that God is at the heart of all we most desire, long for, love, and like. With unusual charm of expression, Julian of Norwich, a fourteenth-century mystic, records these words of God heard in her heart. "I it am; I it am that is highest; I it am that thou lovest; I it am that thou likest; I it am that thou servest; I it am that thou longest; I it am that thou desirest; I it am that thou meanest; I it am that is all . . . I it am that shewed myself to thee here."[14]

In other words, within our human experience, in the day-to-day living made up of joy and pain, fears and risks, movements of intense sharing and moments of intense loneliness, God is intimately present, addressing us as a Word emerging from our inner depth, our innermost heart.

Our Christian formation has not, for the most part, led us to trust or to grow in this realization. We have been inclined to mistrust our own experience and have tended more to lean on other "experts" to provide us with valid criteria of discernment for measuring God's activity within our lives. Our scientific culture has conditioned us to predictable and controlled methodology for testing attitudes and values on almost every level. Expectations from others, the world, the Church, family, and friends often incline us to create a false image of ourselves and one that we know does not coincide with who we really are and desire to be. If we can begin to trust God's loving acceptance of us as we are, then, it is hoped, we can grow in compassion, understanding, and acceptance of one another. John Shea puts it this way:

> The story of God's unconditional acceptance of humankind moves us beyond the need for "cover-stories," i.e., those stories we tell in self-deception to screen out all that does not reinforce the ideal self I aspire to be but what I know in my actual condition is not. With acceptance the need for cover-stories dissolves and the dynamic urge to know is realized.[15]

Spiritual direction requires more than ever the ability to enable women and men to come in touch with, to trust, and to articulate the movements of God in their daily experiences of life. This direction may come from an individual but perhaps more frequently today will come from that kind of sharing that happens when people share a common concern, a common lifestyle, or a support group that enables them to listen prayerfully to one another as they seek to discern and to name movements of God in the experiences of life. Such reflection may concern the action of the group as a whole or that of any particular individual in his or her need for discernment. Its object and purpose is to assist a process of thinking theologically about past and present experience, to verbalize it, possess it, share it, dialogue about it, and finally, to rethink and reverbalize it in an ongoing process that leads to action.

This means that we believe that God is constantly speaking to us and that we can discern the Word of God in our individual and collective experiences. It means that we believe that God's Word can sometimes demand action and sometimes demand restful awe, but that it is always full of compassion. It means that we believe that all of us can hear the Word of God better than any one of us, and that especially today we have to learn nonindividualistic ways of finding God. It means that we believe that in order to hear God's Word more clearly and cooperate with it more efficiently, both theological reflection on experience and spiritual integration are necessary. It means that we believe it is imperative that we reflect together both on our concrete, relevant experiences and on one another's intellectual, moral, and religious horizons. It means, in short, that we believe that the ongoing revelation of Jesus is in the shared faith of the community.[16]

This kind of sharing cannot be separated from the experiences we undergo as citizens of our time, our country, our world. It helps us to realize that we are part of a whole and that the individual calls of God within the fabric of our lives are not unrelated to those of others with whom we share a common heritage and a common destiny. The formation of the divine/human community is the mission of Jesus and the Church. This community realizes the biblical notion of justice in which the relationships we owe to God and to one another are enabled through the abiding presence of the Spirit of Christ Jesus who is both the way and the goal. Our effort to relate more or less consciously to Jesus in the experiences of life calls us to continual conversion, commitment to the oppressed, and effort at reconciliation even with those whose world view stands in opposition to our own. It also invites us to seasons and times of celebration in which present joys and creative hopes are engendered. To hear the Word of God rising out of a depth both prior to and present in our own experience calls for solitary responsibility, contemplation, and reverential awe. To hear that Word in the experience of others, especially in those whose mourning and weeping is a cry for recognition and righteousness, is a summons to liberating praxis. This, for me, is the meaning of spirituality today. It challenges us to create a harmony out of the personal search for spiritual understanding and experience on the one hand, and the discordant, dissonant sounds of human struggle and sacrifice on the other. When and where the two intersect and interact we will be able, we hope, in the words of the psalmist, to "sing [and play] a new song unto the Lord" (Ps. 96:1).

If lyrics were possible they might remind us of the reassuring presence of a God who is the solid ground of our hope and belief that

> All things shall be well
> Thou shalt see thyself
> That in all manner of things
> They shall be well. . . .[17]

NOTES

1. Synod of Bishops, *Justice in the World* (Washington, D.C.: United States Catholic Conference Publications Office, 1972), p. 34.
2. Gustavo Gutierrez, *A Theology of Liberation* (Maryknoll, N.Y.: Orbis Books, 1973), p. 204.
3. Segundo Galilea, "Liberation as an Encounter with Politics and Contemplation," *Concilium 96* (New York: Paulist Press, 1970), p. 20.
4. Bible quotations throughout this chapter are from the Revised Standard Version.
5. Gerard Manley Hopkins, "Inversnaid," *Poems of Gerard Manley Hopkins* (Oxford: Oxford University Press, 1948), p. 95.
6. John Higgins, *Merton's Theology of Prayer* (Cistercian Publications, 1971), p. 92.
7. Michael H. Crosby, *Spirituality of the Beatitudes* (Maryknoll, N.Y.: Orbis Books, 1980), p. 18–19.
8. Ernesto Cardinal, "In Cuba," *New Directions* (1972), p. 277.
9. Lèon-Dufour, *Dictionary of Biblical Theology* (Montreal: Palm Publishers, 1967), p. 490.
10. John R. Donahue, "Biblical Perspectives on Justice," *The Faith That Does Justice* (New York: Paulist Press, 1977), pp. 68–70.
11. Crosby, p. 56.
12. Ibid.
13. Teresa of Avila, *The Way of Perfection: Complete Works of St. Teresa*, translated by E. Allison Peers (London: Sheed & Ward, 1946), p. 114.
14. Julian of Norwich, *The Revelations of Divine Love of Julian of Norwich*, translated by James Walsh (St. Meinrad, Ind.: Abbey Press, Religious Experience Series, 1974), p. 90.

15. John Shea, "Theology and Autobiography," *Commonweal* (June 1978), pp. 358–62.
16. "Spiritual Integration for Ministry Program" brochure (Toronto: Regis College Press, 1980).
17. Julian of Norwich, p. 98.

QUESTIONS FOR REFLECTION AND DISCUSSION

1. Why is an understanding of the world context in which we live necessary for an understanding of spirituality?

2. What is the relationship between the spirituality of the Judaic tradition and the spirituality of Jesus? How do they relate to social responsibility?

3. What does it mean to say that God is not removed or apart from the human experiences that make up the daily fabric of our lives?

4. What connections can you make between your responses to questions 2 and 3?

5. What are the implications of a socially responsible vision of Christian life (and therefore spirituality) for religious education?

16. A Liberationist Perspective on Peace and Social Justice

ADA MARIA ISASI-DIAZ

SOCIAL JUSTICE has been an ever-present concern of the Catholic church since Vatican II. For nearly two decades, church members have been about social justice attempting to help the poor, the oppressed, and hoping to better unjust situations in the world.[1]

With the broadening of the understanding of ministry, social justice has come to be accepted as a necessary and most important ministry in the Church.[2] This has brought about a re-examination of what ministry means. Until recently ministry was understood as something done to others. Social justice, however, can only be a ministry if it is a way of life—a day-to-day living within a community, a struggling to be just. Those involved in social justice ministry cannot be teachers and not doers. What the 1971 Synod of Bishops said about the Church has to be applied to social justice ministers: One cannot speak about justice to others if one is not just oneself.[3]

Because justice is a constitutive element of the gospel, as the same synodal document clearly states, the social justice minister has to be an advocate and an educator, an activist and a thinker. Separation among education, thinking, advocacy, and action in the ministry of social justice leads necessarily to false prophets, to pharisaical attitudes that lay heavy burdens on the people while the ministers profit and benefit from the structures that they publicly denounce.

Social Sin and Social Justice

The Church recognizes social sin as a reality that is in need of forgiveness.[4] Therefore, repentance is required. Social sin is not impersonal. It does not occur aside from individuals. Though one single person might not be responsible for the sin, the sum of decisions made by one or several individuals brings about situations that are sinful. Because individuals are involved in the decision making that causes social sin, individuals can also participate actively in correcting sinful situations.[5] To disengage or attempt to deal with social justice with a different methodology than the one used to deal with social sin questions the full acceptance of social sin as an operating oppressive structure in the world today. To deny personal responsibility for social sin is to deny personal responsibility for social justice, and that denies the active participation of humanity in the day-to-day unfolding of the reign of God. That would imply a fatalistic interpretation of history contrary to the understanding that is accepted by the Church at large of human participation in the continued creation, redemption, and sanctification of the world.

Just as social sin does not happen aside from individuals, social justice is not something abstract. The conditions necessary for social justice to prevail are the responsibility of Christians and all people of good will. Those who in a special way recognize injustice and its causes cannot but be actively involved in its eradication. The social justice minister is a person who is called by the Spirit to place at the service of the community, for the common good of the community, his or her gift of discernment of injustice, its causes, and the ways the community can become engaged in changing the oppressive situation. Social justice ministry is not only a matter of understanding. It has to do with the whole process of dialogue, which requires reflection, analysis, and action. Though this does not apply exclusively to social justice but is true of most ministries, social justice ministry per se requires righting wrong, denouncing evil by pointing to justice—action is intrinsic to social justice ministry. The ministry of social justice demands personal involvement by the minister in the struggle to bring about a just order of relationships. Because of this, social justice ministers have to be integral members of the community that suffers —suffers either by being oppressed or by not realizing how it oppresses or contributes to oppressive situations.

All ministry happens within a community for the good of the community. The sense of social justice as something not immediately related to a definable community places social justice outside the realm of ministry. If social justice is not born of the community for the good of the community, then it can only be considered an advocacy or a lobbying for justice. This in itself has enormous merit but is not to be conceived of as ministry. Undeniably there is a significant need for information regarding social injustice, social sin, and social justice. However, ministry, to be valid, has to be organic ministry—ministry that has its roots in, and immediately relates to, a given community out of which it is born and to which it is accountable.

Social Justice and Liberation

The word *liberation* is widely used and has lost some of its specificity and precision of meaning. Liberation here means the process by which particular individuals become conscientized, coming to understand the oppressive situation in their lives by reflecting on and analyzing that situation and, together with those likewise affected, setting out to change that oppressive situation. Liberation is also a process that is necessary for the oppressors. Part of their oppression is that they belong to a class that oppresses and need to become conscientized and to engage in the process of liberating themselves as individuals. As a class the oppressors can never be liberated. Furthermore, the oppressor cannot liberate the oppressed. In a letter written by Paulo Freire to a theology student, Rogerio de Almeida Cunha, Freire states: "The contrary of love is not, as is thought many times or almost always, hate. It is fear of love, and fear of love is fear of being free. The biggest, the only proof of love that those oppressed can give the oppressors is to reiterate radically the objective conditions which give them power to oppress, and not to accommodate themselves masochistically to the oppression. Only thus can the oppressors be humanized. And this labor of love, which is revolutionary, political, belongs to the oppressed."[6]

The process of conscientization that initiates and remains the backbone of the process of liberation is not an intellectual process divested of or divorced from the day-to-day living of the individual. The process of conscientization has as two of its intrinsic elements an understanding that is born out of an experience and the realization that analysis and action that is political, and therefore not individualistic, is required. These elements are not optional. Though the injustice might be at the individual, interpersonal, or structural level, the process of conscientization is triggered by personal oppression that comes to be understood as nonprivate. In the struggle for liberation the personal is political. What affects the individual is rarely the result of individual action or understanding. It almost always has to do with structures that involve others as oppressors. In life, situations are the result of combined understanding and action and are, therefore, the responsibility of at least several persons.

In the U.S., emphasis on the political, communal aspect of social justice and liberation is needed. The individualism of American society and the privatization that capitalism needs to flourish have resulted in a mind-set that makes corporate understanding and action very difficult. Specialization adds to this mind-set of separatedness that makes the tactic of divide and conquer extremely easy to implement. If the process of conscientization that is an intrinsic element of liberation is to be understood and promoted, there is a need to put aside individualistic understanding and action.

Liberation as a process that eliminates oppression is one of the main means that can be used to bring about social justice. If this is accepted as true and valuable by the Church in the U.S., as it has been by the Church in Latin America, liberation as a whole, with all of its elements, has to be espoused. If, however, liberation is not acceptable to the Church in the U.S. as a viable way to bring about justice, a different method of analysis and action needs to be developed. What can become extremely dangerous is to use—to manipulate —the mind-set, the understandings and elements operative in liberation by accommodating them to what would be acceptable here in this country.

I have repeatedly heard Latin American social justice people protest the manipulation of the concept of the process of liberation that goes on in the U.S. They see this as a cover-up: Instead of liberation they claim that what is sought is equality within present oppressive structures. Though their indictment might be considered a harsh one, their desire to see the process of liberation respected in its entirety is valid and valuable.

Why would accommodating the concept of liberation be extremely dangerous? It is the totality of liberation as an understanding and a methodology that makes it an effective means of social justice. Once some of its elements are not accepted and recognized as operative principles, liberation loses its cutting edge, its prophetic voice. For example, if the sense of community intrinsic to liberation is not acceptable because of American individualism, the result is what Gustavo Gutierrez calls *la salida individual* (the individual way out) *la salida individual* occurs when individuals, because of superior ability, knowledge, money, and so on, are able to extricate themselves from the oppressive situation. The common good does not benefit from this, and *la salida individual* serves to split the community, lowering significantly its corporate effectiveness.

Gutierrez also points out another danger, *la salida facil* (the easy way out). This happens when one or several individuals accommodate themselves to the demands of the oppressor and find a way out of the oppression without struggling to change the structure. The real results are that the individual abdicates an opportunity for liberation while at the same time becoming a participant in the oppressive structure.[7]

Education vs. Activity

The emphasis and the common understanding of education is that of learning based on intellectual transfer of knowledge. Whether that knowledge becomes operative or not in the life of a given individual has not been a major preoccupation of schools and universities. Grades measure the amount of intellectual knowledge accumulated by a student but do not refer to how that knowledge has affected the life of the individual.

Justice, having to do with what each one has a right to and needs to become fully human, is not something that can be taught exclusively at the intellectual level. To understand what is just for others, one needs to enter into their experience and to learn by understanding. The learning of justice is a process that goes far beyond the usual concept of "knowing about" justice.

There are three normative dimensions of justice: "To reorder relations with those in need through alms (Mt. 6:2–4), with God and neighbor through prayer that celebrates forgiveness (Mt. 6:5–15), and with the oppressed through fasting that enables one to experience the depth of need and to respond more easily to the cries of others (Mt. 6:16–18)."[8] Empathy, therefore, is intrinsic to justice education and necessitates personal involvement beyond intellectual knowledge. Mercy has to be part of justice. Caring for others is the way humans image God!

Activity has been seen by many as a doing that follows education and/or understanding. Doing is greatly valued and highly praised in this society. But the activist is not recognized as someone able to do much beyond implementing ideas, carrying out strategies.[9] The separation between thinking and doing is in keeping with the compartmentalization and high level of specialization operative in this society.[10]

But in the field of social justice, the doing has to be born out of a knowing that requires shared experience. Doing in behalf of others without sharing and participating in their lives has led to goodwill-charity and paternalism.

Though often there is no choice but to "give charity" to those starving to death—dying under oppression—charity has often been a band-aid solution that has served to help perpetuate oppressive structures.[11] Charity has served repeatedly to set the consciences of the rich at ease. To be about radical changes of structures is the only thing that gives one the right to resort to band-aid solutions.

Paternalism, a system that keeps people dependent on the parent image, has likewise made it possible for many to believe they are "about justice" while maintaining their distance from the poor and the oppressed. To help others the way those with power or in authority think they should be helped will never change oppressive structures. This is why many of the so-called activists affirm the need to keep analysis as a separate discipline. Likewise, the theoreticians can claim to be about justice without personally becoming involved. By insisting on specialization and compartmentalization they keep far away from practice.

Liberation: A Framework for Social Justice

The elements of education and activism cannot be separated when dealing with social justice. The understanding of liberation, with its process of conscientization and dialogue carried on within a community, offers a way of integrating education and activism in the field of social justice.

Conscientization is a process of education that has the lived experience of the individual as its starting point.[12] What is used as the motivational force is the desire of the individual to understand her or his life and to deal with it in an adequate fashion. Intellectual knowledge is not ignored or belittled, but it is placed in context; it is used by the person to understand who he or she is and what he or she is about. One of the main goals of conscientization is to provide for the individual the tools with which to deal with the situation at hand. The measure of success is not knowing how to do or understanding the why, but the actual doing, which, of course, includes knowing and understanding. Given the complexity of all reality, the conscientized individual knows that the doing has to be communal and not individualistic.

The process of dialogue is likewise an integrative process. To dialogue is not to talk about something. It is not to share in order to place in common. Dialogue is a process of reflection-analysis-action. The telling of the story of each person is but the starting point for a true dialogue. To reflect upon those stories and analyze them so as to understand the points of similarity and begin to formulate a common action—that is dialogue. The process necessarily calls for a vision of the personal as political.

Dialogue understood this way makes both knowledge/understanding and activity integral parts of one and the same process. Though one is not the other, reflection-analysis is part of the same process as activity. The activity is both end result and starting point for the process of dialogue. Reflection and analysis provide the basis for action while at the same time making action effective. They enable action to be liberating since they provide understanding of the oppressive structure.

The action one engages in is not an individualistic attempt, though it is indeed a personal one. Grounded in the understandings of social justice, struggling to identify social sin and call sinful structures to repentance, the personal struggle links with similar struggles of other individuals, thus creating a liberation movement. Intrinsic to the process of liberation is the action in common born out of a common analysis of the oppression experienced at first hand. The action in common is necessary not only because it is more effective but because the sense of community is a constitutive element of Christianity. The community serves as a support. The community becomes the *locus* for doing analysis, reaching understanding. The community calls the individual into accountability, thus becoming a corrective tool when necessary or an encouraging, supportive implement.

Integration in the Life of the Social Justice Minister—A Personal Reflection

Justice is an intrinsic element of the Christian feminist movement. Sexism that operates at all levels of the structural Church and is at the heart of many of the understandings and beliefs that support such a structure is a sin—contrary to God's will, according to *Gaudium et spes* No. 29. Our struggle is not to be equal with men within an oppressive structure. Struggling to liberate ourselves because we as women are Church, we seek to change such a structure radically. It is difficult to call the Church to justice for women when those who control the Church—all males—refuse to understand our struggle as a struggle for justice. As oppressors who hold power, they seek to define the liberation struggle of the oppressed in order to be able to control it. Denying that it is a matter of justice, they appeal to theological understandings that they claim are based on Scripture and tradition.

Our struggle as Christian feminists has the added difficulty that we are dealing with a structure that exercises control over the consciences of people. The Christian feminist always struggles under the possibility of excommunication.[13]

Because the struggle is one of liberation, our social justice ministry as feminists is not a profession but a day-to-day living and struggling. As feminists we struggle constantly to operate in a patriarchal world that attempts to dismiss us at every level: personal, interpersonal, and structural.[14]

If we consider our intense struggle as a job, we run the risk of burnout. If our liberation process is not integral, necessary to our lives and benefiting all aspects of it, and yet is constantly before us—and it cannot be otherwise given our patriarchal world—we become consumed by the job. Because we resent the job and do not find personal satisfaction in it in comparison to the amount of time we spend on it, burnout can easily happen.

But if we consider and understand our ministry to the Church—to call the Church to justice for women—if we understand it as integral to our liberation as women, our ministry becomes a life-giving struggle and not a sure road to burnout. Of course we all need space and distance from the details of the movement! But social justice ministry, as well as the liberation process, demands reflection and analysis as well as action. We cannot turn our minds off when we leave the office. Reflection and analysis are something that go on in our minds and our hearts constantly. They make our lives extremely uncomfortable at times. The feminist sings: "I wish my eyes had never been open." How true! Reflection and analysis, however, give us the constant satisfaction of knowing that we are growing in the process of conscientization. That assures use that the struggle for liberation continues—that the possibility for our becoming agents of our own history is becoming a reality.

I remember that in my own personal story the process of conscientization was sparked by not being able to find a job in a parish in the southern U.S. because of being a laywoman. Reflecting on my own experience of oppression, I began to analyze why I could not function as a minister in the Church. Initially I found no answer to my question and no solution to my problem. Years later, friends recognizing in me the gift for ministry enabled me to become involved in Women's Ordination Conference. But it was not until I began to understand the social justice dimension of our struggle in the Church that I was able to move in my own process of radicalization. Sensing that my treatment was not right, that it was unjust, my resulting reflection and analysis led me to understand that sexism is antigospel. Once I saw the struggle as integral to my own liberation, I was able to see my life as a whole, and have been able to dedicate endless hours and energy to the movement without being afraid of being consumed by the job or suffering burnout.

Conclusion

Social justice, if it is to be understood as a ministry, has to be grounded in a community. The perspective provided by liberation integrates the elements of education and activism that are part of social justice. Conscientization and dialogue provide tools for such integration.

The tension between the job and the rest of the life of the social justice minister are also resolved by understanding social justice ministry as part of the minister's own process of liberation.[15] Social justice ministers have to understand that they are not only teachers and proclaimers of justice but also doers.

Social justice is a constitutive dimension of the gospel. Therefore, it is a requirement for participation in the reign of God. Social justice ministers, like everyone else, in order to participate fully in the reign of God have to enter into the process of continual conversion—a process operative in the life of the believer at all times, at all levels. To fail to see social justice as an intrinsic part of life will lead those involved in the ministry to a pharisaical attitude. Faithfulness to the task of establishing a new order of relationship, establishing social justice, and re-ordering society requires "to walk humbly with your God, to love goodness [and] to do the right" (Mic. 6:8,7,6).

NOTES

1. Many who read this essay might find the lack of references to published works disturbing. This essay is the result of years of experience, sharing with others, and struggling for liberation. It is impossible to give credit to all those who have helped me come to these understandings. As a Cuban who lived in Peru in the late sixties, I have been influenced by the early liberation theology and Freire's work. But the refinement and constant redefining of many of the understandings here presented have happened through my involvement with the feminist movement during the last five years.

    The academicians will excuse the almost total lack of academic footnotes. The activists will excuse the academic footnotes even if they are few. Those who struggle for liberation will know that as a sister-in-the-struggle, my organic understandings belong to all. They will accept my sense of gathering the knowledge of the people—of being a voice through which their voices and minds speak. I do not, however, relinquish responsibility for what I have here written—especially for the grammatical shortcomings for which my English-As-A-Second-Language might be an acceptable excuse!

    As a Hispanic, I would like to honor our custom and dedicate this to those who allow me to call them sisters and friends.

2. I do not attempt to deal here with ministry in a restricted sense in spite of the NCCB's latest attempt to use this word only in reference to ordained ministry. Ministry is the placing of the gifts of the individual at the service of the commu-

nity for the common good. The gifts the community needs are brought forth by the Spirit in different people as the Spirit sees fit. The discernment process on the part of the individual is a communal experience and therefore requires that the ministers be an integral part of the community. The recognition of the gifts of the Spirit by the larger community—the Church—is necessary to help the community understand itself within, and related to, the world at large. Such recognition brings to the community the richness of the faith tradition alive since the very beginnings of the Christian community.

3. "Justice in the World," *The Pope Speaks* 16 (1972).

4. The attempt here is to point out parallels that exist in the methodologies used to understand and explain both social sin and social justice. This is not intended to be an exhaustive explanation. I intend to simply point out some of the elements to be considered when discussing social sin and social justice.

5. An example of this is the *corporate social responsibility* movement. Different religious congregations who own stocks in some of the main international companies have united to use their power as stockholders to correct the abuses brought by such companies all around the world. Their individual power is small. But their willingness to bond and act as a block has begun to have an impact on these gigantic multinationals.

6. Excerpts of this letter were published in a *folleto popular* (a people's pamphlet) published by Creatividad y Cambio, a feminist publishing/conscientization house in Lima, Peru.

7. Gustavo Gutierrez often talks about these dangers. I heard him explain them at the "Theology in the Americas" meeting that took place in Detroit during the summer of 1980.

8. Michael H. Crosby, O.F.M.Cap., *Spirituality of the Beatitudes* (Maryknoll, N.Y.: Orbis Books, 1980), p. 131.

9. In the summer of 1980 I was told by the organizers of a national conference that I was not being invited to be one of the speakers because I was an activist and did not qualify as a theoretician.

10. Jamie Phelps, O.P., a black feminist, recently commented that many of the black women leaders have a multiplicity of talents. The problem is that this multiplicity is not recognized, and they are called upon to share their talents in only one field.

Personally, I find it difficult to convince people that I have expertise in the fields of education, social justice, feminism, spirituality, ministry, and the Hispanics in the U.S. Church. I have successfully lectured in all of these fields and published in several of them.

11. Marjorie Tuite, O.P., feminist and renowned strategist, shared with a group of us the following story.

There was a peaceful, prosperous village by a river. One day a body came floating down the river. The people of the village took it out and buried it. Since bodies kept coming down the river, the villagers had to organize themselves for the task of burying them and set aside a plot as a burial ground. Then one day one of the bodies was still alive, so the villagers took care of the person. Others kept floating down the river barely alive, so the villagers had to set up a hospital. Some of the ones they were able to save were children, so they also organized a school.

One day one of the villagers said to the others: "Let's go up the river and find out why the bodies keep coming down the river." But the rest of the villagers did not want to do that. "We are taking care of the bodies, what else do you want?" But the villager insisted and decided to go alone. No one ever heard from the villager that went up the river. Some time later the villagers picked up from the river the dead body of their friend who had gone to find out why bodies had been floating down the river.

12. I propose here some elements for a working understanding of conscientization. This is not an all-encompassing definition and does not use Pablo Freire's words. However, this understanding of conscientization does not contradict Freire's.

13. Sonia Johnson, convicted feminist from the Mormon faith tradition, was excommunicated from her church because of her unwillingness to obey church leaders and work secretly against the ERA. Though in the Roman Catholic church we feminists have not been excommunicated, we have already received the first warning. We have been fired from church jobs and have lost friends of many years, and bishops across the United States have refused to dialogue with us.

14. Barbara Zanotti, a radical feminist from Cambridge, Massachusetts, explained to me how we have to constantly "go out of our minds" as feminists in order to operate in this patriarchal world.

15. People working on the issue of El Salvador, for instance, see their work as integral to their own liberation because they understand that their living in the U.S. makes them unwilling participants in the unjust structures that the U.S. maintains in that country.

QUESTIONS FOR REFLECTION AND DISCUSSION

1. Discuss a specific situation in which you have experienced oppression.

2. When in your life have you taken *La salida facil? La salida individual?*

3. What is the relationship between the story related in note 15 and the understanding of dialogue presented in this essay?

4. Is there any validity to separating the job from the rest of one's life if one is a social justice minister?

5. In what ways do you consider the questions raised by feminists, in and out of the Church, issues of social justice?

About the Contributors

MARY C. BOYS is a native of Seattle, Washington, and assistant professor of theology and religious education at Boston College's Institute of Religious Education and Pastoral Ministry. She is the recipient of the M.A. and the Ed.D. from the Columbia University/Union Theological Seminary joint program in religion and education. Among other works, she is the author of *Biblical Interpretation in Religious Education* (1980).

MARGARET BRENNAN is a Sister of the Immaculate Heart of Mary from Monroe, Michigan. She is director of continuing education and associate professor of pastoral theology at Regis College in the Toronto School of Theology. She is a native of Detroit, Michigan, and has published articles in the areas of spirituality, ministry, and religious renewal as well as lecturing to a wide variety of audiences on these topics.

RUSSELL A. BUTKUS received his B.A. from Saint Lawrence University, Canton, New York, and his M.Ed. in religious education from Boston College. He is currently a doctoral candidate in religion and education at Boston College's Institute of Religious Education and Pastoral Ministry. He has taught in Catholic secondary schools in Connecticut and is married and the parent of a little boy.

VIRGIL ELIZONDO is the president of the Mexican-American Cultural Center in San Antonio, Texas. Among other degrees, he is the recipient of both the S.T.D. and the Ph.D. from the Institut Catholique in Paris. He has lectured widely and is the author of a number of books, including *Tensions Between the Churches of the First and Third World (1981)*.

JOSEPH J. FAHEY is director of the Peace Studies Institute and associate professor of religious studies at Manhattan College in New York City. He received his B.A. and M.A. from Maryknoll Seminary and his Ph.D. from New York University. He is a former Honorary Research Fellow in Peace Studies at the Queens University of Belfast, Northern Ireland, has taught at Fordham University and Maryknoll School of Theology, and has lectured and written widely on justice and peace concerns.

MARGARET GORMAN, a native of Kingston, New York, and a member of the Religious of the Sacred Heart, is adjunct professor of theology and psychology at Boston College. She was chairperson of the department of psychology at Newton College of the Sacred Heart (Newton, Massachusetts) from 1960 through 1975. She holds the doctorate in educational psychology from Catholic University of America and is the author of numerous articles on moral development and the book *General Semantics and Contemporary Thomism*.

THOMAS H. GROOME, associate professor of theology and religious education at Boston College, received the M.Div. (equiv.) from Saint Patrick's Seminary in Carlow, the M.A. in religious education from Fordham University, and the doctorate in religion and education from the Union Theological Seminary/ Columbia University joint program. He has lectured widely in this country, Canada, and Australia and published in various journals. He is the author of *Christian Religious Education: Sharing Our Story and Vision* (1980).

MARIA HARRIS is a native New Yorker whose doctorate in religious education was received from Union Theological Seminary/Columbia Teachers' College. She is the author of over forty articles; the most recent of her five books is *Portrait of Youth Ministry* (1981). Harris is professor of religious education at Andover Newton School in Newton, Massachusetts.

DAVID HOLLENBACH is a Jesuit and associate professor of theological ethics at Weston School of Theology in Cambridge, Massachusetts. He holds the Ph.D. degree from Yale University. His published writings include *Claims in Conflict: Retrieving and Renewing the Catholic Human Rights Tradition* (1979), several articles in *The Faith That Does Justice* (edited by John Haughey), and a number of articles in journals such as *Theological Studies, Theology Today, The Human Rights Quarterly, The International Bulletin of Missionary Research,* and *America.*

KATHLEEN HUGHES is a Religious of the Sacred Heart, born in Shaker Heights, Ohio, educated at Newton College of the Sacred Heart (B.A., philosophy), Catholic University of America (M.A. in religious education) and the University of Notre Dame (M.A. and Ph.D. in liturgical studies). She is assistant professor in liturgy and preaching at Catholic Theological Union in Chicago. Hughes is a member of the advisory committee of the International Commission on English in the liturgy and chairperson of the subcommittee on Translation, Revision, and Original Texts. She wrote her dissertation on the opening prayers of the Roman sacramentary and has written articles for *New Catholic World, Pastoral Musicians, Spirituality Today, Celebration, Assembly,* and other journals. Her current work includes preparation of a ceremonial for her religious congregation and research on the correlation of the Myers-Briggs personality types to preaching styles.

ADA MARIA ISASI-DIAZ was born in La Habana, Cuba, in 1943 and came to the United States as a political refugee. From 1965 to 1967 she was involved in teaching and other pastoral work in Peru and subsequently spent three years working in Louisiana. Since 1974 she has worked in religious education and pastoral ministry in Rochester, New York. She is presently a member of the ministerial team of the Women's Ordination Conference. In this capacity she lectures widely throughout the United States on feminism, spirituality, and Hispanics in the Church in the United States. She has published articles in *Prophets Without Honor* (Orbis Press), *Missiology Review, El Visitante, New Women/New Church,* and other publications.

CLAIRE E. LOWERY is a native Californian and a member of the Religious of the Sacred Heart. She has served as a school administrator, in formation positions within her congregation, and in campus ministry. She is at present assistant professor and coordinator of the pastoral ministry program at Boston College's Institute of Religious Education and Pastoral Ministry. She is the recipient of the M.Div. and D.Min. from Andover Newton Theological School in Newton, Massachusetts. Lowery's field is pastoral care and counseling, and she is preparing a manuscript based on a symposium on spirituality conducted by the Institute of Religious Education and Pastoral Ministry.

RICHARD P. MCBRIEN, a priest of the archdiocese of Hartford, Connecticut, is chairman of the theology department and Crowley-O'Brien-Walter Professor of Theology at the University of Notre Dame. McBrien is an internationally recognized systematic theologian and ecclesiologist, who has written innumerable articles and books. His most recent book is the highly acclaimed two-volume study *Catholicism*.

MAURICE MONETTE is a member of the Oblates of Mary Immaculate who was, until recently, director of the Catechetical and Pastoral Institute of Loyola University in New Orleans. Subsequent to this service, Monette spent sabbatical leave in Latin America studying *communidades de base*. A graduate of Columbia University Teachers' College (Ed.D. in adult education) and Weston School of Theology (M.Div.), Monette has published in such journals as *Adult Education, Religious Education, Living Light, PACE (Professional Approaches in Christian Education),* and *Ministries*.

GABRIEL MORAN is a native of Manchester, New Hampshire, residing in New York City, where he is associate professor of religious education at New York University. Moran received the Ph.D. in theology and religious education from Catholic University of America. He is the author of innumerable essays and books; his most recent books are *Education Toward Adulthood* (1979) and *The Interplay of Religion and Education* (1981).

PADRAIC O'HARE is a native New Yorker educated at Saint Francis College, Brooklyn (B.A., history), Fordham University (M.A., political science), Manhattan College (M.A., religious studies), and Union Theological Seminary/Columbia University Teachers' College (Ed.D. religion and education). He is associate director of the Institute of Religious Education and Pastoral Ministry at Boston College and the author of essays in *Religious Education, New Catholic World, Professional Approaches in Christian Education, Momentum, The Living Light,* and *Parish Religious Education* (edited by Maria Harris) as well as the editor of two collections: *Foundations of Religious Education* (1978) and *Tradition and Transformation in Religious Education* (1979).

MARGARET WOODWARD was born in New Castle, New South Wales, Australia. She has studied theology and religious education in the United States (M.Ed., religious education, Boston College) as well as in her native country, where she is at present pursuing doctoral studies. Woodward has been engaged in school teaching, religious education coordination, diocesan educational efforts, and adult education. She is currently involved in projects related to justice education with adults.

Index